A Miraculous Journey

The Life of Vernon L. Bowlby

Jesus said, "Let your light so shine before men, that they may see your good works, and glorify your Father which is in Heaven."

Matthew 5:16

Published by Mount Hood Publishing Company
First Edition: October, 2014
Editor: Betty Thompson

Cover photo of Mount Hood and Lost Lake by Brent Bradley,
Oregon Scenics. Used by permission.
http://www.oregonscenics.com

About Cover Photos

Mt. Hood

Growing up in the Hood River Valley, Vernon recognized God's power in the creation Mt. Hood and Mt. Adams, and he has always felt that he would be empowered by experiencing this energy from the mountain tops. Vernon realized at an early age that his soul would never be satisfied until he climbed both mountains. Accordingly, in 1949, when he was 18, he climbed Mt. Hood with his best friend, Dick Minor. In 1953, he climbed Mt. Hood and Mt. Adams with his brother, Bob.

Vernon and his dog Buster in 1939

When he was three, Vernon saved his dog, Buster, from death at birth. In return, his dog saved him from drowning twice. Buster remained a faithful partner until he died in 1951, shortly before his master joined the Army.

Rainbow over window where Vernon wrote *A Miraculous Journey*

Returning home after his diagnosis with stage 4 metastasized cancers, Vernon observed a rainbow over his office window. He believed it to be a message from God that he should write about his life, and that God's promise to him was that he would complete his story virtually pain-free, despite his doctors' prognosis of an early and painful death.

Wedding picture of Ruth and Vernon

The wedding picture symbolizes the love of Vernon's life for over fifty-eight years.

Gifted the power of the Holy Spirit to heal himself and others

Many cultures believe that, to become a healer, a medicine woman or man, a shaman, or a kahuna, one must heal himself first, as Vernon healed himself on January 22, 1990. The Holy Spirit gifted him with this power, and hundreds of people, with various maladies, have been sent to him for healing.

The crystal bowl in the picture was bequeathed to Vernon and Ruth from their special friend of forty-two-years, Linda Neider, who died on Christmas Eve 2002. Vernon believes that the crystal bowl revitalizes every cell in the human body, which speeds healing, and he employs it often with his patients.

DEDICATION

TO MY WIFE, RUTH, WITH WHOM I FELL IN LOVE THE MOMENT WE FIRST MET, IN MARCH OF 1956, AND WHOM I HAVE CONTINUED TO LOVE FOR THE FIFTY-EIGHT YEARS OF OUR MARRIAGE.

Acknowledgments

Ruth Bowlby, for her patience, understanding and advice during this book writing process and journey.

Rebecca Friesen, who spent three days in August 1997, typing the story of Vernon's life journey of sixty-six years.

Maia Fischler, who organized hundreds of pages of notes and stories into a readable form.

Jennifer Richter, who gave strong moral support as well as technical assistance and gave key suggestions.

Irene Gresick, who has contributed keen insights to the book production.

Cindy Yonck, who contributed her amazing gifts and moral support.

Edith Bowlby, who helped with pictures and other support.

Sherry Kilpatrick, who assisted in editing and helped resolve computer problems.

My granddaughters, **Kimberly, Jennifer, Elise, Angie and Danielle,** and my grandson, **Andrew Wilson**, who assisted in the production of the book in many different ways.

Susan Hayes, who provided computer assistance and support at just the right time.

Betty Thompson, who was happy to employ her English degree for my project, and Doug Thompson, who helped with his wife's computer problems and in other ways.

Nancy K. Bowlby Magee Boatwright, who came on board to provide invaluable computer and secretarial services to conclude the book.

Mike Magee, who worked till midnight improving the cover photos.

Jeff Winders, who provided picture changing skills of photos.

Taylor Huck, who contributed the picture of **Andrew** and myself.

Jeff Weger, who brought a photo to useable condition.

Patrick Magee, who, with relentless Spirit, gave assistance from beginning to end and enlisted his wife, **Lani Magee**, to "pinch hit" when needed into the wee hours of the morning.

Foreword

My story could not be told without relating the countless miracles that have spared my life at every turn, and it has been my life-long search to understand what has made so many amazing miracles possible.

Describing the journey that led to this moment is like standing at the peak of Mt. Hood after a long arduous climb, looking back at the past through its many steps, twists, and turns. The struggles along the way enrich the appreciation of the view from the top.

It is my hope that, by reading my story, you will better understand the view from the top of a journey that has lasted for over eighty years.

The beauty and the wonder are in the eye of the beholder, and the journey has changed me into one who can appreciate the miracle of the view.

Many things that occurred in my life are, quite frankly, hard to believe. They become believable only when we realize that Saint Michael has made me the conduit of his unlimited power to protect unknown people from death, to heal people whom he has selected at his direction, to suspend gravity as needed, and to carry out a master plan for every phase of my life's journey.

The key to the success of my journey has been the faith with which I have obeyed Saint Michael's messages, instantly as they were received.

My hope is also that my journey will help you to realize that you can call upon the power of Saint Michael at any time, and he will respond. The bottom line is: why not have Saint Michael on your side?

Why struggle through life, going into one dead end after another, when you can surrender yourself to the guidance of God's master messenger, Saint Michael?

My Life's Messenger, Saint Michael

Archangel Michael played a key role in my life, so it is imperative that one have some background on his role in God's work. Archangel Michael is the only angel mentioned by name in all three of the major sacred texts of the world's religions that place the most emphasis on angels, including the Bible, (Christianity), Torah, (Jewish), and the

Qur'an (Islam). In all these faiths, believers consider Michael to be a leading angel who fights evil with the power of good.

Michael brings us, directly, the Creator's pure messages of love, wisdom, and power. The books of Daniel and Revelations describe how Michael provides protection during times of trouble.

Michael does not want to be worshipped. He gives all the glory to God, and does not need our prayers. He is, instead, an intercessor between the Creator and the created. We can call upon him without praying to him, which is a subtle but important distinction. You can ask Michael for a comforting message simply by thinking or speaking your request.

He loves all people unconditionally, just as God does. Yet as powerful as he is, Michael is only allowed to intervene in your life if you give him permission, since he cannot violate your free will. He does need you to ask for help before he can offer it. The only exception to the free will that angels must obey is that, when people are about to be killed before it is their time, God and the angels can intervene and save a life, without someone's permission. Sometimes, they do it directly, and at other times, they give the person divine guidance to follow.

From an early age, I believed that I received messages of guidance from Michael, and I responded dutifully with whatever request Michael made to me, as his voice was perfectly loud and clear. We became like partners as Michael gave me the messages and I obeyed him.

Michael, like other angels who do not have physical bodies, is completely unaffected by gravity, time, and other aspects of physics. He can move instantly, from point A to point B, like an automobile, as he performs his magic when it is necessary in order to save lives. Michael's miraculous strength and gravity-defying powers may also protect us by blocking the source of our fear.

Michael watches over everyone on the entire planet, at the same time, and when requested, he can always provide individual attention. Michael is an exceptionally strong angel who protects and defends people who love God. He is concerned about truth and justice. Believers say that Michael communicates boldly with people, whom he helps and guides.

The Bible describes Michael in Revelation 12:7-12: he leads armies of angels, who battle Satan and his demons during the world's last conflict. Michael and the angelic troops emerge victorious, says the Bible, which also states, in 1 Thessalonians 4:16, that Michael will accompany Jesus Christ when he returns to Earth. The Qur'an warns, in Al-Baqara 2:98: "Whoever is an enemy to God and his angels and his apostles, to Gabriel and Michael -- lo! God is an enemy to those who reject the faith."

Muslims believe that God has assigned Michael to reward righteous people for the good they do during their Earthly lifetimes.

In Catholic tradition, Michael also escorts people's souls to heaven after they die. The Seventh-day Adventist and Jehovah's Witness churches believe that Jesus Christ was the Archangel Michael before he came to Earth. The Church of Jesus Christ of Latter-day Saints believes that Michael is now the heavenly form of Adam, the first human created.

(It is interesting to note that my first great-grandson, born since I was diagnosed with stage 4 cancer and incurable, was named Adam, without my input.)

Constantine's Connection to Saint Michael

The **Michaelion** was one of the earliest and most famous sanctuaries dedicated to Archangel Michael in the ancient and medieval Near East. According to tradition, it was built in the 4th century by Emperor Constantine the Great (306-337 A.D.) over an ancient pagan temple, and was located just north of Constantinople in the village of Sosthenion, modern İstinye.

The pagan temple which had existed there had been previously associated with healing and medicine, and the Christian tradition continued to associate the location and the Michaelion with healing waters.

Michaelion was a magnificent church and became a model for hundreds of other churches in Eastern Christianity.

According to a widespread tradition, current already since the 6th century, the Church of Saint Michael at Sosthenion was founded by Constantine the Great, who visited the temple, erected by the Argonauts and dedicated to Zeus Sosthenios or a winged deity. Constantine interpreted the winged statue of the temple as a Christian angel. After sleeping the night in the temple, Constantine reported a vision that the angel was the Archangel Michael, and converted the building into a church to honor him.

Spirit Meaning

The term Spirit as used in this book means direct Communication from heavenly sources including God, The Holy Spirit, or Holy Ghost, the third person of the Divine Trinity as manifested as Father, Son, or Holy Ghost. Archangel, which means in Greek, "The Greatest messenger of God, and such special powers vested in Saint Michael from God that includes the power to heal, the power to suspend gravity, and the power to protect people from harm."

The Holy Spirit has the power to bestow nine special gifts upon whomever is Divinely designated.

Saint Michael has the power to dispense his special gifts upon whomever he is directed from God.

The term "near-death experience" includes an experience where one came within seconds of dying but survived to live another day.

Names of persons in testimonials and healing stories in this book have been changed to protect their privacy, except for those who have given permission to include their names.

CONTENTS

Part 1: Roots and Influences

Looking back at my family's history, it is clear that divine Providence, combined with strength of character, has steered our paths for many generations. My father's heritage has been traced to John Alden and Priscilla Mullins, two of the best-known passengers on the Mayflower's crossing from England to Plymouth Rock.

My mother's family, the Piatts, settled in New Jersey, and with its roots in the earliest days of America, it had ancestors who fought with General George Washington.

My father's family, the Bowlbys, arrived in New Jersey in 1727, about the same time, and in the same place, as the Piatts.

In 1727, Thomas Bowlby waved goodbye on the docks of London, to seven of his children and his wife, Martha Barker Bowlby, whose father, Samuel Barker, had died in New Jersey with an estate. Thomas left on a journey to New Jersey with his three oldest sons to establish a home for the entire family. Thomas died before the home was complete and never saw his family again. Martha Barker Bowlby is the source of about ninety percent of all Bowlbys in the United States and Canada.

Martha Barker Bowlby Painted at Age 13 in 1684

Wayne Bowlby of San Diego, California contributed the following poem.

1727 - Our Bowlby Forefathers Come to America

After Grandpa Samuel Barker's will was read
Thomas gathered his family around and said
My time has come to sail to the New Jersey shore
Taking George, John, and Richard, but no more.
So they arranged to sail off one fine English day
Filled with excitement, yet some fear and dismay
Anxious to see their new American homeland
While aware they might never return to England
After tearful goodbyes to family and close friends
Began a voyage that seemed it would never end
But after at least six long weeks on the Atlantic sea
They finally arrived on the shores of New Jersey
After welcomed baths, clean clothes, and fresh food
A long rest gave each of them a rejuvenated mood
Then traveling by coach over miles of new land
They arrived at Burlington, West Jersey, as planned
Thomas Bowlby lived only three or four more years
Which surely brought his three young sons tears
But from Burlington the three eventually did leave
Settling farther north on lands they each had received

My life has been strongly influenced by those who came before me. I would like to introduce my family and to describe the events that led the Bowlbys to Oregon.

The Vision of Life in the Hood River Valley in Oregon

My family's history begins in Oregon, when my grandfather, Frank J. Simpson, nineteen years old, first viewed the spectacular Hood River Valley, anchored by 11,245 foot majestic Mt. Hood on the south and 12,500 foot Mt. Adams on the north, the surrounding mountain vistas, and the mighty Columbia River, which runs through the northern edge of the little town, Hood River.

He envisioned that one day he would marry, have children, and bring his family to the Hood River Valley to raise. He had grown up in

Michigan, and when he finished high school in 1900, he and two friends decided to explore the west for six months. They worked their way across the country until they arrived in Hood River. When Frank Simpson experienced the beauty of the valley, he said, "I want to inhale the beauty of this place with my family until my dying day." Frank Simpson married Lottie Mae Piatt in Cooperstown, North Dakota on January 25, 1903. Frank and Lottie built a house on the Sheyenne River in North Dakota, on the 640 acres that Lottie Mae's father and mother, Charles Carroll and Charlotte Piatt, had homesteaded in 1881.

Lottie Mae and Frank Simpson, January 1903, Cassopolis, Michigan

Their first four daughters, Olive Grace, Allene Beth, Madge Irene, and Pauline Carol, were born in that home. A fifth daughter, Kathryn Blanche, was born while the family lived in Mishawaka, Indiana. Kathryn's birth was very difficult for Lottie Mae, and Frank was bedfast from an illness at the time, so Frank's sister, Blanche Doane, raised Kathryn. She also raised another child, Bruce, whose mother (Frank's sister-in-law) had died in childbirth. That was a fairly common practice within the families of those times. My grandfather was born at the perfect time in history for him, when inventions were changing people's lives at an amazing rate, and the possibilities were wide open for inquisitive men like him. Cities were beginning to get electrical service, but, at the turn of the century, most rural areas, including the farm community of Cooperstown, North Dakota, were still using candles and kerosene.

Grandpa Simpson's 1910 car in front of home he built in 1903 in Cooperstown, North Dakota, where his first four daughters were born.

My grandfather and his wife's father, CC Piatt as he was known, and brother-in-law, Chester, decided to build a power plant. The company was named the Piatt, Piatt, and Simpson Power & Electric Company. Frank sent away for plans and parts, including the enormous gasoline - powered flywheels that would produce the electrically powered energy. The site was in the middle of town, and Frank knew that it could be dangerous to the surrounding homes if there was an explosion. As a safety precaution, he built the plant about eight feet below ground level. Once the plant was operational, he installed power poles, wired the town and charged people to provide electricity to their homes and farms. Gasoline to run the plant was shipped in on riverboats from refineries in the south, and eventually trucked to town.

My grandfather always looked for a new challenge. In 1903, his brother-in-law, Chester Piatt, acquired the first auto dealership in Cooperstown, when cars were first becoming available, and Frank became a car salesman for the new business. At the dawn of the radio age, Frank bought a kit to build a radio receiver, and he received the first radio broadcast from Chicago. Eager to see new places, he moved his family to Mishawaka, Indiana, St. Paul, Minnesota, New York City, and Three Rivers, Michigan. In St. Paul and New York, Frank worked as a policeman, and tinkered with inventions in his spare time.

My mother related to me later that, while in New York City, she and her sisters loved to explore Central Park. On June 24, 2014, my twenty-seven-year-old granddaughter, Kimberly, flew from Oregon to New York City to seek her future as a Broadway performer, one hundred years after my mother lived there. Kimberly enjoys the solace of Central Park, as did my mother!

The family moved to Michigan, and in 1925, Frank decided that it was time to move the family to Oregon. His vision of the Hood River Valley had remained with him for twenty-five years, and he wanted to share it with his wife and daughters. Frank designed and constructed a "house-car." Built on a flatbed truck, with windows, a toilet, kitchen, and sleeping bunks, it was the forerunner of today's RV.

Simpson Family with House Car

The trip took sixty days, via great-grandfather's farm in North Dakota, as help was needed with the harvest. Next, there was a trip south to Colorado, to visit the site where my great-grandfather, CC Piatt, in 1868, fought in a famous Indian battle, known as The Battle of Beecher Island.

A difficult decision had to be made as to whether Kathryn, then fourteen years old, should join the family for the great trip west. At the last minute, it was decided that she should stay with her aunt Blanche, who had raised her from infancy. The separation was traumatic for everyone, and the entire family felt the burden for the rest of their lives. At age sixteen, Kathryn married a very nice man, and together they raised five children. She died from Alzheimer's disease, at age sixty-two.

As the house-car took shape and the trip planning began in earnest, three of the daughters had boyfriends that they did not want to leave, so it was decided that the three boyfriends would join the family on the trip, along with a touring car owned by Dan, one of the boyfriends. The family left Michigan on June 25, 1925 and arrived in Hood River August 25, 1925. Some of the family slept in the house-car, while others slept in tents. My mother's sister, Olive, maintained a daily detailed diary, and she described lots of breaks for ice cream, and sometimes dances in the auto parks. It was a grand adventure posing many challenges, such as having to deal with muddy roads and bridge washouts.

When the travelers finally arrived in Hood River to buy gas, one of my mother's sisters, Allene, fell in love with the gas station attendant. Her boyfriend Dan knew immediately that he had lost her. The next day Dan headed back to Michigan in his touring auto, which unfortunately broke down in The Dalles, twenty-five miles from Hood River. (Dan was right: Aunt Allene and the gas station attendant, my uncle Ted, had been married for sixty-three years when Ted passed away!) The next day, another boyfriend, Don, began hitchhiking to Michigan. Dan's auto was repaired, and in southern Idaho, Dan observed Don hitchhiking and gave him a ride.

Fifty years later, my dad and I returned to Michigan to visit relatives, Dad met Dan in the front yard of his brother's home, and they shook hands for the first time in fifty years.

My parents were married eighteen days after their arrival in Oregon, September 12, 1925.

My grandfather got a job with the Pacific Power and Light Company. His primary duty was to drive around Eastern Oregon in a car with aerials on top, sensing where the power leaked, so that repairmen could shore them up.

Meanwhile, my grandfather, Frank, explored new hobbies and areas of interest. He raised turkeys at his yard in Hood River, and he strove toward the goal of a forty-pounder. (The largest turkey that he ever raised weighed thirty-nine pounds.) For every Thanksgiving and Christmas, my grandparents invited their four daughters, with their husbands and children eventually totaling twenty-five for dinner.

When he was fifty-seven years old, Frank decided to learn to fly, so he journeyed about seventy-five miles west of Hood River to Vancouver, Washington, where he learned to fly solo. He flew over the Hood River Valley and Mt. Hood, seeing the vistas from a different perspective, and his ability to fly a plane enabled him to aid in searches for people lost in the woods and mountains.

Frank also pursued photography. If he were alive today, he would be a computer wizard. He loved to explore everything new and he challenged himself to understand how things worked.

All his life, my grandfather dreamed of becoming a doctor. In those days, the vast majority of doctors were self-taught; and in 1910, about ten percent had formal medical training. In Hood River, Frank bought the medical library of a doctor who had died, and he studied extensively about the human body, including drugs that were available by mail order. Frank became a passionate mountain climber, and he became the first-aid man for the Crag Rats, the original mountain search-and-rescue group in the United States. That group still thrives, nearly ninety years later. At age sixty-eight, Frank still pursued his love of healing. His last job was with the Buck Ambulance Company in Gresham, Oregon where he was a medical emergency assistant in ambulance runs.

Craig Rats Climbing Mount Hood, July 1929. Taking rope to the top for annual Legion Climb involving hundreds of climbers.

To become a Crag Rat, one had to climb a certain number of the snowcapped peaks in the Cascades. Frank, aged forty-five, wanted to become an immediate member of the Crag Rats. Frank, and two fellow

Crag Rats, Mace Baldwin and Kent Shoemaker, planned a sixteen-day trip, and to achieve their goals, they enlisted the help of their intrepid wives.

The trip started at the southern side of the South Sister. Their wives deposited them, and then drove on to the north side of the North Sister to wait. When the men arrived at the appointed location north of the north sister, their wives had dinner waiting. In four days, the three men had climbed the South, the Middle, and the North Sister, all in excess of ten thousand feet, including many miles between the mountains.

The next day involved a climb of the 10,500 foot Mt. Jefferson with its pinnacle of class four and five rock. The women drove to Mt. St. Helens, while the men slept. Fifty-two years later, in 1980, the mountain erupted with the force of five hundred Hiroshimas. The top thirteen hundred feet of the mountain exploded into the sky with hurricane force, a wave of scalding gases and fire-hot debris traveling at two hundred miles an hour.

The three men then climbed the 14,411 foot Mt. Rainier, a two-day climb. They then headed toward home, and climbed the 12,500 foot Mt. Adams in Washington, which is across the Columbia River to the north of the Hood River Valley.

Starting after work on a Friday night, these three men had climbed seven mountains in sixteen days, plus their travel time between the mountains, and they were back to work the following Monday morning. It must have taken careful planning to arrange for the food and hike icy mountain slopes that they had never climbed before. Their wives' contribution was almost as outstanding as had been their husbands'. The women had traveled on many rut-filled roads, and most faithfully, were ready with food and rest, and met the hikers at the prearranged locations.

Frank's work with the Crag Rats kept him very busy and, over the years, he climbed Mt. Hood sixty-five times, most of them after he was fifty years old. In one incident, he helped rescue nine people, who, roped together, had fallen into a crevasse. The other Crag Rats had lowered him into the crevasse, and there he set bones, cleaned wounds, and doctored everyone. Only one person died, a man who had been impaled by his ice-ax. Frank was also a mountain guide, and on a weekend, he was involved in taking several hundred people to the top of Mt. Hood.

For those times, my grandparents were considered quite prosperous, as my grandfather had a well-paid job with the Pacific Power & Light Company. They bought a new car every year, and enjoyed vacations at the coast and many other places.

My grandparents owned about ten acres of land, including a pie cherry orchard and a very large barn, whose second story was somewhat finished. Whenever we went to visit them, Grandfather always had something fun for us to do. One favorite activity was to pick pie cherries from the trees and throw them, one-by-one, to about a dozen 150-pound hogs. The hogs squealed and ran as fast as they could to chase down a single cherry. We almost died laughing as they came back to beg for more cherries.

Every year my grandfather had a huge lighted Christmas display, complete with a very large Christmas tree, which was a rare treat in those depression years. Santa and the reindeer were on the roof, and there were lights all over the property. To see this Christmas display, people drove there and lined up for long distances.

When golf became my grandparents' favorite sport, they sold the property. My grandfather built a golf course with five greens around their new home. I had the privilege of mowing this lawn on the riding lawn mower my grandfather had built, and then I played a round of golf with my grandparents. We played five holes forward, and then played four holes backward, in order to play nine holes. Those were, indeed, fun times!

My grandmother was very spunky and she wanted to do anything my grandfather did. Although she may have climbed a couple of mountains, in that realm, she focused primarily on making sure that my grandfather had everything he needed. She was often involved in searches and other kinds of rescues in the area. Once, a Boy Scout was missing at Eagle Creek and after everyone had given up the search, my grandparents went back to the area. My grandmother spotted him in the depths of the Eagle Creek punch bowl, which became one of the most photographed falls in Oregon.

During the time that my grandfather was a policeman in St. Paul, there was a rapist in the area, and my grandfather used my grandmother as a decoy. She walked in certain places while my grandfather followed at a distance in order to guard her. What a courageous lady! (It was probably a good thing that the rapist never showed up.)

Grandmother was an excellent golfer and she often played with her best friend, Frieda Adams. Once, the two of them played in a tournament and, at the end of two days, they were tied for the club championship. The last hole was one of about 350 yards. Frieda shot first, and then she hit a second shot within a foot of the hole, for a sure birdie and, most likely, the win. A large crowd had gathered around the green, my grandmother's shot went into the hole for an eagle, and she won the match. The crowd went wild in disbelief of what they had seen.

I also have clear memories of my great-grandmother, Charlotte Millard Piatt, who died when I was nine years old. At the end of her life, she lived with my grandparents, and she was a strong character in her own right. She grew up at the time of the Indian Wars, during the Civil War, and as a young woman in frontier Kansas, she must have had some exciting times.

In 1872, Charlotte and my great-grandfather, Charles Carroll, were married in Lecompton, Kansas. She bore five children, two of whom died, before they moved to a homestead in North Dakota in 1882. Seven more children were born there, five of whom lived to adulthood. Great-grandmother was a very strong-willed woman, and family lore has it that, when she boarded the train to move to Oregon, she took her rocking chair with her into the passenger car. The conductor told her that it was not allowed, but, she caused such an ado that he let her keep it. When she alit from the train, her rocking chair came off first.

Vern and Madge Bowlby Set Up Housekeeping

After my parents married on September 12, 1925, they lived in a farm tenant house where my father worked in the apple orchard near Odell, in the center of the Hood River Valley.

My mother was pregnant and in those days, most babies were born at home. My mother chose to give birth in my grandparents' home, near Hood River on Alameda Way, and it proved to be a very difficult labor. After many hours, the doctor in attendance announced that with the current situation, he could not deliver the baby alive.

To save my mother's life, he asked permission to crush the baby's skull, rather than to risk losing both of them. It was a difficult decision and my father and grandparents opposed the idea. My grandfather then recalled that there was a local doctor who specialized in difficult births, and he was called. Dr. Chick arrived and delivered my brother in about five minutes, just twelve days before my parent's first anniversary! When the newborn was weighed, it became clear that the birth was difficult because Wayne Frank Bowlby weighed almost twelve pounds! Coincidentally, twenty years later, Wayne began married life with his bride, Evelyn, in a converted garage next to the home where he had been born.

Vern and Madge Bowlby

Four years after Wayne's birth, my dad was unemployed, and a job was needed to support his family, including Lillian, who was twenty-two-months-old. My parents must have been excited when they received a letter from my father's brother in Michigan, which said that my father could have a job where he worked in a machine shop in Three Rivers, Michigan.

My parents borrowed money from my grandparents, who grieved about losing their daughter and two grandchildren for an indefinite period of time, with the probability that it would be permanent.

In October 1930, with sixty dollars in cash, my parents commenced the 2,200 mile journey in a 1920, two-seater vehicle, and drove on many miles of unimproved roads from Hood River, Oregon to Michigan, their car loaded with luggage. The travelers were my mother, four months pregnant with me, my sister Lillian - a toddler who sat on me all the way to Michigan, and my four-year-old brother Wayne, who lay across the back window ledge.

My grandparents, Frank and Lottie Simpson, must have been devastated with the decision of their daughter and their son-in-law to return to Michigan. My parents lived next door to my grandparents, where Lillian was born. My grandparents dearly loved my brother,

Wayne, their first grandson, whom they had nurtured from the time of his dramatic birth a little over four years before.

My parents must have been bitterly disappointed after they had traveled two thousand two hundred miles to my dad's new job in Michigan to find when they arrived that the machine shop had closed and there was no job for my father!

My great grandmother, Lilla Bell Johnson Blanchard, seventy years old, lived on a small farm on the edge of town in Constantine, about twenty miles south of Three Rivers, Michigan. Lilla Bell was the mother of my grandmother, Flora Arbell Blanchard, who died in 1920. Lilla Bell's husband, my great grandfather, Henry Alden Blanchard, died in 1909.

My dad exchanged his work for the rent on a small farm in Constantine, where I was born on March 26, 1931. My mother told me the doctor charged thirty dollars to deliver me, but they never had the money to pay him.

When they arrived, my father's first paid job was to drive a school bus for forty dollars a month.

I now have evidence that the farm may have been owned by my great-grandmother, Lilla Bell, and that the home where I was born may have been the same home where my grandmother, Flora Arbell Blanchard, was born on September 9, 1878, over fifty-two years before, and that it might well be the same farm where my Father, Galen Lavern Bowlby, was born on November 3, 1903.

In May 1932, when I was fourteen months old, my parents decided to return to Oregon, probably with another loan from my grandparents. My mother was to rejoin her parents, three sisters, and their families, from whom they had parted over a year previously. In Michigan, they left behind my grandfather, Claude Curtis Bowlby, and his second wife, whom they would never see again.

Also left behind were my father's two brothers, Forrest and Hiram Bowlby and families, my great-grandmother, Lilla Bell Blanchard, my mother's sister, Katherine, and her family, as well as many other relatives from all sides of the family.

My maternal grandmother, Flora Arbell Blanchard, the daughter of my great-grandfather, Henry Alden Blanchard, was a descendent of John and Priscilla Alden. Flora died in 1920, along with her daughter, Lillian, my father's sister, at age twenty-one, in the Spanish flu pandemic which killed an estimated 50,000,000 to 100,000,000 people around the world, and which infected 500,000,000 people.

When our family returned to Hood River and my grandfather first viewed me, he said I had explosive energy. He named me, Dynamite, which became the only name he ever called me.

We moved into a rental home on fourteenth street on the heights, next door to the Earl and Mary Minor family, who had a two-month-old son, Dick. When they played cards, our parents put us into a crib together. He became my life-long best friend and we are still best friends more than eighty years later.

In the summer of 1933, when I was a little over two years old, the Bowlby family moved to 810 June Street, in Hood River, our home for the next two years. A block west was the home where Lillian was born, next door to my grandparents, who lived on May Street. Eight years later, our home was a block south, at 915 Pine Street. All these homes were across the street from the then junior high school, which all the Bowlby children would attend.

My earliest childhood memories on June Street, and the names of my neighbors and playmates, are locked in my mind to this day! Next door was the Clark family, four boys and one girl, and next door to them was Lee Nance, who became a regular playmate. The Sheldrake family was across the street. One block away was the Christian Missionary Alliance Church, where I became a Christian when I was twelve. Across the street was the garage where I met one of the greatest companions of my life, my dog, Buster.

Wood was our source of heat in this home, and my mother cooked on a wood stove. When I was three, I loved to help my dad stack the huge loads of wood that were dumped in the front yard. By the time I was four, my father relinquished all responsibility for stacking the wood, as he knew that I derived great pleasure from the job. This early adventure in organizing scattered loads of wood into their logical sequence must have been an early indication that, one day, the accounting profession would become my life's endeavor.

A Boy's Best Friend

During those financially difficult times, people explored ways to earn money in any way they could. Our neighbor across the street decided to earn money by raising collies and he sold puppies for profit. This breed of dog was in much demand at the time. At great cost, he had acquired a purebred female collie and we shared in his excitement as we anticipated the birth of the puppies.

One evening, my father and I noticed great activity in the neighbor's garage, and we scurried across the street to watch as, one by one, nine perfect collies were born. Half an hour after the last puppy was born, the mother began to convulse. Suddenly, she gave birth to a tiny puppy that looked entirely different from the other nine.

The neighbor decided to kill this runt, rather than to jeopardize the profits to be made from his nine purebred puppies. I was horrified and Dad asked if we might take the runt. The neighbor agreed, reluctantly, based upon my father's promise that we would never tell prospective buyers that this puppy had come from the same litter as the others. I was in heaven as we carried the puppy home, and we were up most of the night feeding him milk with an eye dropper.

I named the puppy, Buster. He grew into a beautiful smooth collie. Buster became a huge part of my life, always right at my heels. He taught me many human traits such as bravery, fearlessness, devotion and, most of all, love.

Buster was always ready to protect me, no matter how big the threat. He considered that any dog that came into our presence must be a threat, and his hair rose straight up, and his lips pulled back in a loud snarl. Otherwise, he was a very happy, friendly dog.

Buster stayed when he was told to, but he liked to sit on the porch, and then, when I called him, he raced to meet me.

In 1936, when the Hood River movie theater showed *The Trail of the Lonesome Pine*, the first movie in color, Wayne, Lillian and I walked downtown to see it. In those days, a movie cost ten cents, and with cartoons and newsreels, the movie lasted for hours. The route home was totally dark once we left the city where there were no streetlights. When we reached the gravel pit, about half a mile from our home, we yelled "Bitta-Boy!" Buster heard our call and, in total darkness, he ran like a race dog to meet us, expressing his great joy.

Buster had an amazing internal clock. When we moved to 915 Pine Street, we were across the street from the athletic fields of the junior high. Every day, at exactly 11:45 AM, Buster sat up and walked to the door, with my brother's dog, Blackie, behind him. My mother let them out the door, and they trotted the five hundred yards or so to the school, where they sat, side by side, and waited for me to appear. When I came out the door for lunch at 11:55 AM, the two dogs jumped for joy at seeing me. The other kids could not believe it.

Buster ate store-bought food one time only in his entire lifetime. There was a fire at the Safeway store, and my sister, who worked there at the time, brought home many scorched boxes of dog kibble. Buster's regular food was chicken bones, along with other table scraps. Now, veterinarians advise you not to give dogs chicken bones, but, Buster must have eaten the bones of thousands of chickens. Buster was never sick, and he never saw a veterinarian or received any shots.

Buster lived to the ripe old age of seventeen and died on May 22, 1951, the same day that my grandmother Simpson died. Two weeks later, the Korean War raged and I left home to begin training with the United States Army. Throughout my childhood, Buster was a great companion.

Near-Death on the Columbia River

On July 4, 1935, my family joined over a hundred others for a picnic at Koberg Beach on the Columbia River. I was four years old and thrilled to be at such a festive occasion. There were lots of contests and games, and I enjoyed watching them with my parents. After a while, with the crowd focused on a contest of women hammering large spikes into 4x8 timbers, I began looking around for something more exciting to do.

Buster was with me and the two of us wandered down the sandy beach to the river. A two-foot wide float, made of chained-together logs, enclosed the swimming area. Unobserved by any adults, Buster and I walked along the wet logs until we got to the end of the float, which was in one of the main channels of the Columbia River. Suddenly, I slipped on a wet log and fell into the deep river.

Buster dove in after me. I was a non-swimmer and I was sinking fast. Buster finally caught up with me and clenched his teeth on my ankle. I can still vividly recall the entire scene: the pain of Buster's teeth while he was dragging me to the surface, the feel of the current pulling me away from him, sunlight beaming through ten or fifteen feet of water, and my short life flashing through my mind.

By chance or Divine Providence, a man saw Buster jump into the river and surmised that I had fallen in. He yelled to my dad, who was a superb swimmer. He raced to the beach and dove in to find me, catching up with Buster and me downstream. Buster was doing his best to pull me toward shore, but I was on my back and taking in a lot of water. Dad helped keep my head above water. Together, he and Buster overcame the current and got me to shore. A crowd had gathered as my dad pressed the water from my lungs. A short time later, I was on my feet.

Buster taught me many facets of character in his seventeen years of life. He was loyal and fearless, and without hesitation, would risk his own life to protect me. I have always had an intense love of animals. In my childhood, Buster was clearly my live Angel of Protection and he was aided by Saint Michael, who intervened when Buster and I disappeared into the Columbia River.

Near-Death at a Gravel Pit

A second time Buster rescued me from nearly sure death was when I fell into a murky pond in the gravel pit. I was nine years old and I had not yet learned to swim. As I waded in the muddy pond alone, I stepped into a deep gravel trench and sank into fifteen feet of water. My lungs filled with water and, again, my life flashed like a movie through my head. Buster caught my heel and dragged me some thirty feet to the shore. I lay there coughing out water, as my body was wracked with spasms. The runt whose life I had saved six years before had repaid me.

The Bowlby Family Homestead

In 1934, with a job on the Bonneville Dam and with three children, my parents were ready for their own home. They purchased three acres of land which bordered a gravel pit to the west of Hood River, at a price of nine hundred dollars. The terms were ten dollars down and ten dollars a month, with an annual interest rate of one percent. That was quite reasonable for the times, when a man thought that he did well if he earned a few dollars a day.

If measured against today's standards, the house that my father built on that property would have been condemned before occupancy. There were no interior walls - just 2x4s. The exterior wall was lumber, which lapped one board over another, with no siding. There was no insulation anywhere in the entire structure. Our water came from a tap one hundred feet away and a privy in the yard served as our toilet. Kerosene lamps provided light and there were none of the electrical appliances that we now consider essential. We lived in that home for eight years. We had two stoves, one to cook on, and one to heat the entire house. There was so much love within those walls that it never occurred to me that we were poor.

I was four years old when we moved in and I joined my older brother, Wayne, and my sister, Lillian, in doing daily chores. We were responsible for getting water to the house, carrying it in a bucket, and placing it on the kitchen counter, where we could use a dipper to drink. After two years, around the same time that we got electricity, my father dug the trenches for the pipes necessary to bring water into the house from the street.

We had the outdoor privy until we moved into town when I was twelve. My father could never have guessed, when he dug the hole and built the privy, that, seven years later, it contributed to the war effort. One day, an army of over a thousand soldiers appeared suddenly and set up camp on the neighboring acreage as well as on our property. The first thing that the soldiers did was to dig deep, narrow trenches, place a wall of tenting around the spot, and that became their toilet (which required spread-eagling across the ditch.)

At once, our privy became the one of choice and, to use it, the men queued up in a line over a hundred feet long. Whenever we needed the privy, the men, most graciously, allowed us to go to the head of the line. We were proud when our privy became famous! After the Army departed, my father dug another hole and moved the privy to a new location.

Bathing involved heating water on the wood stove and filling a galvanized thirty-inch tub. The kitchen was our bath area and it was off limits when anyone bathed. The wood stove was also used for cooking and, in the summer, my mother used it to can about six hundred quarts of fruits and vegetables.

We three children brought in wood for the wood stove and for the kitchen stove, the warm heart of our home in all seasons. Winter is harsh in the Columbia Gorge and when the wood burned out at night, the indoor temperature could drop below zero.

For the eight years that we lived in this house, I had all rights to stack the huge piles of wood, as had been established when we lived on June Street. To stack the wood was a very important part of my childhood. When my parents told me that a load of wood was to arrive, I was excited, and I could scarcely wait until I could get my hands on it. I loved the smell of the wood. I organized the piles of wood into stacked tunnels and hideaways, including steps within the pile and a lookout on the top. I did not arrange the wood in the same way twice.

Before I began to stack the wood, I sat and envisioned what I wanted to build, which included bracing the wood so that it would not cave in on me. Over the years, my brother, Wayne, five years older than I, must have been very happy that my enthusiasm for stacking mountains of wood eliminated any need for him to be involved with that chore.

Wayne, Lillian and I shared a bed in the upper part of the house, which we reached by climbing up a 2 X 4 ladder.

One of my fondest memories was that, every night after the lights were out, my brother, Wayne, told me endless stories about Jocko, an imaginary monkey. I listened to these stories until I was fast asleep and I never heard the end of a single story.

My brother, Bob, was born in 1936, and when he became a toddler, my father lifted him up the ladder to his big brother, Wayne, who hoisted him into the upstairs. Bob was handed down the same way. To stay warm in the winter, we huddled together under eight inches of blankets.

Nancy, Wayne, Lillian, Bob, Vernon and Buster, July, 1939.

My mother let me give birthday party invitations to all my grade school friends, which always included Donna Koberg and her best friend, Helen Ridgley. When I was six years old, I fell madly in love with Helen the first time I saw her with her long black hair. I never again felt such love for anyone, until I met Ruth, nineteen years later, when I was twenty-five and Ruth was seventeen and a senior in high school. (I was shocked when I received the newsletter for our thirty-fifth high school reunion and discovered that Helen had died of an illness at age fifty-two.)

On more than one occasion, when children attended my birthday party, and on other occasions, too, my grandmother Simpson appeared suddenly, colorfully dressed as an old woman, and toe-danced and sang Old Pompeii died and laid in his grave. All the children were eager to return the following year, as most of them had never seen anyone dance or sing with such vigor and flair as she had.

After all these years, my grandmother's singing at all our birthday parties still reverberates in my head, as it does for my sister, Lillian.

Grandmother Simpson sang and danced this song two times, and the children laughed non-stop the entire time. Those were happy times, indeed.

One my favorite childhood memories is my being allowed to play barefoot. Our shoes came off as soon as school was over for the summer. On a sunny afternoon, with a picnic lunch in my wagon and Buster at my side, I wandered in the acres of tall grass, taller than I was, we lay on a blanket and I dreamed of the future. I remember looking up thinking that, somehow, the whole world revolved around me. I think of it now as the development of self-love: such an important concept! If you are to share love with others, you must first have self-love.

As I watched clouds float across the blue sky, I thought deep thoughts of love, and Buster was the perfect companion for a lazy afternoon in the sun. Snow-covered 12,500 foot Mt. Adams towered to the north; the Columbia River appeared to be at the mountain's feet; timber-covered mountain vistas appeared in all directions.

I still remember how excited we were, about 1939, when modern communications began and our first telephone, number 5807, was installed. Eight families shared the party line and they could listen in on one another's conversations!

Lyrics from Old Pompeii Folk Song

Old Pompeii was dead and he lay in his grave
Lay in his grave, lay in his grave.
Old Pompeii was dead and he lay in his grave,
Oh, ho, ho.

There grew an old apple tree over his head
Over his head, over his head.
There grew an old apple tree over his head,
Oh, ho, ho.

The apples got ripe and begun to fall
Begun to fall, begun to fall.
The apples got ripe and begun to fall,
Oh, ho, ho.

There came an old woman a-picking 'em up
Picking them up, picking them up.
There came an old woman a-picking 'em up,
Oh, ho, ho.

Old Pompeii got up and he gave her a pop
Gave her a pop, gave her a pop.
Old Pompeii got up and he gave her a pop,
Oh, ho, ho.

And made the old woman go hippity hop,
Hippity hop, hippity hop.
And made the old woman go hippity hop,
Oh, ho, ho.

Another exciting event was when we inherited two of our grandparents' hand-me-down appliances, our first refrigerator and a washing machine, as they had purchased the latest models for themselves. In the summer, my mother dried our clothes on the clothesline and, in the winter, she dried them on a wooden rack.

My dad had a green thumb. He always planted a huge garden and grew all the produce that sustained us through those Depression years. In addition to the family's garden, he sold the strawberries and potatoes which he had planted on one acre of our property. My job was to wash the potatoes and place the baskets of strawberries in neat rows. Wayne,

Lillian and my mother sold these door-to-door, my mother driving, and Wayne and Lillian going separately to each door.

We all helped grow, pick and preserve our fruit and vegetables. We canned yellow beans, green beans, carrots, corn, peas, beets, tomatoes, squash, raspberries and rhubarb. With the conveniences we have today, it is difficult to believe the amount of work required to can on a wood stove! We cleaned and cut up big bowls of beans; we shelled peas; corn was cut off cobs; strawberries were hulled; rhubarb was cut up; pie cherries from our grandparents' orchard were pitted. My mother kept a large vat boiling on the stove, and she sealed quart after quart of fruits and vegetables and, sometimes, salmon.

My mother canned so much that there was no place to store the many quarts of food. My father solved that problem: he dug a cellar six feet deep under the house. We got into the cellar from the kitchen by climbing down a ladder to a gravel floor, and we carried countless quarts of food up and down that 2 X 4 ladder.

From neighboring orchards, we picked windfalls of apples, pears, peaches, cherries, and apricots, which cost about fifty cents a box. Mother always bargained for better prices. Money was always tight and my parents were very careful with what little they had. Whenever possible, we bartered instead of paying cash. For example, we offered to exchange our apples for salmon, fished by the Indians at Celilo Falls. At the grocery store in Hood River, we purchased only the staples that we could not raise ourselves, such as coffee, sugar, flour and oatmeal. The store was called Cash and Carry; they accepted only cash - no checks - there was no credit and no credit cards! -

My father staked out a 20 x 20 foot garden spot for me, and I planted and raised my own vegetables. I was proud to provide occasional items for our family's meals. As a married adult, I have always found a garden spot and, whenever possible, I have planted grapes as the first fruit to be grown. I still have about forty feet of grapes to share, as well as one of the largest gardens in our development.

On the farm, we had a large chicken coop and many rabbit pens. Providing feed and water for the chickens and rabbits was a daily chore.

One of the highlights of growing up in Hood River was the annual Memorial Day parade. It was always led by Chief Tommy Thompson, Chief of the Celilo Falls Indian Tribe, followed by his wife, Edna, who, in full Indian regalia, rode bareback over a mile to the Idlewilde Cemetery, where the Memorial Day speeches were given. One year, my brother,

Wayne, dressed in his Boy Scout uniform, recited from memory President Lincoln's entire Gettysburg address.

Oftentimes, we purchased eggs from a neighbor for seven cents a dozen. Once, I was sent to buy eggs and the neighbor told me that she had raised the price to eight cents. She gave me the eggs and told me that on my next trip I was to bring another penny from home. My mother would have no part of that! She sent me back with the eggs and the message that she could not afford the eggs at that price! The neighbor backed down and the price stayed at seven cents.

Every year, my parents ordered one hundred fifty baby chicks, to be delivered to the Post Office, along with those for many other small farms. I remember how strongly the Post Office smelled of ammonia during delivery season each Spring! Until I was six years old, chicken was the only meat our family ate. When I was seven years old, I bought six rabbits, using money that I had earned picking beans and strawberries. It was not long before we had hundreds of rabbits and a never-ending supply of rabbit meat.

We were almost never sick but, when we were, my mother had a host of home remedies for us. Every day we were given a spoonful of cod-liver oil. It tasted awful, but it was considered essential for good growth and to prevent illness. It must have worked because we seldom visited a doctor or a dentist.

When we were sick, our mother was our doctor. When she thought we were coming down with colds, she immediately covered our chests with mustard plasters, wrapped us in heavy blankets and placed our feet in nearly scalding hot water. She literally killed the bugs before they could get started.

Now, in Germany, that very type of heat therapy has been developed to kill cancer cells, since it is known that cancer cells cannot stand excessive heat, as can healthy cells. To kill these cancer cells the body is heated to one hundred four degrees.

My grandmother Simpson was mortified that we lived in such primitive conditions. When Wayne turned thirteen and was a freshman in high school, he went to live with my grandparents. He had his own room and indoor plumbing facilities. As their first-born grandchild, Wayne was their favorite, much to the chagrin of one of my aunts, who lived close by. She tried, at first, to have her daughters spend as much time as possible at my grandparents.

My younger brother and sister were both born in our farmhouse, with the help of Dr. Chick. Robert was born on January 31, 1936, and

Nancy Carol was born on December 23, 1937. Aunt Maude Piatt, my grandmother's brother's (Paul) wife, was the midwife for both deliveries. On October 2005, Nancy died in her home, within one hundred feet of where she had been born.

My Brothers and Sisters

As a middle child, I was in a great position to have relationships with all four siblings. We loved and protected one another and I had many very fruitful times with them.

As a child, Wayne was the one with whom I spent the most time. In my eyes, he was fearless, strong, imaginative and kind. I idolized him, as many younger brothers would do. Together, we had countless adventures as we explored the Hood River Valley and visited many mountain lakes, including our favorite, Lost Lake.

Our mother always inspired us to invent money-making schemes. One of our most beneficial efforts resulted from Wayne's idea of establishing a paper route. He signed up to receive *The Grit* newspapers from Chicago and he sold them door-to-door. Wayne moved on eventually to higher challenges, and Lillian and I took over his paper route. We took turns carrying the big sack of newspapers, walking the entire route of several miles.

Vernon, Wayne, Bob, Lillian, Mother, Dad and Nancy

The unsold newspapers became a treasure trove of knowledge, as I read every issue cover-to-cover. At an early age, the newspaper taught me a lot about the world.

When I was twelve years old, Wayne recruited me for the Boy Scouts. Wayne became an Eagle Scout and received the Gold Quill award for having written and published over ten thousand words. Sports became my priority and I settled for merit badges attaining the rank of Life Scout, my highest rank.

Wayne was a great favorite of the teachers at our school and he had a strong reputation in the community. Without a doubt, Wayne raised the bar of expectations for his younger siblings. Wayne was a tough act to follow! But, I did follow his footsteps into many endeavors. Whenever Wayne left a job, he suggested to the employer that I should be hired in his place. When I followed Wayne into one job, the boss told me that if I performed half as good as my brother, Bo, he would be happy to hire me. I always aimed to be twice as good as Wayne, which raised the bar for my little brother, Bob, who always achieved the same level of performance as had his big brothers. The standard of performance that Wayne set me undoubtedly carried me through the challenges of my Army career and strengthened my determination to graduate from college.

I remember one incident in particular that illustrates our close relationship. I was about eight years old and Wayne was about thirteen. We were burning out yellow jackets' holes in the big grassy field by our house. Suddenly, a wind arose and the fire raced through the tall dried grass. In seconds, it was eight feet high and moving fast. Wayne grabbed a small mattress and, as I ran after him, I grabbed a couple of gunny sacks and dunked them in a bucket of water. Speedily, he raced along the high point of the flames and stamped out the main part of the fire. I ran behind him, swung the gunny sacks with both hands and smothered what fire remained.

The fire burned about an acre before we could finally extinguish it. We worked as a team and barely communicated throughout the entire incident. When Wayne left home, my younger brother, Bob, then became my daily companion until I went into the Army on June 6, 1951.

Throughout the fifty-four years that we shared, Wayne and I had an amazing bond. We often received the same messages from Spirit and we communicated without words.

Wayne was discharged from the Navy, at age 19, in August of 1946. Two days later the family of seven squeezed into a 1936 Chevrolet and began the 2,200 mile trip to Michigan to visit relatives. The next day a postman came by and took the following picture. Thirty years later, the postman died and his wife developed some old film. She found the picture of our family and liked it so much she had it framed and it sat in her living room for several years until my aunt came by to visit and recognized the picture. She asked for a print and sent our family a copy about 35 years after the picture was taken. Thanks, unknown Angel!

In 1966, Wayne became the Executive Director of the Oregon Gasoline Dealers Association, and he was instrumental in guiding the state and nation through the gasoline crisis of 1974. In the early days of the crisis, we talked about the problem of long waiting lines at gas stations, and one night I dreamed of a simple solution. When I called Wayne to suggest a system of flags, green for "gas available," yellow for "service only," and red for "no gasoline available," he told me that he had had the very same dream. Due to Wayne's influence, that system was very quickly adopted by service stations throughout the nation.

For nineteen years, I called Wayne when I was in Portland on business. We would meet at a restaurant, and discuss business and political issues. Almost always, we thought the same way and arrived at the same solutions for the problems of the day. In August of 1977, with no prior discussion, both Wayne and I, on the same day, purchased the identical Buick and model of car.

In September 1977, I walked across my office and I was temporarily frozen by a sharp pain in my lower back, so that I could not move. At that same moment, Wayne, in his office in Portland, underwent a very similar experience. I consulted a chiropractor, who suggested massages and bed rest for three days. I was mobile again after five days. Wayne was taken by ambulance to a hospital, where he was administered pain medication and kept in traction for three weeks.

Wayne died from a heart attack on July 30, 1985. We did not know, until after the autopsy, that the back pain he suffered eight years earlier was a major heart attack, which had healed on its own. Some years later, my heart also repaired itself, without a heart attack. When my arteries became blocked, my body created a bypass system. Our brotherly bond connected us, even after our earthly ones were broken.

Lillian, like Wayne, was an inspiring older sibling. She was a natural athlete, and growing up with boys had made her fast and fearless. Long before Title IX required schools to give girls equal access to athletic opportunities, Hood River had one of the early girls' track teams. Lillian got her start in a meet with The Dalles, one of the top teams in Oregon State. She entered six events and won first place in five. The event in which she placed second was the shot put; before the meet, she had never thrown a shot put.

Many times I played with Lillian at the gravel pit. At the rim of the pit was a layer of soft dirt about five feet thick and from there down it was pure gravel. One day, we dug in the gravel on the side of the hill and the whole dirt rim, about twenty feet wide and five feet thick, broke off. The entire massive chunk came down on us and with all that dirt, probably a ton or more, we rolled all the way down to the bottom of the pit. Fortunately, it did not bury us. We were fine, but filthy. However, we had breathed in a lot of dirt. The cloud of dust made a huge plume into the sky and we coughed out the dust for days.

The family enjoyed watching my brother, Bob, play football and baseball his senior year of high school. Bob and I had been very close after I returned from the military and, together, in the summer of 1953, we climbed both Mt. Hood and Mt. Adams. In the fall of 1954, as a twenty-three-year-old freshman, I commenced my college career at

Oregon College of Education in Monmouth. As a nineteen-year old freshman, Bob joined me for winter and spring terms.

I was nearly seven years older than Nancy, who was thirteen when I left for the Army. I missed her teenage years when she was a slim high school majorette. Eventually, Nancy and her husband, Robert, purchased a home about one hundred feet from where our old homestead had stood before it was razed.

A Friend for Life

Aside from my brothers and sisters, one of my most constant companions was Dick Minor. We met in the cradle when our family lived on fourteenth Street and we were reunited when we went to the same high school. Our birthdays were just four days apart, less one year, so we celebrated them together several times. We were Boy Scouts together, fished and camped, and climbed Mt. Hood for the first time in 1949, when I was eighteen years old.

I have always said that, if everyone in the world were like Dick and me, there would never be another war. We both wanted to do the very best for other people and we encouraged that in each other. To have someone mirror your values as you grow up is a blessing, indeed.

Dick was not a church goer, but he had had a strong moral upbringing. His father worked for the railroad, and he drove up and down the railroad tracks on a handcar to make sure that there were no rocks or trees on the tracks.

In the Depression years, many unemployed men traveled the rails and Dick's father sometimes invited one of them home to dinner. These men were dirty and shaggy from weeks on the road, yet they were brought to his family's table and his wife served them.

Dick was the same kind of generous, loving person as his father. I remember one time when Dick accidentally broke a cup at our house, and he had felt so bad that he cried. He did not want to harm anyone or anything. I have always felt blessed to have had him as a friend. He lives now in The Dalles and every time we get together, we connect to the years of the past. Recently, Dick suggested that we climb Mt. Hood together; an impossible feat for either of us, in our states of health.

The year I graduated from high school, Dick's father got us jobs working on the Mt. Hood Railroad, a twenty-six mile line that served the fruit and logging industries of the Hood River Valley. We were gandy dancers, the slang name for the men who laid and maintained the railroad tracks. The tracks were held in place by ties and by the mass of the crushed rock beneath them; however, each time a train traveled around a curve, the vibration shifted the tracks a tiny bit and, if the rails were not maintained, there could be a derailment. Our job was to lever the rails back into place, using heavy steel pry-bars, pushing the crushed gravel ballast underneath to level them out. When an engine and cars derailed, the rails and railroad ties were completely torn apart. We had but a few hours in which to put them back into place, using special sledge hammers called spike mauls to drive the spikes into the rails.

We earned fifty-five dollars a week, which was an excellent wage in 1949. It was very intensive labor and, although I did not know it at the time, the repetitive stress on my shoulders destroyed both my rotator cuffs. I discovered this many years later, when a doctor looked at my x-rays and said that he was amazed that I could even raise my arms. I was missing the rotator cuffs and major tendons that control ninety-five percent of the job of lifting. From the outside, both my shoulders feel as if they have been smashed by a hammer, but I do not have any pain. To compensate, my body produced a whole system of smaller muscles, tendons, and tiny bones, which replaced my shoulder joints and allowed my arms to work normally.

When the Korean War began in June 1950, I decided to follow in my big brother, Wayne's footsteps, and enlist in the Navy for four years. I convinced Dick and two other good friends to enlist in the Navy with me in Portland, Oregon. During my physical exam, the doctor said, "You're sick. You've got a temperature of 101." I said, "I don't feel sick." They took my temperature again and it was still 101. He said, "You must have a sinus infection and that would never work on a Navy ship." He stamped me 4F and I returned home. Dick and my other two friends joined the Navy for a four-year enlistment.

Dick just laughed and called me an SOB. He always said that if you could not call someone a name like that and laugh about it together, you really were not friends. Happily, it all worked out for both of us. A year later, I was drafted into the Army and Dick began a successful Navy career, topped by meeting his beautiful wife, Patricia. They have now been married for fifty-nine years. I was Dick's best man at his wedding in the summer of 1954 and Dick was my best man in September 1956.

Inspiring Parents

My mother and dad were can-do people. Through their words and actions, they gave us a clear message: it does not matter what the job is, find a way to get it done. We were taught that, if we did things to the best of our abilities, we could overcome any obstacle and accomplish whatever we wanted. My dad's attitude was that, no matter how bad things got, you could always find a way. The most natural trait that seems to run in our family is the love of selling, which my mother especially liked to do.

Money was always scarce and it was a challenge to earn enough money for whatever we wanted to buy. My two brothers and I have never received an unemployment check. With our mother's guidance we always created new ways to earn money.

In many ways, life was easier during the Great Depression days than it is now. There were fewer financial choices to make. First, money was needed to buy the food for the table; second, money had to put a roof over your head; and third, money was necessary to clothe you. Everything else was a luxury that had to be paid for with cash, except for your home and property, which was often paid for with a land sales contract, as there was almost no commercial financing of real estate.

Credit was almost non-existent. My dad's job at the dam paid a good wage, fifty cents an hour, four dollars a day, and he supplemented his income with his strawberry and potato crops. My mother helped by selling the produce, and at times, both my parents sold door-to-door for the McConnon Company, a distributor of household and health products. Their territory covered the Hood River Valley.

My dad came from a family of healthy men and we children inherited his genes. He had two brothers, Forrest and Hiram, and an older sister, Lillian. His sister died in sad circumstances at age twenty-one. In 1920, she returned home from the first day of her honeymoon in order to take care of her mother, who had contracted the Spanish flu. When she arrived home to help her mother, she caught the flu herself and died within hours. Her mother died a few hours later.

My mother was also an incredibly durable person. When we were young, our car was a Ford, which had to be cranked to start. She was always the one, when my dad was not there, who had to lean down in front of the car and turn the crank. It took a lot of strength to start the motor, especially when the motor was cold. Sometimes, the engine backfired as she cranked and that jarred her entire body. She built a huge bicep cranking that old Ford.

One of my mother's most important adages was, "The world is your oyster." We could accomplish anything we wanted to, and we should not let peer pressure cause us to do things that did not make any sense to us. She made sure that we all got a good head start and made the most of our skills and talents.

With all of us, she focused on mathematics and memory games. I was not even aware that she taught me at the time - it seemed like fun! We memorized the forty-eight states and their capitals in alphabetical order, and I remember them to this day. She also taught me the multiplication tables, starting before I entered the first grade. I was always selected first in the class math competitions. I have loved numbers ever since and I credit my mother for putting me on the path to becoming a CPA.

I have been blessed with two absolutely superior cooks in my lifetime, first my mother and then my wife, Ruth. My mother always had big bowls of food in the refrigerator: carrot salad, orange Jell-O, rhubarb, potato salad. There was always something nutritious to eat for a snack anytime we were hungry.

One of the highlights of my life will always be the delicious dinners my mother prepared every Sunday afternoon after church. Sometimes, my dad splurged and spent gas money to take us for a country drive to explore the Hood River Valley, always a memorable occasion.

My mother was a great giver, happy to pass things along to anyone who needed them. During the Depression, men came to our door to ask for food and she always had a sandwich or something for them to eat. Our house was one of two houses on about twenty open acres and word must have gotten around that a generous woman lived there. Later, she collected rummage for veterans: clothing, old appliances, anything that we were not using. Mother asked us to give unwanted items to her so that she could pass them on to others in need. I guess that my mother practiced the old saying, "One man's junk is another man's treasure." My big brother, Wayne, felt the same way and our three children are extremely giving as well.

Our parents instilled in us a sense of honesty (a strong characteristic of my wife, Ruth) as they were quick to teach us the difference between right and wrong. I remember one of my early lessons when I was about four years old. My mother took me to the grocery store and, as we entered, I noticed a display of strawberries in neat rows of four, at eye-level. I asked if we might buy some and I was told that they were too expensive.

They tempted me and when my mother was not looking, I popped one into my mouth. My mother looked at the strawberry container, she saw immediately that one strawberry was missing, and she knew what I had done. I was given a penny and told to pay the grocer for the strawberry. I was terrified as I handed the penny to the grocer, who was stern as he accepted it. On the way home, she told me that I would have many opportunities throughout my life to choose between right and wrong, and doing something wrong that I knew to be wrong, might lead to painful consequences.

That lesson remained with me and it helped me to resist temptation many times over the years. When I was in third grade, on the way home from school, one of my friends produced a pack of his father's cigarettes. All the other children eagerly accepted his offer of a smoke.

My favorite picture of my mom at age 18

I knew that this was exactly what my mother had warned me about! Clearly, this was a choice between right and wrong and so I refused to participate. My friends' teasing only strengthened my resolve and I have never smoked a single cigarette in my entire life. From then on, whenever peer pressure raised its ugly head, I resisted immediately and took the course that I knew to be right. This may have been my first message from Saint Michael, one that has lasted for a lifetime.

Fun and Games

There were about thirty children in our neighborhood, and the boys and girls played together. We never thought of not letting girls play -- our older sisters would not have allowed that! On long summer evenings we played softball, football, Kick the Can or Annie-Annie-Over the Roof, a team game you played with a big rubber ball. We used to climb the black walnut trees and pretend that we were Tarzan and his apes. Hours were spent playing in the gravel pit and, along with the snakes and frogs, we swam in the ponds.

One of my favorite things to do was to run off the edge of the gravel pit as fast as I could, fly out into space, hit the gravel, and roll down toward the bottom, some thirty feet below. I never hurt myself. It taught me to relax when I fell and this was a skill that I later put to use on the football field. When you play football, the key to avoid injuries is to relax when you fall.

When I was eight years old, my dad was given a three-story commercial building in downtown Hood River in exchange for hauling it away. He brought the disassembled building to our property and spread the multi-shaped pieces over one-half acre, with the plan to build us a new home. The many differently shaped pieces of wood became my "Tinker Toys", which I built into airplanes, cars, castles and anything else that I could dream up. I learned to use a board as a lever to move wooden boards that weighed twice as much as I did. My dad never finished the home that he envisioned, but I enjoyed an endless source of creative problem-solving.

During the 30s and 40s, radio programs were very popular. Our family listened together, although sometimes we could barely hear the radio signal, as it faded in and out. My favorite program was *Gang Busters*, which dramatized actual FBI cases with a barrage of machine guns and other sound effects. We also gathered around the radio to listen to President Roosevelt's fireside chats. In September 1937, the president came to Hood River, after the dedication of Timberline Lodge and the Bonneville Dam. I was in first grade and joined hundreds of other school kids from the entire county who lined Oak Street in Hood River, waving American flags.

At home we played games almost every night. In the early years before we had electricity, we played by kerosene lamps. Sometimes, it was a classic board game like Monopoly or Parcheesi, but often mother would get creative and we made up our own games. My brother, Bob, and I had a huge map of the world, and we could entertain ourselves for hours with the map. We both would write the names of five cities and exchange the names. Whoever found them first won the game. As we searched for the five cities, we learned a lot about the cities of the world.

Our life was simpler than families have today, without heavily scheduled after-school activities and the outside intrusions of television and computers. We did not have a telephone until I was eight years old! One of our favorite family times was when we fished in the sloughs around the Columbia River or swam in the river on beautiful sandy beaches, usually with no one else around.

Often in the evening, my parents would lay out a blanket on the grass and we would all lie down, watch the stars together and talk.

When I was twelve, my parents sold the three acre farm and we moved to a home at 915 Pine Street in Hood River. It was only a block from June Street, where I had lived from age two to four. Best of all, the new home had indoor plumbing - no more trips to the privy in the howling wind and snow!

As I moved into adolescence, sports became my main outlet for fun. I was very competitive and played a sport every season: football, baseball, basketball, boxing, golf, track - I sampled them all. My best sport was baseball, where I could focus the same kind of concentrated energy that I brought to fruit-picking. When I lived by the gravel pit, I would pick up a stick, throw a rock in the air and hit it. I would hit a rock many times in a row, training my eyes and arms to focus on the ball. Sometimes I practiced fielding, throwing a baseball as high as I could, chasing it as far away as possible, still trying to catch the ball, while falling to the ground, if necessary, to make the catch. I played center field on the high school baseball team and I made many catches that required my body to do a roll, or whatever it took to catch the ball.

Our football team uniforms were a lot different from those of high school players today. We wore helmets made of hard leather, a leather vest that came around to protect our ribs, and hip pads. We had no face masks, except for players who wore glasses.

Organized sports were not the only thing that a boy could do to burn off energy. We lived in one of the most beautiful recreational areas of the country, and we loved to take advantage of the mountains and streams. With our grandfather as a model, we developed a love for hiking and climbing, and we spent many weekends camping and fishing.

Early Influences

My family members shaped my character. I also owe a debt of gratitude to a number of influential adults, who helped steer me on a strong path to adulthood.

Mrs. Sunday

The first non-related person to take a special interest in me was my Sunday school teacher, Mrs. Sunday, at the Christian Missionary Alliance Church. It was at least a year later that I learned that Sunday School was named for the day of the week and not for her! I was a little over two-years old when I began to attend her classes and I was always excited to go. When my family moved out of town to our home in the country, church members came by to take me to Sunday school. I can still picture her, with her close-cropped white hair, and the little room where she read us Bible stories from a colorful picture book. I firmly believe that she laid the foundation for my Christian faith.

Henry Schweigert

When I was six, I moved from Mrs. Sunday's Sunday school class to that of another wonderful teacher, Henry Schweigert, who was a businessman in our community. He had a golden touch in everything that he did. A true Christian, he gave to other people in countless ways, and the more he gave, the more came back to him. Henry was never without a smile on his face and always had a Bible in his hands. He knew what was important to young boys. He supported us with a basketball team and drove us to games in neighboring towns. That gave him an opportunity to talk to us about the Bible, building on the groundwork laid by Mrs. Sunday. I had the pleasure of visiting Hank Schweigert and his wife about five years ago, when he was 101 years old, and they had been married for eighty years! He still preached the same message that he had when I was a child!

Peter Mohr

Among the people who showed me the Christian way was Pete Mohr, one of my parents' McConnon Product customers. Very thin, he was a tall fellow with a big Adam's apple, like the stereotype of a hillbilly farmer. Pete really liked me and, for many years, he brought me presents. Coming home from school, I would find that Pete had been there, leaving a box of apples, peaches, or some kind of fruit that he had raised. I believe that one thing a person needs to learn is how to accept gifts graciously. It honors the giver and the recipient enjoys the pleasure of generosity. I believe that Pete was an angel sent to teach me the joy of receiving.

Annie Sloat

When I was four to twelve years old, our next-door neighbor was Annie Sloat. She, too, was a big influence because she taught me, at an early age, the give-and-take of good conversation. My mother used to send me to her house to buy eggs, and I spent hours talking to her and listening to her radio. Annie was married to the chief of police and she did not have children so she had lots of time to herself. Annie became the "frosting on the cake", along with the knowledge that I gleaned by reading *The Grit* newspaper and exchanging thoughts with her. In hindsight, to discuss the issues of the day with an adult like Annie, hour after hour, contributed mightily to my maturity and to my future achievements.

Annie lived in that same house until she died at ninety-four. Every year for thirty-five years, she sent me a birthday card and an occasional note. Through my Army and college years, her cards and messages uplifted me. She was like an angel from heaven, who reminded me of the good times we had spent together.

History repeated itself when my daughter, Cathy, three years-old, had a similar relationship with Hazel Millard, the woman next door, and Cathy spent countless hours talking and discussing life with her.

Cecil Hickey

After completing high school in June 1949, jobs were hard to find, and I was blessed to acquire a summer job on the Mt. Hood Railroad for the wage of fifty-five dollars a week. I was then hired by Cecil Hickey, a local small-town grocer, for the sum of thirty-five cents an hour for a sixty-five hour week (about twenty-three dollars a week). This was approximately a sixty-two percent cut in pay from my work on the railroad and I had to work an extra twenty-five hours to earn that much.

However, my primary incentive was that, if an opening occurred, I could learn the meat-cutting trade. After eighteen months on the job, with only one raise of two and a half cents an hour, I was drafted into the Army for the sum of sixty-eight dollars a month, which was even less than Cecil paid me but, I did get room and board. When I returned from the Army two years later, a meat cutter, who had worked for Cecil for many years, decided to retire. I was hired to learn the trade, as I had manifested nearly four years before.

Learning this trade led me to the love of my life, Ruth Ann Grady, and it provided me with a job that, three years later, paid me eight hundred dollars a month. Financially, it supplemented my college career until I hung up my knives for good. A month after I completed my junior year of college, I took a job as an accountant in a CPA firm, for three hundred dollars a month.

Needless to say, the opportunity that Cecil gave me to become a meat-cutter was instrumental in funding my college career, which, in my life's journey, made me feel very grateful towards Cecil.

Roy Webster

Roy Webster was another extraordinary man. He came to Hood River from the east coast and bought a number of orchards, eventually totaling several hundred acres. In the late 1940's, he organized a group swim across the Columbia River and that event continues to attract hundreds of participants from around the world. Roy was about six feet three inches tall and he had incredible stature in whatever task he undertook. By chance, his son, Wayne, was in Army Leadership School with me at Camp Roberts, California, and after the military, Roy asked me to pitch for a softball team he was organizing. He was the kind of person who uplifted those around him.

Becoming a Christian

When I was twelve, a traveling evangelist preached at the Christian Missionary Alliance Church, which I had attended since age two. With his white hair flowing, he delivered his "fire and brimstone" sermon on salvation. My two friends and I went forward to become Christians. I can still recall his voice, as he told me that the Spirit of the Lord would speak to me, and guide me forever, and that His angels, led by Saint

Michael, would watch over me and protect me from all perils. The Lord would bless me with abundance in the riches and treasures of the universe.

The evangelist declared that we would be cleansed of all sin and I immediately felt as if my entire body were being scrubbed from the inside out. I felt a glow and a sense of rising to a higher level of being. Along with this physical sensation came a very strong feeling that good things would happen to me soon.

The next day, I found a dime on the sidewalk. The message flowed to me that this was one of the blessings prophesized by the evangelist. I used the dime to buy myself my favorite candy bar. As I walked out of the store, a friend met me. I was eager to eat the candy bar but, I thought that I could not eat the candy bar without giving him part of it. My next thought was to save the candy bar for later so that I would not have to share it.

Suddenly, I received a strong message that I should not only share the candy bar but give my friend two thirds of it, which I did. I was promptly filled with a profound feeling of euphoria, and I had the sensation that a cloud had come down from heaven and cloaked me with the Holy Spirit. Free from stress, I no longer had to concern myself with the future and the worry of not knowing what it might bring. Whenever there was a question concerning what path to take, I need only have a conversation with Saint Michael and let it happen. The messages received from Saint Michael constantly exceeded my expectations with a supernatural result.

After that incident, blessings really started to flow and I received regular messages from above, to the point that I had daily conversations with the higher power. I was filled with the Holy Spirit and, from that point on, I never wavered in my total faith and confidence that my angels were to take care of me and fill my life with abundance, beyond my mind's comprehension.

The very next week, my parents received an offer for their home. We soon moved to town and experienced the joy of an inside bathroom for the first time in eight years. I was sad to leave my boyhood home, where I had had so many happy memories, but the entire family felt that we were moving up in the world. The message came to me that this was more abundance dispensed to me from the Holy Spirit.

Several weeks later, I had a dream in which I drowned. My Spirit seemed to float up to the ceiling of a local funeral parlor, where I had never been. Below me, I observed my family and friends in mourning. My body, dressed in my Boy Scout uniform, lay in an open casket. The next week, one of the boys in my scout troop drowned and he wore his Boy Scout uniform in his casket. I was selected as one of his pallbearers. Everything, including the funeral parlor, was identical to my dream, except that I lived. The message came to me from Spirit that anyone may die without a moments notice, but I was protected by my Guardian Angel.

I received the message from Spirit that, to have a better understanding of what religions were all about, I should attend different churches. Over the course of about three years, I sampled almost every church in town: Catholic, Methodist, Baptist, Mormon, Episcopal, and the local Riverside Christian Church, where my Boy Scout troop met, and where my little sister, Nancy, would one day marry. I attended the various youth groups and made friends in all of them. I was fascinated by the different messages and traditions, and I tried to understand the deeper meanings behind them. Gradually, I came to the conclusion that all faiths made major contributions to the community.

The important unifying message was that each of us receives many blessings and we can share those by doing well for others.

Of all the churches that I attended, the one that left the longest impression on me was St. Mark's Episcopal Church, which was across the street from Coe Primary School where I began first grade. The youth group had a series of classes on the Saints of the Church, which included Saint Michael. The thought occurred to me: who would not want him as their Guardian Angel: with his super powers of suspending gravity, as it is in heaven; with his ability to find lost objects; with his ability to heal; with his power to protect people from harm; and with his ability to watch over one. Saint Michael seemed to me to be the best arrangement, to get the most "bang for a buck." Or, to put it another way, a little prayer for Saint Michael to come into your life might well be worth the time invested.

School Days

My elementary school was about two miles from our home. Our stop was the first one for the bus and that made it a very long ride. Most of the time, I walked to school with my sister, Lillian, as that was quicker, and I enjoyed the walk, the bus ride was always extremely monotonous to me.

The Columbia Gorge is known for dramatic winter weather, as Arctic storms from the east whip westward down the Columbia River, with bitter cold and strong winds, accompanied by ice and deep snow.

School must have been cancelled sometimes, but I cannot remember that ever happening. Many times, I walked to school in drifts three feet deep. When I played on sports teams, we never thought to cancel a game because of weather. To play basketball, we drove all the way to Maupin, in eastern Oregon, and to all the little towns in between, and no matter what the weather, we would go.

In elementary school, I had the honor to serve as a school crossing-guard. I think that that was the principal's way of recognizing students who had leadership potential and keeping them on a positive track. I was chosen the first time it was available to my age group and I was proud to be given that special responsibility.

In elementary school, I was blessed to have some truly outstanding teachers, who helped to channel my energy, and who taught me how to organize my thoughts. Miss Andrews, my third grade teacher, was the first. We developed a special relationship when the school administered the Stanford-Binet test, which measured our natural intelligence. I took the test and, afterwards, I raised my hand to say that I thought that the test was faulty. Miss Andrews wisely suggested that we discuss this matter after school. I met with her and tried to convince her of my way of thinking.

The Stanford-Binet test measured what I had learned, I said, but it did not measure my potential. I pointed to one question on the test, "On which side of the plate do we place the fork?" How could that question measure my intelligence? She was firm in her own opinion that the test was valid and I was never able to convince her of my viewpoint. However, I appreciated the fact that she took me seriously, and I learned a great deal from the encounter; mainly, that no matter how right you think you are, someone else thinks that they are just as right, but for different reasons!

From reading *The Grit*, a weekly newspaper published in Chicago, I developed a great curiosity about the world and I held many strong viewpoints. For the rest of that year, whenever I tried to express my opinion, Mrs. Andrews would say, "I think we should discuss this after school." She suggested this to my fourth grade teacher, Marie Sigenthauler, and to my fifth grade teacher, Mrs. Davis, and they agreed with her. They never stifled me, but instead they challenged me and made me feel that I was worth listening to.

In the fourth grade, we were introduced to the Civil War and to many of the great battles, which included the crucial Battle of Gettysburg. I thought that someday I would like to visit as many of those battlefields as possible. At that time, I could never have guessed that I would write a tax manual that would take me on journeys to give taxation talks and to sell my tax manuals. On our many trips, we visited nearly all the Civil War sites, including Gettysburg and Appomattox, where General Lee surrendered to General Grant and ended the Civil War. Once again, the dreams of a ten-year-old boy became real, over forty years later, and I believe they were influenced by the presence of the Holy Spirit.

My sixth grade teacher, Paula Clark, went further. She was a strict disciplinarian, and when I met with her after school, she made me hone my position and back it up with facts. She never smiled and she was all business. She taught me an invaluable lesson on how to argue my point in a more effective way. In so doing, she laid the groundwork for my CPA practice, where a great number of my clients' problems were solved by my sitting down with one of my female accountants and brainstorming a solution.

In the sixth grade we studied China and I can still remember the colored pictures of life in China, with oxen working in the rice fields. I dreamt of going to China someday, to see the Chinese life in action, as one of my best friends, Hoover Lee, was Chinese. Forty years later, my wish came true.

With hindsight, I was blessed by these four teachers, who took under their wings a small boy from "the other side of the tracks" and nurtured him into a level of thought that few students ever reached. They gave me confidence and self-respect, which probably led to my strong belief that I wanted to teach, and teaching has remained one of my primary pleasures in life.

In the seventh grade, I had a wonderful social studies teacher, Harriet Blashfield, who stated that some of us in the classroom would earn as much as $300,000 in our lifetimes! That thought never left me.

I rationalized that there must be a way to earn this enormous sum of money. My head spun, as I quickly calculated that from four dollars a day times two hundred and fifty work days a year would equal one thousand dollars a year times forty years would equal forty thousand dollars, a long way from $300,000 dollars. After high school, I worked six days a week in a grocery store, and earned thirty-five cents an hour for a sixty-five-hour week, which came to twenty-two dollars and seventy-five cents a week (about three dollars and eighty cents a day).

My boss assured me that if I did a good job, he would give me a raise. I worked as hard as I could and when the raise came, it was two and one-half cents an hour, bringing my wage to thirty-seven and one-half cents an hour. At that time, I thought that I should think of a way to go to college and become the boss, if I were ever to earn $300,000 dollars in my lifetime.

In the eighth grade, I had an exceptional math teacher, Mrs. Killbuck. I have always said that, in her class, I learned everything that I needed to know to pass the math part of the CPA exam. She taught her students how to think, rather than to memorize the cause and effect of mathematics and that made a huge difference to my success in math.

Building a Work Ethic

My mother always said that she raised only chiefs, not Indians. What she meant was that she expected us to become leaders, and not always to be followers. She encouraged each of us to be self-sufficient and in control of our own lives. When my sisters grew up, they both owned their own businesses, Lillian as a clothing store owner in Corvallis, and Nancy as a daycare operator in her home in Hood River, a hundred feet from where she was born and died at sixty-seven. I was always impressed to see Nancy at work, with up to twenty children in her home, a baby on her hip, and loving her job every minute of the day. The newborns related to Nancy better than to their own mothers, who worked all day.

My brothers were equally successful. Wayne led the Nation through the great gas crisis of 1974 as the Executive Director of the Oregon Gasoline Dealers Association.

Wayne's effort is one of the primary reasons why the State of Oregon is one of only two states in the Country that do not have self-service gasoline.

In 1956, Bob, aged twenty, went to work for the Guy F. Atkinson Company as a heavy equipment oiler on The Dalles Dam. This company was one of the largest construction companies in the world. He held many positions in the company such as Paymaster, Labor Relations Manager, Purchasing Manager and Safety Engineer. Bob worked in locations in South Dakota, Missouri, Northern California, Seattle and Hanford, Washington and the company's world headquarters in South

San Francisco. He also spent three and one-half years building the Mangla Dam in Pakistan in 1963.

Bob became so knowledgeable about the company operations that he was consulted regularly by managers on other jobs, and it became a common joke that the company could not survive without him. When he retired on his sixty-second birthday, after forty-two years with the company, he was one of its oldest employees. The company was bought on that same day and Guy F. Atkinson Company ceased to exist! Bob now lives with his wife, Carol, in Cannon Beach, Oregon.

My dad set a high standard for the family work ethic. Starting in 1934, he was a laborer on the Bonneville Dam, among four thousand men who worked eight-hour shifts for four dollars a day. It was considered a well-paid job during those Depression years. Dad learned to be a plumber and that became his profession after the dam work was finished in 1937. To get to the construction site, he drove twenty-four miles one way, a trip that would be less than twenty miles after the freeway was built in the early 1950s.

My dad and my mother continued their door-to-door sales of products, including Electrolux vacuums and Nutrilite food supplements.

At a very young age, we children all learned the meaning of productive work. My first paid job was when I was six and picked beans for a neighbor. Paid by the pound, the first day I earned just nine cents. I noticed that a much older child made thirty-eight cents that day and I was determined to earn that amount by the end of the week. It was all about intensity: if I were fast in moving my hands, I could pick more beans. By the fifth day in the field, I earned thirty-nine cents! I learned to concentrate my mind on the task before me and I moved my hands quickly. This was a skill that I continued to develop for many years, as a fruit and vegetable picker, and later, as a meat-cutter.

After my bean-picking experience, I graduated to a job in the strawberry patch. With my earnings there I bought six rabbits, which may have been the best investment I ever made! We soon had more rabbits than we had pens and I started selling the extras. Rabbit meat became one of our family's staple foods.

When I was seven, my sister, Lillian, and I took over Wayne's newspaper route. He delivered the *The Grit*, a weekly newspaper published in Chicago and popular throughout the United States. It cost ten cents and was about forty pages long, with news, comics, women's and family issues, and stories. *Grit* was a great source of unbiased information and I read it from cover to cover every week.

When I was twelve, I needed a lot of dental work, but there was no money for all the work that was needed. My mother and I looked up the home addresses of two local dentists and drove to see their homes. My mother noticed that there were a lot of weeds growing in a very large peony patch around one dentist's house. We returned home and, that evening, she called the dentist and asked if he would trade dental work for my work in his yard. He said, "Sure, send him tomorrow at 8:00 A.M., and I will see what he needs." For the next three summers, I worked many hours in his yard before my dental work was finished.

Another time, driving up the street, my mother noticed a local attorney mowing his very steep lawn. She stopped the car and said, "Let's get you a job mowing this man's lawn." Without hesitation, she suggested to him that I would mow his lawn for $2.50, and he said, "That's a deal." Once a month I went to his legal office and was invited into his main office, where he brought out a big check book and wrote a check for my pay. I was very impressed with all the law books that covered all the walls in his office.

That was just the beginning, as my mother insisted that I go door-to-door and offer to mow lawns. In a short time, I had twenty-five lawns to mow, which resulted in my earning a considerable sum of money. When I no longer had time to mow, Bob, my younger brother, took over my lawn business.

My next effort to earn money was when my mother observed a man working in his yard on a hillside, with dirt in big piles. Mother stopped the car and asked him if he needed help, and he quickly agreed. I helped him dig a trench beside his house. I was curious what his line of work was that afforded him such a huge house, with a beautiful view. When I asked him about his employment. He said that he was a CPA, and he explained to me what was necessary to become one. The seed that he planted in my mind that day lingered for many years and it came to fruition years later, when I switched my life's game plan to become a CPA, instead of a teacher.

Wayne constantly schemed on ways to earn money and I joined him in a number of successful ventures. For many years we harvested trees from public lands and sold them as Christmas trees. Wayne had a two-seater car with a rumble seat, and we completely buried the car in trees, selling them for between thirty-five cents to a dollar each. In the summer, Wayne and I earned money selling fireworks, which we ordered from the Zebra Fireworks Company. Those were the days of real firecrackers: you could cause severe injury with one firecracker! We built a little stand by the side of the road and sold a wide variety of fireworks.

Hood River is one of the nation's richest fruit-growing regions in the world. There was never a shortage of seasonal picking and thinning apples, pears, cherries, and apricots. I became a regular part of the crews that harvested the bounty of our beautiful valley, getting to know the migrant workers and their lifestyle. Hard work was balanced with good times and friendship. At the lunch hour, the women played guitars and sang. They taught me to value simple pleasures: accomplishing a tough job, appreciating nature's beauty, and sharing meals with family and friends.

Most of the time, my good friend, Dick Minor, joined me on the picking crews. One year, we were part of a crew of eight or nine people who picked three acres of cherries. The following year, when I was twelve and Dick was eleven, none of the other crew members were available because of World War II, so, Dick and I picked the entire three acres alone! These cherry trees were about twenty-five feet tall. The two of us put up a twenty-foot extension ladder, and then climbed through the branches, trying not to leave a single cherry unpicked. The pay was five cents a pound, and we earned about twenty dollars a day on good days, a huge amount in 1943. Only five years previously, my dad worked for four dollars a day.

One year, I worked thinning apples with about ten other children. At the end of the first week, the orchard owner fired us all and gave us checks for that week's work. There were still many apples to be thinned, and we could not understand why he had fired all of us at once. I went home to tell my dad and he was shocked, to say the least. Half an hour later, the phone rang, and it was the orchard owner, Ernie Hukari, who said, "Say, how about I will pick you up in the morning and you and I will finish the orchard together?" The two of us thinned the rest of the apple orchard and I received a substantial increase in pay. My training in the bean fields had paid off handsomely.

When I was a teenager, I set a personal goal of picking five hundred boxes of apples in one day, but the best that I ever could was four hundred ninety-five boxes! It was always satisfying to look down the rows and see all the boxes full of fruit that you had picked. I routinely picked over one thousand pounds of cherries in a single day. When I graduated from high school, I had $1,300 in the bank, a princely sum for that time, all earned from various jobs, and with the thought that, someday, it would be a start towards college and the sum of $300,000 that I hoped to earn in my lifetime.

My Angel of Ancestral Guidance
Showing me how my forbearers survived and thrived through life's challenges.

My Angel of Protection, St. Michael
Shielding me from bodily harm.

The Angel of My Christian Path
Showing me the way to surrender my will in service to God.

My Angel of Education
Guiding me toward the knowledge that I most need for whatever situation I'm facing.

My Angel of Friendship
Bringing people into my life whose divine influence gives me strength and great pleasure.

My Angel of Numbers
Reminding me through numerical messages that a Band of Angels is watching over me.

My Angel of Patience
Reminding me that I can manifest the things I want, and they will come to me in divine timing.

Near-Death Experiences

Near-Death in the Woodpile

One day, when I was four years old and living on June Street, we received a load of firewood, which always excited me, as I loved to pile the pie-shaped sticks in order (which must have been the accountant in me showing up an early age.) I quickly stacked the load of firewood, and was down to the last two splits of wood that had sharp edges, and being too short to reach the top of the stack, I called several times for my brother, Wayne, to come help me. When he did not arrive, I pulled a small bench beside the woodpile, climbed on the bench and reached with the log over my head. The shifting weight caused the bench to tip. I fell backwards and struck my head against the sharp corner of the last remaining log.

My parents were horrified as I ran into the living room, blood streaming from the gash in my head. I was more angry than hurt, shouting, "goddamn Wayne," who had not come to help me when I called. My parents rushed me to Dr. Chick, who stitched up the back of my head without anesthetic. He said that I must have a very thick skull to have gotten away without more serious damage. That assessment proved to be true. In the nearly eight decades since that accident, I have survived many deadly blows to the head and I have never had any serious repercussions.

Near-Death in a Dark Alley

I have had numerous "banana peel" falls in my lifetime, but my thick skull has saved me every time. One dramatic fall happened on a dark rainy night in October of 1964. Leaving a client's office via a dark alley in downtown Corvallis, I stepped on a slippery piece of wet cardboard. My feet flew up, higher than my head had been, and my head struck the concrete. I rolled into a puddle of water, regained my feet, and walked away wet but otherwise unscathed.

Famous Relations

Most schoolchildren have read or heard the story of Priscilla Mullins and John Alden, who were among 111 passengers aboard the Mayflower. Henry Wadsworth Longfellow, a poet and descendant of John and Priscilla, wrote the story of how Priscilla attracted the attentions of the newly widowered Captain Myles Standish. Captain Standish had asked John Alden to find out if she would marry him and Priscilla had replied, "Why don't you speak for yourself, John?" Their romance began and a marriage ensued that lasted about sixty-five years and produced ten children.

John Alden was a bit of a rabble-rouser and he served in a variety of civic capacities, including twice as deputy governor of Massachusetts. According to the genealogists, John and Priscilla had more than 1.5 million descendents in 1970 and we are among them, on my dad's side of the family. Priscilla was a young teenager when the Mayflower landed and she was the only member of her family to survive the first winter at Plymouth Colony. John and Priscilla were the last two survivors of the Mayflower. Priscilla lived to be eighty-three and died in 1685. Two years later, In 1687, John died at eighty-eight.

Another famous ancestor on my dad's side is Major Henry L. Bowlby, a West Point graduate and engineer, who played an important role in the development of Oregon's highway system. Bowlby, a mathematics specialist and professor at the University of Nebraska, came to the Northwest at the request of his friend Sam Hill, and he was appointed highway commissioner for the state of Washington in 1909. Hill took him to study road construction in Europe and, in 1911, Henry Bowlby experimented with numerous innovations and engineered the three miles of road known as the Maryhill Loops near Goldendale, Washington.

In 1913, Bowlby was hired as Oregon's first state highway engineer, at an annual salary of three thousand dollars. At the time, the state had no oiled or paved roads. He developed the first highway plan, which was adopted by the Oregon Highway Commission in 1914. Later, Bowlby helped to fulfill Sam Hill's vision of the Columbia Gorge Highway, a highway that, in addition to being well-built and extremely innovative in its design, promoted the scenic beauty of the Columbia River Gorge. Bowlby and his wife lived in a tent during the construction of the highway and she cooked meals for a number of men. The famous Mitchell point tunnel, five miles west of Hood River, was once named Bowlby's Tunnel, but it was destroyed when the new freeway was built in 1952.

Bowlby also engineered the first highway from Portland to Astoria, Oregon. Henry L. Bowlby's name is engraved on a shovel displayed in the Maryhill Museum near Goldendale, Washington.

One of the English Bowlbys made an important contribution to the field of child development. John Bowlby studied psychiatry at Cambridge, and he was particularly interested in the importance of the attachment of mother and daughters. His studies, beginning in the early 1940's, with a report on how children who were separated from their parents responded to their mothers, after living in the subways of London during World War II. Bowlby left a lasting impression on psychology, education, child care and parenting. Researchers extended his research to develop clinical treatment techniques and prevention strategies.

On my mother's side, one of our most famous relatives is Captain William Piatt, my sixth great grandfather, who crossed the Delaware with George Washington on Christmas day, 1776, to a battle that turned the tide in the Revolutionary War. Along with Washington, William was among the founding members of the Society of the Cincinnati, which preserved the ideals and fellowship of the officers of the Continental Army. In 1791, he was involved in raising a company of volunteers to serve in the Indian War and he joined the army of General St. Clair.

Captain Piatt was killed at Fort Recovery, Ohio, along with fifteen hundred others in the major battle of that war. His name is on the memorial at Fort Recovery, Ohio.

The Piatts came to America in William's father's generation to escape religious persecution. They were Huguenots, French Protestants, a group that had been hounded for generations by the majority Catholics. William's father, John, immigrated to Holland, England and then to New Jersey, where he established a business. From there, he moved his wife and growing family to St. Domingo in the West Indies, where he built a sugar plantation.

Due to an uprising of workers, Piatt sent his wife and five sons back to New Jersey. About two years later, William Piatt, the oldest son, and a brother, returned to St. Domingo to locate their father. They discovered that their father, John, had been killed. Barely escaping with their lives, they boarded a ship bound for New Jersey. On its return, William fell overboard during a typhoon, but he survived by clinging for hours to a floating chicken coop until he located the ship and was able to climb aboard. Without that bit of divine Providence, we, his ancestors, would not be here today!

A great grandson of William Piatt, Charles Carroll Piatt, had an equally dramatic brush with death. He was involved in the 1868 Battle of Beecher Island, an Indian attack on an elite team of fifty cavalry scouts. The scouts were camped on the Arikaree River in Colorado, when they awoke at dawn to find that they were surrounded by over one thousand Indian warriors. Isolated on a sandbar in the middle of the river, the scouts used their tin cups to dig for cover in the sand and they began to defend themselves with their Spencer rifles.

Chief Roman Nose attacked the island with five hundred Indians on horseback. The sharp-shooting scouts killed him and repulsed the charge. The siege lasted nine days, rations ran out and the scouts were forced to eat the decaying horseflesh that surrounded them. Finally, a rescue party arrived, and amid the horse carnage, they found many dead Indians, including the chief. All but five scouts survived.

Vignettes

Root trips

While on my way to Lawrence, Kansas, to give a Christmas Tree Taxation talk, I visited Lecompton, Kansas, where my great grandparents, Charles and Charlotte Carroll, were married in 1872 (four years after Charles had fought in the Battle of Beecher Island - as described under Famous Relations). Ruth and I went on a "roots" trip to Ohio in June 2013, and visited the house where Charles Carroll was born in 1848. It is the oldest house in Columbus, Ohio, that is still inhabited.

Numbers

Numbers have always played a huge role in my work and my personal life. My mother started me on this path by teaching me the multiplication tables when I was five years old. The flow of numbers that she inspired within me continues to dwell in me nearly eighty years later!

I am convinced that angels communicate with me through numbers. The number of letters in my first, middle and last names, Vernon Lee Bowlby, are 6-3-6, and that combination adds up to 9 backwards and forwards. Its factors and multiples show up in an endless array of message forms. License plates are one of the most common. I frequently find myself following a car with the license numbers 636, or sometimes 326, the month and date of my birth, or 926, my half-birthday or often 631, which is the IRS code section that was the basis for the Christmas Tree Taxation Manual that I authored. Another number that shows up often, sometimes several times a day, is 444, which means that Saint Michael is with me!

Three is a sign of the Trinity. My mother was the third-born of five children, my father was the third of three boys and I was the third of five children, and the middle one of three boys. I was born on the 26th of the third month, my two brothers were both born on the 31st, and my two sisters were both born on the 23rd. Divine number timing!

Recently, I experienced a classic incident of divine communication through numbers. I found an old phone credit card, which I planned to use to make some long-distance calls while on a trip to Portland. But, five miles from town, I remembered that I had left the card behind. I used my cell phone to ask Ruth for the number on the card. My cell phone always tells me how many minutes that I have left and I noticed that I had 333 minutes. That, in itself, is unique. When I got to Portland and used the phone card number that I had received from Ruth, I heard the message, "You have 333 minutes on this card." Was this an amazing coincidence or a message from above? On my way into Portland, the last car that I had followed off the freeway was 636. When I was back onto the freeway, the car in front of me was 636. I consider that this is how I know that Saint Michael watches over me.

Picking up Pennies

When I find a penny or any other coin, I always pick it up. I consider the coin a blessing from heaven for the moment and, even though it may be small in amount, my blessing its presence indicates that I am open to receiving gifts from above. The more a person accepts the blessings that are sent their way, the more will come and they may well be beyond all expectations.

I frequently receive communications from the Holy Spirit in the form of coins or paper money. Pennies, nickels, dimes: the message is that I must humble myself to accept graciously whatever gift Spirit wishes to share with me at any given moment.

One morning, I checked my stocks and found that I had made a profit in the market, overnight, of over five thousand dollars. When I arrived at the golf course a few hours later, I opened my car door and saw a dark object on the ground. It was a burnt penny, a message to me to remain humble and gracious, and to bless all the gifts that flow to me from Spirit.

Cousin Connection

The grandchildren always had a wonderful time together at the Thanksgiving and Christmas dinners that my grandparents hosted. Of the Simpson's twenty-two grandchildren, seven of them attended our fiftieth wedding anniversary, nine were deceased, and two live in Michigan. We still see several of them regularly, I prepare income tax returns for two of my cousins and, through my healing practice, I have helped them with pain management.

Near-Death Experiences of my Father and Son

When my father was eleven years old, he accepted his friends' dare to climb a thirty-foot tree and touch an 11,000 volt wire. Blown downward through the tree, he landed on the ground with no signs of life. The friends rushed to get my grandfather, who carried him inside, laid him on a couch, and covered him with a blanket. However, to everyone's surprise, my father awoke, with a few assorted burns, but with no broken bones or other medical problems. More than a hundred of his descendants are thankful that he survived this dangerous escapade!

Our son, Bruce, also survived a dangerous fall. While at Pacific University in Forest Grove, Oregon, he leaned out a second-story dorm window to speak to someone looking out another window. The window frame suddenly came apart. Bruce fell head first, together with the broken window, to the concrete twenty feet below, landing on his arms and striking his heels on the metal window seal. Both arms and legs were bruised by the concrete and scratched by broken glass, but no bones were broken. Bruce's three daughters are thankful for his survival with no lasting effects.

Part 2: Finding My Path

Two Years in the Army

In June 1950, my brother, Bob, and I were at a Portland Beavers baseball game at the old Vaughn Street Park, when newspaper vendors came through the stands announcing that North Korea had invaded South Korea, an American ally. Our first thought was, "Where in the world is Korea?" We soon found out and, a year later, June 6, 1951, I was drafted into the United States Army.

Vernon in US Army, Camp Roberts, December 1951

After being declared 4F by the Navy, I thought that I was not qualified for military service. However, when it came to Korea, the draft board had lower standards. They needed "bodies" to fight in Korea and of the eighty-eight men who arrived for a physical in Portland the same day that I did, only one was not accepted.

The standard protocol was, that each soldier received fourteen weeks of basic training, after which he received a ten-day leave before being sent to Pittsburg, California, where he was deployed for a boat ride to Korea: known as FEACOM (Far East Command).

Basic training was grueling. We were being prepared for brutal warfare, in extreme heat, fighting over mountainous terrain, and the training regime and maneuvers were designed to mimic the conditions that we might experience in Korea.

The fear of combat was instilled in every soldier by such methods as the infiltration course, where trainees crawled through barbed wire, strung haphazardly along the dusty ground for a hundred yards. Live machine gun bullets flew thirty inches above their heads, in daylight and nighttime, tracer bullets left their red trail. Depth charges of live TNT, surrounded by wire, were also laced through the course, with ear-popping explosions that rained dirt and small rocks on the trainees. Occasionally, a soldier stood up from more fright than he could handle and he became a casualty of basic training. Another exercise, which put shivers rippling through our bodies, plus the fear of God deep into our souls, was when two hundred men with fixed bayonets charged over the hill, screaming bloody murder.

I was chosen by our company's Master Sergeant Zimmerman, as one of the ten out of three hundred men in our company, to be recommended for the eight-week Armed Forces Leadership School when our basic training was completed. If we were selected for Leadership School, we were promoted automatically to private first class and this included a pay raise from sixty-eight dollars a month to ninety-two dollars a month. Upon graduation, the top three men advanced to the rank of corporal and their pay increased to one hundred and thirty-two dollars a month. In addition, after successful completion of Leadership School, these three men would be assigned to train trainees, and they would not be flown to Korea. If one flunked out, his rank would be reduced to E-2 (the sixty-eight dollars a month pay rate). He would also receive three weeks of KP (kitchen police), ten days furlough and a boat ride to Korea. This was almost as undesirable as being on the front lines even sooner. Needless to say, the Army offered as many incentives as possible for each person to do his very best, for their desired result, with undesirable consequences, if we did not complete Leadership School.

As I entered my last week of basic training, I looked forward to the change and the opportunity to attend Leadership School. I exerted all my energy in order to obtain one of the top three spots and, for good measure, I tossed in a few prayers.

Spirit had a different plan for me. Later, when I looked back at my two-year Army experience and, at how many times I had come to a crossroads and chosen a plan, I would suddenly find myself going in an altogether different direction. Each time that I had made a decision to go one way, I would move another way, like a puppet on a string. The unplanned route always turned out to be better than the one I had chosen. That is when I learned the concept of surrender to a higher power. When you release yourself to the Divine, you no longer have to worry about what is going to happen. You lose your sense of fear and anger: those feelings emerge when you try to control things that you really cannot control. Surrender grants you peace of mind, in the knowledge that everything will be all right, and that you flow with the power of the Holy Spirit.

On the second-to-last day of the fourteen-week basic training course, we were assigned a maneuver that was supposed to duplicate live warfare, with real dynamite going off around us, as we climbed a long, steep hill. A rock that I had not seen, twice as big as my head, bounded down the mountain and, as I turned my head, it struck a glancing blow to my eyebrow. A doctor told me later that, if it had hit me a quarter-inch closer, it would have killed me.

Blood burst all over my face and I could not move or speak, although I remained conscious. Taken to the hospital, I recovered from the head wound in about three days. While I was in the hospital, I was given an overdose of a sulfa drug, which caused severe side effects. Three more weeks I remained in the hospital for observation and to recover from the drug overdose.

Since I had not finished basic training, my orders to attend Leadership School were cancelled.

The military sometimes acts stupidly, as anyone knows who has ever spent time in the armed services. When I was discharged from the hospital, I was placed in basic training with another training unit that was in their tenth week of a sixteen-week cycle. I was required to spend six extra weeks in basic training to make up for the one day that I had missed.

Sometime, during that second round of basic training, while walking across the parade ground, I chanced to meet Sgt. Zimmerman. He was surprised that I was not in Leadership School and, when I told him what had happened, he said, "I'm going to get you in if it is the last thing I do."

He went to Battalion Headquarters and, somehow, made it happen. This time, when everyone in my second basic training company received orders to go to Korea, I went to Leadership School at Camp Roberts, known as the "non-com West Point of the West."

Camp Roberts was modeled on West Point tradition and its aim was to develop non-commissioned officers for leadership in Korea. The commandant was a West Point graduate and a former World War II combat officer. His approach was to push us to our limits, both physically and mentally, in order to see what we could manage, with as much stress as the instructors could create. To survive, you had to be in extremely good physical condition and able to make good decisions under extreme mental duress.

One of the most important things that I learned in Leadership School was the value of focusing my energy. We were challenged in dozens of ways, and it was critical to know how much time should be consumed in meeting each challenge, without wasting time or effort. For example, we had brass insignias on our collars and some soldiers spent excessive hours shining their brass. Mine was never the shiniest, but it was always good enough to pass inspection. My shoes were not the shiniest, but I was never downgraded. Some candidates spent too much time doing things that were not that important, they lost sight of the big picture, and failed to complete another requirement.

It was in Leadership School that I developed my great love of teaching. We were trained in various activities and then we taught them to each other or to trainees. My first assignment was to teach the basics of the hand grenade to a group of about one hundred trainees, who did not want to be there. I stood on the side of a hill in 110-degree heat and taught my first class.

I had learned to kill with my bare hands (probably the last thing I ever wanted to know), and my second class was to teach this skill of unarmed combat. Even in those conditions, and with those topics, I realized that I loved teaching! When it came time to be assessed, I was the first man volunteering to be tested for my teaching skills. I got a sixty-five grade, and I passed by just one point, but it was more than a week before anyone else received a passing grade. Focusing time and energy in the right proportions paid off, handsomely, for me.

The final test of Leadership School was simulated combat. We were chased by "aggressors" night and day for forty-eight hours, over rugged terrain, and without any breaks or planned sleep. Then, the last twenty-four hours, under exhausting conditions, we ran through combat

54

situations and were graded upon our reactions. Several of the non-commissioned candidates were exhausted, mentally and physically, and they dropped out of training during the three-day final grind. I felt blessed, as my body, somehow, always performed strongly the more difficult the challenge, such as climbing Mt. Hood the first time when I was eighteen years old, and this situation was not an exception.

I completed Leadership School as one of twenty-eight men who finished, out of over one hundred soldiers who had begun the training. As I placed number two, I received my corporal stripes and an increase in pay to one hundred thirty-two dollars a month. With hindsight, I have no doubt that the Almighty had played a significant part in the many twists and curves that completed my manifestation of not only finishing the leadership course, but graduating in the top three. I was pleased that I would be training trainees, which would advance my teaching skills, instead of being flown to Korea.

After a month or so of training trainees, I discovered that training raw recruits was a lot more stressful than I had ever imagined, but I loved every minute of it, even though it allowed very little time for sleep.

A short time later, one of my fellow cadre men (non-commissioned officers who trained trainees) told me that he had had a wonderful time in the airborne and that he was sure I would enjoy it. Realizing that I was not acrophobic, from the experiences of my boyhood, jumping off the cliff of the gravel pit, climbing tall fruit ladders, climbing like a monkey around tall walnut trees, or walking on top of 11,245 foot Mt. Hood (which was as exhilarating a thrill for me as it had been for my grandfather), I decided in a flash to sign on for the airborne.

The next day, I obtained the necessary papers to become a paratrooper and signed my request for a transfer to Fort Bragg, North Carolina. I had never known the Army to operate with such speed, as two weeks later I received orders for a ten-day furlough, and orders to report to Fort Bragg to begin training as a paratrooper. Again, I was very excited and I began to get ready for my departure in ten days. I wondered then if the Army knew something that they were not telling me, such as an airborne invasion of North Korea?

Two days before my first furlough was to send me home, my orders were cancelled because I had only fourteen months and three weeks to serve. The airborne training required fifteen months of service at the time I entered training. Therefore, for the lack of a few days to serve, I realized that I was to remain a trainer of trainees at Camp Roberts, California. Once again, Spirit had changed my plans.

After training trainees for a month or so, I visited an Army friend, who had become an MP (Military Police) at Camp Roberts and he told me how exciting it was to be an MP. He suggested that I consider requesting a transfer to the MPs. That sounded like a good idea and he took me to visit his company commander, whom I instantly liked. He said that he had an opening and that he would love to have me join his company. I thought, wow! This is too good to be true! I signed the necessary request forms, which were sent to Regimental Headquarters to complete the transfer within a couple of weeks! I was in seventh heaven, thinking that this was splendid! I returned to my basic training company and thought that I had robbed a bank when someone had left an open door.

Two weeks later, my company commander called me in to discuss the transfer. Much to my dismay, he asked me why I wanted to leave the Infantry, when it was the backbone of the Army and the most glorious experience of a lifetime. He told me then that I was just too valuable a trainer of trainees and he refused to sign the transfer. I felt as though I had been hit in the head with a baseball bat from behind. I walked out of his office and wondered why Spirit had done this. Three weeks later, nearly all of my friend's MP Company, including my Army friend, received orders for Korea. Once again, I concluded that Spirit watched over me.

After serving seventeen months in basic training and training trainees, I was mentally ready for a change. I then decided to ask for a transfer from Camp Roberts to Ft. Benning, Georgia, where I was to enter Officer Candidate School, which required my resignation from the military upon completion of the twenty-two-week course. I would have to re-enlist for two more years as an officer. It sounded as though it would be a good thing to have in my resume.

I received a ten-day furlough and orders to report to Fort Benning for training. The barracks there were the nicest that I had ever seen, with almost metallic bright green floors and plenty of privacy. I guessed that this must be part of being "an officer and a gentleman."

I quickly discovered that there was a downside to the officers' training area, as the barracks were heated by coal and thick, acrid black smoke was always present. It was quite cold in Georgia at night, beginning in September and continuing through the winter months.

A week later, I came down with an inflamed sinus infection that was extremely painful. I continued in the program for the next sixteen weeks, and I suffered numerous infections and splitting headaches, during the entire time. I was excited to receive blue cloth bars which signified that I had six weeks remaining in officers training. Unfortunately, upon awakening, my sinuses hurt so badly that I was dizzy and I could barely walk. I decided that I had endured all the pain my physical body could stand, and so I went straight to the commandant's office and asked to resign from officers' training. This the Army frowned upon, after its having spent seventeen weeks training me as an officer. Fortunately, the commandant's wife also suffered from the coal smoke and, sympathetic, he granted my resignation.

Once again, there was an unplanned change of course in my life's journey. The black coal-smoke was a blessing in disguise, as it affected my sinuses, which had kept me out of the Navy, and I did not have to serve two more years in the Army. Most likely, I would never have met my wife, Ruth, and I would never have guessed that the black coal smoke was to be directly responsible, forty years later, for six more years of pain that would lead me to the role of healer. Additionally, I might have made the dreaded trip to Korea and, perhaps, I would have become just another Army casualty of war.

I served my final five months in the Army with the military personnel division, completing the paperwork for promotions and transfers of other military personnel. I enjoyed the last months of my military service and I left on weekend passes to visit the white sandy beaches in Florida, as well as to visit other interesting sites, such as President Roosevelt's private hideaway in Warm Springs, Georgia, and the Masters Golf Course in Augusta. My office was next door to the military courtroom and, in my spare time, I watched the military court proceedings. It was fascinating to watch and hear the prosecution, as well as the attorneys for the defendants in action, which later encouraged me to serve as an expert witness for court cases, after I had become a CPA many years afterward.

My Army experience raised my personal growth to a level that I never could have achieved in any other manner. It made me aware of the constantly changing crossroads of life and the fact that a wrong turn at any point could have huge repercussions later in life's journey. It also helped me to understand that, no matter what decision I made, guidance from above would move me to a better resolution than I could have imagined.

The Korean War was the first United States engagement in which men would openly admit that they had no desire to serve their country during war. This attitude was the opposite of the servicemen who served in World War II, completed less than five years before, when Japan had surrendered officially on September 2, 1945. In general, the public maintained a positive attitude towards servicemen, but it disliked the thought that another war was to begin that was termed, officially, a "Police Action."

During the Korean War, 750,000 American soldiers served in Korea, compared to 1,500,000 men and women who served in World War II. In Korea, about 55,000 died and over 8,000 were missing in action, according to Oregon's Korean War Memorial in Wilsonville, Oregon.

When the North Koreans attacked South Korea, they quickly surrounded the South Korean Army and massacred 400,000 men, committing one of the most brutal atrocities in the history of mankind. In a short period of time, the North Koreans captured all of South Korea, except for a small area around the Pusan Harbor, on the southern tip. Fortunately, the Americans arrived in timely fashion, and they slowly held back the North Koreans. In the Pusan Harbor battle, 4,280 American soldiers were killed, 12,377 were wounded, 2,107 were missing in action, and 401 were confirmed captured.

Where do you think the world would be today, if it were not for the Americans, who took the brunt of the cost of the war in both men and money, other than the South Koreans, who suffered extreme losses both in the military as well as the civilian population?

A possible answer to that question is that the entire world may have been laid waste long ago, as North Korea would have had all the productive energy of the entire Korean nation. It is a known fact that the goal of North Korea is unchanged and it still attempts to develop nuclear rockets that can destroy the West Coast of the United States.

Another huge benefit to our country from the Korean War is the hundreds of thousands of Koreans who have immigrated to the United States and who have contributed mightily to our nation's success.

Many years later, a counselor told me that my soul was completely opposed to hurting people in war, or at any other time. In the Army, I was trained to kill with my bare hands and I became an unarmed combat instructor. I have prayed, over the years, that I would never find the need to use my hands and feet for destructive purposes. As I grew to develop my life's healing mission in the world, I learned to use my hands to heal people and, in that capacity, my soul has flourished.

Mountains to Climb

I was honorably discharged from Ft. Benning on June 5, 1953. Rather than returning home directly, I took the train north and toured with some Army friends. After a few days in Washington, DC, I went to New York City, where an Army buddy, Richard Riker, gave me a weeklong tour. We stayed in his mother's tiny apartment at 5 East 51st Street, across the street from St. Patrick's Cathedral in Manhattan.

On the train ride home from New York, I stopped to visit relatives in Constantine, Michigan, where I was born. I have always felt a strong connection to Constantine, despite the fact that my family lived there for only fourteen months after my birth. The town is named for the Roman Emperor Constantine the Great, a significant figure in the history of Christianity.

When I returned to Hood River, I was astounded by the beauty of the area in which I had grown up. There is nothing like a two-year absence to increase one's appreciation for one's home town! My brother, Bob, and I had always talked about our climbing Mt. Hood and Mt. Adams together and now seemed a perfect time. Our grandfather Simpson, seventy-two years old, made us promise to carry his ice ax to the top of the mountains, which was the ice axe he had used to climb Mt. Hood sixty-five times as the first-aid man for the Crag Rats.

We arranged to climb Mt. Hood with some very experienced climbers and another friend, and we left for Mt. Hood a few days later. At 11:00 PM, Bob and I, along with about five other climbers, left Timberline Lodge, at the 6,000-foot level, to ascend the southern trail to the top of Mt. Hood. At 11,245 feet, it is the highest peak in Oregon. There was a full moon and the bright snow made it easy to see the trail. Our spiked shoe crampons dug into the ice and made an eerie clanking sound as we walked, single-file, behind our leader. We were soon stretched out over a hundred yards and I had the sense that I walked on a distant planet.

The leader stopped the group quite frequently, and Bob and I felt our legs tighten up in the long rest periods. Our blood surged and we were eager to expend our youthful energy. I had climbed Mt. Hood once before, with my good friend, Dick Minor, the summer after I had graduated from high school, so I asked the leader to permit Bob and me to move ahead of the group. He consented and Bob and I, quite quickly, left the rest of the climbers behind. As we looked back down the mountain, the other climbing groups looked like dark centipedes, wending their way slowly up the mountain.

After four hours of vigorous hiking, we reached the most difficult part of the trail. Bob and I tied ourselves together with rope for the last five hundred feet up the icy chute, one of us anchoring with the ice axe, while the other climbed. We both crawled the last few feet to the top of the mountain, where we could look five thousand feet down to the north side of the mountain, one thousand feet to the south. To the east was a narrow ice trail, about six feet wide, with steps carved in from the crampons of previous climbers. About one hundred feet along the trail, the mountain top widened.

When I stood up to walk the ice trail, Bob told me to untie the rope. He knew how fearless I was and he did not want to be bound to me for the icy traverse. I walked, while Bob crawled and, for dear life, I clung to each icy step. He thought that I was crazy to walk across the icy trail and to risk falling. He still says so to this day!

Bob and Vernon Climbing Black Crater in 1992. Mt. Jefferson in Background

The remaining climbers joined us about an hour later and we watched the dawn break at the summit. We could see nearly all the way to the Oregon coast and to the wheat fields of Central Oregon. When the sun rose, we could see the shadow of Mt. Hood to the west, a very interesting view.

A message came to me of how insignificant is man, compared to God.

On the way down the mountain, we glissaded at terrific speeds down the snowfields, our ice axes controlling the descent. Our pants and packs were burned from the friction! We arrived home that afternoon and we were back at work the next Monday morning.

That same summer, Bob and I climbed Mt. Adams, which has four false summits: you think that you have reached the top, because you cannot see anything higher, and then, when you walk a little farther, you see that you still have a long way to go! My grandfather's spirit animated us through that climb as well. Bob and I had both inherited his extraordinary capacity to create oxygen for energy in high altitudes. In October 1953, grandfather Simpson died, a few months after our two climbs.

The Gift from Spirit to Learn the Trade of a Meat-Cutter

While sitting atop Mt. Hood, I tried to envision how I might accumulate enough money to last through four years of college. It was obvious to me, that, to increase my present nest egg, I needed to earn more than a minimum wage. I also needed to earn more money during the summer college breaks. No sooner had I this thought, than Spirit provided an answer that had lain dormant in my mind! I was to visit Cecil Hickey, whom I had worked for in his grocery store before my Army service, and I should ask him if there was a chance to learn the meat-cutter trade. I knew that it would pay substantially more than a minimum wage.

Upon my returning home from climbing Mt. Hood, I ventured to Cecil's store and I broached the subject of my learning that trade. Much to my elation, Cecil said that my timing was good, as one of his two meat-cutters was retiring on August 1, 1953, and that I could begin August 3. Once again, divine timing and spiritual direction were given me. Learning the meat-cutter trade would allow me to save a tidy sum over the next fourteen months and it would eventually lead me to my bride-to-be. Spirit, as usual, provided a gift for me, far in excess of my wildest imagination.

Car Tales

My 1934 Chevrolet

I can remember, as if it were yesterday, the purchase of my first car in summer of 1949, after I had graduated from high school. I paid two hundred dollars for a 1934 Chevrolet. While I was in the Army, my mother sold the car to my best friend's brother for seventy-five dollars. She loaned this money, very promptly, to my brother, Wayne, who needed money to finance an inventory for his bread route.

My 1952 Two-Toned Metallic Green Chevrolet

When I returned from military service, I purchased a two-tone metallic green 1952 Chevrolet, a two-seater. One time, I took my brother, Bob, and three of his friends, to ski at Timberline Lodge. We took the magic mile chair lift up one thousand vertical feet from Timberline Lodge, over the snow fields of Mt. Hood, and we skied down to the lodge, in nearly three feet of blowing powder snow. It was a total whiteout: you could not see your hand in front of your face! When we finished skiing for the day, we got back in the car and headed around the mountain towards Hood River.

At the turnoff to Hood River, there was a sign saying, "Highway Closed for the Winter." So, I said, "Let's open it up!" The men got out of the car, moved the barricades and, after replacing the barricades, we drove on. It snowed and blew so hard that you could barely see the road. Several times, I slid off the highway and, each time, the fellows got out and pushed the car back onto the road, and away we went. The highway was closed for fifteen miles, but we made it to the plowed highway and, with no chains, we were the only car on it. Because of my extensive experience driving on snow, and my faith, it never occurred to me that we would not make it around the mountain.

My 1956 Red & White 4-Barrell Pontiac

My next car came into my life when I first moved to Goldendale, as the head meat-cutter for Safeway. I received a call from a fellow that I had known, who worked for a Pontiac dealer in Hood River. He had received a super-good buy on a brand new, red and white, two-toned 1956 Pontiac, for a price of eighteen hundred dollars. The listed selling price had been nearly three thousand dollars. But, having had a disagreement with his boss, and now working for another dealer, he could not drive a Pontiac. It was not difficult to talk me into buying the car, as it was beautiful, beyond my wildest dreams and it had many extras. My Angel of Abundance had come through again. In my entire lifetime, that was the only occasion when I have paid personal interest on any purchase, as I always believe in saving money and paying cash for personal items.

The following winter, I loaned my car to one of my fellow employees at the Safeway store in Goldendale so that he might take his "dream girl", Ruth Grady, whom I had never met, to their high school seniors' Valentine's Day dance.

The First Call to College

I was in a foxhole in the Army with trainees when I recalled that my seventh grade teacher had said that some of us would earn $300,000 in our lifetimes, and I thought that I should go to college, if I were ever to earn that sum of money. I decided that I should pursue that idea when I returned to Hood River after my honorable discharge.

At that time, many returning veterans took advantage of the GI Bill, a law that provided a single person one hundred ten dollars a month toward college expenses. The first step was a test, administered by the Veterans Administration, to help GIs determine which aptitudes best suited the careers that they wanted. I had already experienced the love of teaching during my Army leadership training and I had a strong desire to teach at the high school level. When my test scores arrived, I met with a Veterans Affairs counselor, who told me that, realistically, I would not make it through college. It would be a waste of my time and the government's money, for me to try. Of course, his attitude motivated me! I argued with him that the tests had missed something essential - my desire and determination to succeed in college. In the fall of 1954, I enrolled at the Oregon College of Education in Monmouth and I completed that first year as one of the top five students in my freshman class.

I was twenty-three years old when I entered college at the Oregon College of Education (now known as Western Oregon University) from which, many years later, my granddaughter, Jenny, would graduate.

My brother, Bob, five years younger, joined me at the Oregon College of Education after his graduation from high school the following year. What a great time we had! We lived together off campus, paid fifteen dollars a month for rent, and about the same for food. Tuition was forty dollars a quarter and that included a ten-dollar student body card. Despite the difference in our ages and experience, Bob and I had that special brotherly bond that allowed us to joke around and tease each other in cheerful comfort. Whenever we cooked a steak, one person cut it in half and the other could choose which half he wanted. Obviously, neither of us got the short end of a steak! We played a lot of pinochle while in college, sometimes until 2:00 AM.

There were some wonderful professors at Monmouth, and I especially enjoyed my world literature and history classes. Bob and I both appreciated history, and later, both Bob and I explored Civil War battlefields and historical sites in many foreign countries. Bob circled the Earth with his family of five, while he worked for the Guy F. Atkinson Construction Company and he visited the Taj Mahal in India.

Everyone warned me not to take too many classes in college so, my first term, I took only sixteen hours. The second term, I took nineteen hours and, in the spring, I took twenty-two hours. I studied in quite a different manner from my brother. He was methodical, reading and reviewing every day. I tended to study just before a test and I focused intently on preparation for an exam. I always garnered one of the highest grades in the class. My brain is at its best when under pressure to complete a task and, for better or for worse, I have seen that trait in some of my grandchildren, while some are like my brother, Bob.

I left Monmouth in June and planned to return for my sophomore year in the fall. My brother-in-law worked on The Dalles Dam and, for the summer, he had obtained a laborer's job for me. After my second day of work on the dam, as we were going out the door to work, I received a phone call from the Safeway manager in Hood River to ask if I were interested in going to Goldendale, Washington, to cover for the meat-cutter, who was on sick-leave for three weeks. My training as a meat-cutter at Hickey's Market now led me to Ruth, the love of my life. The manager of the Hood River Safeway, Paul Sandstorm, knew me and he had recommended me for the job. Thanks, Spirit.

Safeway offered me a salary twice what I earned as a laborer on the dam, so I borrowed a white shirt from my brother-in-law and headed to Goldendale, where I had never been before. The three-week stint turned into a regular job as a meat-cutter substitute, working vacations for all the area Safeways. I had planned to work the summer for Safeway and return to school in the fall, as I was accumulating money for my college education at a good pace.

Before fall arrived, Safeway offered me a substantial pay increase if I would stay the rest of the year. In October, they told me that I had turned the meat market's loss into a profit and that they would give me still another increase in pay, if I continued to work until March, when I could return to school. In February, they told me that I had sold more sides of beef, adding substantially to the bottom-line profit, than any other of their several hundred stores in the Pacific Northwest. Safeway paid me a bonus that I was happy to receive, and then I was offered eight hundred dollars a month, with additional bonuses, if I continued to cut meat for them until the following fall.

When I added up the money that I could make working for the next six months, it was easy to see that it would be more than enough to carry me all the way through college. This offer was too good to decline and I agreed to work until the middle of September. With hindsight, it was a wise decision, in many different ways as, three weeks later, I met my life's mate, Ruth Grady, in Goldendale.

With bonuses, I earned over five dollars an hour, which was a lot more than when I had started at Hickey's Market, six years previously, and had earned thirty-five cents an hour. I calculated that about fourteen hours of work at Safeway paid me more than I had earned for several months when I was drafted into the Army. My Guardian Angel and my Angel of Abundance conspired to plan for my future in a divine manner.

Ruth Comes into My Life

To drive to Goldendale from The Dalles, where I intended to work that day on The Dalles Dam, I took the historic Maryhill Loops Highway, which rises from the Columbia River. It was built under the direction of Sam Hill, between 1909 and 1913, as an experiment in road-building techniques and surfaces. I later learned that one of my relatives, Major Henry L. Bowlby, was an engineer on that project. The road rises 850 feet in a series of twenty-five curves, eight of them hairpin turns and on the weekend of June 28-29, 2014, there was a world event for skateboarders from twenty-three countries, with hundreds of participants racing down the loops.

Shortly after I reached the top of the Maryhill Loops, four miles from Goldendale, a green 1948 Hudson Hornet drove out of a driveway right in front of me. The driver was so short that I could not see her head above the seat. She drove by, looking through the steering wheel! I tried to pass the car several times but, each time, the Hornet sped up. Finally, we reached town and I thought no more of it until nine months later, when I met Ruth Grady. I discovered that her grandfather owned the green Hornet and that Ruth had been the driver.

I met Ruth in March 1956. A high school senior, Don, who worked for me at the Safeway, had a crush on Ruth and, for months, he had told me about his wonderful girlfriend.

One day, he decided that I should meet Ruth in front of the Goldendale Safeway. When he introduced us, it was love at first sight for Ruth and me. Don knew it too. Later, he said that he had looked at Ruth, then he had looked at me, and he knew that it was ended for the two of them.

Ruth and I had actually had two previous encounters. One was the four-mile drive into Goldendale that first day that I had come to town, ten months before. The second was at a high school basketball game in February. It was an icy night, but some of my friends wanted to go to The Dalles for a beer. Growing up in Hood River, you did not let a little ice stop you, or your social life would be non-existent for five months of the year! We decided to stop by and watch the second half of the basketball game on the way to The Dalles, twenty-five miles away. It was 9:00 PM, and there were never charges after half-time, so, we walked past the girls who were selling tickets, trooped to the top of the stands, and sat down to wait for the second half to begin. Suddenly, Ruth appeared and said, "Hey, you guys didn't buy tickets!" It seemed that the other team was delayed by the ice and, therefore, the game had not yet begun. As everyone in town watched, Ruth ousted us from the bleachers.

Ruth was seventeen years old, and a senior in high school, when we had our first date on April 15, 1956. I took her to her senior prom in June. (These days, the authorities probably would not let a twenty-five year old man take his girlfriend to her senior prom!) In July, I gave her an engagement ring.

I had never had a serious relationship before Ruth, although for years, my mother had tried to involve me with blind dates. All four of her other children were married by age twenty, but my mother was still doing my laundry when I was twenty-five! She had never found a good match for me and, when I met Ruth, my mother was very happy.

I was not Ruth's first boyfriend, but I was the first that her grandfather approved of for Ruth to marry! He wanted Ruth to attend Behnke-Walker Business College in Portland, which his two sons attended, before she went to college. That gave me the idea to switch my major to Accounting, so we both decided to attend Behnke-Walker.

66

Her grandfather's practical advice helped to speed our courtship along. Initially, Ruth and I thought that we would wait a year to marry. We planned to go to Portland and attend Behnke-Walker Business College for nine months, and then to marry in June 1957. Ruth's grandfather convinced us that we should marry right away. "You kids should get married before you go," he said, "otherwise you'll have to rent two different places to live in Portland."

In August, Ruth and I were baptized together, with full immersion, in the Goldendale Baptist Church and we married September 2, 1956.

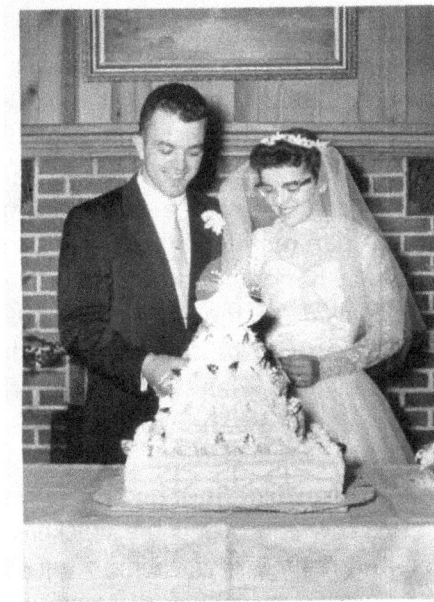

Vernon and Ruth Wed in Baptist Church, Goldendale, Washington, September 2nd, 1956

Our honeymoon began in one of my favorite places, Timberline Lodge on the south slopes of Mt. Hood, followed by a trip to Cannon Beach, Oregon.

Ruth gave me a Bible as a wedding gift and her Uncle, Ed Grady, wrote in the cover sheets two Bible verses, which proved to be very prophetic: "A good name is to be chosen rather than great riches, and favor is better than silver or gold." (Proverbs 22:1)

Less than nine years later, this came true, as my name allowed me to borrow one hundred percent of the money needed to build an office building.

Jesus said in Matthew 5:16, "Let your light so shine before men, that they may see your good works, and glorify your Father which is in Heaven."

My intent to heal people brought me many more, as directed to me by Spirit.

The Safeway district manager told me that he disliked losing me as an employee, but he understood that to go to college was a better option for me. When I told him that we were going to college in Portland, he offered to call the Safeway office in Portland and set up a system for me to work, whenever a meat-cutter was sick, in one of the fifty neighborhood stores in the Portland area. That was perfect, as I could go to school every day at 8:00 AM, take classes until I received a phone call to start work at 1:00 PM and finish at 10:00 PM. That was a long day, considering that I did not get home until 10:30 PM and that my next day started at 6:00 AM.

Although Ruth was young, she was much more mature than most people her age. Both her parents died when she was two and one-half years old. She was raised by her grandparents on the family's farm.

Her grandfather had lived on the farm since 1895, when he was twelve years old and had arrived by stagecoach with his parents and older sister. Because the highway was so icy in winter, Ruth often lived with her unmarried great-aunt Nora, her grandfather's sister, who had a house in town.

Beginning as a very young child, Ruth had many responsibilities. She got up early to milk the cows and tend the chickens and rabbits. She worked in the garden and helped her grandmother can. She learned a farm girl's skills, which has paid off handsomely in our married life.

When I left college in June, 1955, I had every intention to work that summer on The Dalles Dam and to return to college in the fall. With what appeared to be an amazing series in synchronicity of events, and clearly the work of the Holy Spirit just as it had been in the Army, I was moved around like a puppet on a string, for a far better result than I could ever have imagined, manifesting in Eugene and the University of Oregon.

Our first home in Portland was Ruth's cousin's remodeled garage, which had a little kitchen in the space where two cars were designed to park, a tiny bathroom, finished walls, and it rented for fifty dollars a month. Every morning we left our home around 7:00 AM and drove to downtown Portland, where Behnke-Walker Business College was located. Ruth took classes all day long and I took classes until I received a phone call from Helen, at the Safeway office, telling me which of the fifty different Safeway stores needed me that day. We loved our life in Portland and we both felt lucky to move into our future together, with a good part-time job to support each of our business college's tuition of eighty dollars a month.

When Ruth graduated from Behnke-Walker in June 1957, she was hired by a Portland doctor's office. One evening, when I was cutting meat at a Safeway, a divine golden message came to me that I should leave Behnke-Walker and transfer to the University of Oregon. I had heard about a business professor there, a Dr. Johnson, who was supposed to be the best in the country and I knew, suddenly, that I would prosper under his tutelage, and that to become a CPA was my best plan.

That night, I told Ruth of this message to leave Portland and to move to Eugene. She was quite surprised at first, but she adapted, very quickly, to the idea. We found an apartment in the downstairs of a remodeled house, close to the Oregon campus and we moved to Eugene in August 1957. I registered for classes and then I returned to Portland to work at Safeway. I continued to go to school until classes began at the University of Oregon.

Ruth was an excellent secretary and she soon found a job. Our rent and food budgets were each forty dollars a month. Ruth's salary, along with our savings, my summer work at Safeway's meat departments, my two veterans' education allowances of fifty dollars a month from the state, $135 per month from the federal government and my full-time job in a local CPA firm, when I completed my junior year of college, beginning in June, 1959, allowed us to save money during our thirty-month adventure at the University of Oregon. (What a difference fifty years makes. Today, most college graduates finish college with a mountain of debt, whereas we never thought to borrow money for my education, and we saved money at the same time. Of course, we lived a very frugal life.)

Ruth worked at first for Karl Onthank, who was involved with dozens of different conservation organizations. Onthank spent the whole day dictating to Ruth and she never had time to type his dictation. Today, she calls that phase her Ph.T: Putting Hubby Through. She then became the secretary for the Department of Economics, until August 31, 1959, when she was due to have our first child within a couple of weeks.

I continued to work summers as a meat-cutter for Safeway stores in Eugene, Corvallis and Albany. The GI Bill also helped defray our costs, once I resolved a small obstacle. When I went to Behnke Business College, a non-accredited school, I received $135 a month from the federal government and $50 from the state of Oregon. The GI Bill prohibited switching a second time between a non-accredited and an accredited college, and the University of Oregon was the latter.

So, when I enrolled at the University of Oregon, it was simultaneously with the Business College of Eugene. The tuition was thirty-five dollars a month and I was not required to attend classes. I could collect my GI Bill payments, because I was still enrolled in a business college, and I had access to the business college if I ever needed specialized help. For the most part, I used it as a quiet place to study. It was one of those impossible problems that found a simple solution. Indeed, Spirit must have worked overtime to come up with a plan for me to be paid while studying.

My year at Behnke-Walker gave me a considerable head start on my accounting degree at the University of Oregon. The school, founded around the turn of the century, was one of the top business schools in the country. It had a generous donor, who had made it possible to hire an excellent teaching staff. When I joined the University of Oregon business program as a sophomore in September 1957, Behnke-Walker had prepared me well to make the most of this educational opportunity.

As always, I could not have earned the grades that I did without the help of certain angels, who came to me when I needed them. One of these angels was Marie Mason, an older mathematics teacher, who saved me when I had difficulty with algebra. I had not taken an algebra class since I was a freshman in high school, twelve years before, and I competed against high school graduates who had extensive training in algebra.

In my first class, I could not understand my instructor, a Japanese graduate student who barely spoke English. When he talked, he turned his back to us and faced the board. I left his class and wondered how I was to pass the algebra requirement when I met a person whom I had met the prior month during registration. I told him my dilemma and he said, "Go to Deady Hall and talk to Marie Mason. She loves to teach algebra to veterans." Marie was a truly outstanding teacher, a beautiful person with a passion for teaching which bordered on the divine. I completed my algebra classes with no difficulty: As and Bs. Once again, Spirit had matched me with a person who had guided me to Marie Mason.

The divine timing of meeting such a person, walking across campus, whom I knew only casually a month before, while waiting in line, who could direct me to the one person on campus who could teach me algebra, was clearly the work of my Angel of Education. And Marie Mason was an angel of a person to boot!

Dr. Charles Johnson, the professor whose reputation had brought me to the University of Oregon, was another of my angels. His outside-the-box thinking validated my own right-brained approach to accounting and life in general. Following his heart, he had left a lucrative job in the private sector to teach at the University of Oregon. His technique was to involve the class in complex real-world accounting problems. I remember clearly my first day in his classroom, when he covered the entire front blackboard and half the side blackboard, with one single problem, which he went over in finite detail.

In those days, the CPA exam consisted of problems submitted by professors like Dr. Johnson and he was responsible for many of the questions on the CPA exam. He used us for practice on the questions that he submitted for the CPA exam in his classroom. His students were challenged daily, on a high professional level. One needed a fifty percent score in order to pass one of his tests. I received a score of fifty-five percent on the first test (a D grade) but I felt fine about it, as there were only two other students who scored in the fifties and the rest of the class received Fs!

The Passing of a Great Mentor

I had a surprising experience the day Dr. Johnson died. He had become the active president of the University of Oregon at a very difficult time, when there was a great deal of student unrest on college campuses regarding the Vietnam War. On June 17, 1969, exhausted and distracted, he was killed when, on the McKenzie Highway, his VW veered head-on into the path of a log truck.

I was in a tax class in San Francisco that day, along with about three hundred other CPAs from all over the country. Eight people were at my table for lunch and we began to talk about our most influential teachers in college. Amazingly, we had all had Dr. Johnson for accounting, and we all agreed that he was the most dynamic teacher that we had ever had, and worth the price of our college education. We found out later on the evening news that he had died that morning. It was a complete coincidence that his name had come up for discussion and that all of us had graduated from the University of Oregon - a divine tribute to a great mentor.

Ruth in support

Ruth, of course, was my foremost angel, who worked to support us so that I could devote myself to my studies. While she served as secretary to the Department of Economics, she learned to play bridge, a skill that she has developed over the past fifty-seven years. Now, she plays bridge several times a week and she serves as a substitute for several bridge clubs. Ruth learned from associations, while I was in college, that bridge is a social grace which will take you a long way. That certainly has been true for Ruth, who, over the years, has made hundreds of friends through her bridge connections.

We enjoyed a nice social life in Eugene and we spent our free time together, going for walks, sometimes picking up English walnuts and gathering other seasonal fruits. Ruth is a wonderful cook and a frugal homemaker. We both had extensive experience with canning and we took advantage of the valley's bounty to fill our pantry with delicious preserves.

Ruth was interested in and supported my school work. One time, I decided to give her an opportunity to participate. She was to gather information for a paper that I needed for a health class and the topic was leukemia. She worked hard and assembled fifty-five pages of information, which I condensed into a paper of five pages, for which I received an A-plus. Ruth could have been a terrific student, but she chose to be a great mother, the heart of our household, and I will be forever grateful for that.

The Right-Brained CPA Experience

Our first child, Catherine Irene, was born September 18, 1959. Ruth had worked through the end of August and she was more than ready for the baby to arrive. My mother was determined to be there for the birth, but she had other commitments that day and my parents did not arrive at the hospital until 9:00 PM. Ruth had been in labor for over twenty-four hours. The moment Cathy was born, she gave a wild whoop, which my mother heard upon her arrival.

At the beginning of my senior year at the University of Oregon, I needed only twenty-six more credits to complete my degree in accounting, as I had taken extra hours each term. The previous June, I had commenced auditing and other accounting work for a small CPA firm in Eugene. Since I had such a light academic load, I continued to work for the CPA firm throughout my senior year, until March 13, when I completed my college career. I divided my time between attendance at the Eugene Business College, the University of Oregon classes, work for the CPA firm, homework and the our new family. (My time at the Armed Forces Leadership School and Army officers' training had prepared me well to manage multiple tasks at the same time.)

The small CPA firm was a partnership of two CPAs, one right-brained, the other left-brained. Twenty-two students were interviewed for the job, as both CPA partners needed an assistant. Ed Ruby, the right-brained CPA, chose to work with me and the left-brained CPA found someone like himself. Being able to observe the two very different approaches to accounting made this an ideal learning experience, together with accounting challenges that I encountered.

Ed Ruby was a people person, his desk covered with loosely towered piles of paper, where he could find, instantly, anything that he wanted. I do not know how he could do this. The other CPA's desk was pristine, his every move methodical and he focused on completion of each task before the next began. Ed was very outgoing, had high energy and worked on many projects simultaneously. It was Ed who brought much new business to the firm and I loved to work with him and observe his multi-tasking skills.

The CPA firm did much accounting for timber-related companies in the area, and I learned later that few CPAs adequately understood the complex issues of the timber tax code. Timber investing turned a profit only when timber was harvested, but the harvest might be decades from the time that the trees were planted. I was fortunate to have been hired by Ed Ruby, as I learned the timber tax laws early in my accounting career, and it was instrumental in my being hired by a national CPA firm that did a lot of timber tax work.

Ed Ruby wanted me to stay with his firm and become a partner, and I would not have minded that because Ruth and I both loved Eugene. As a senior, I had been interviewed by recruiters from large CPA firms and private businesses in Portland and all around the Northwest. Anyone who had received C's in Dr. Johnson's class was considered a top student. My three straight C's from Dr. Johnson, together with my timber tax experience, was the key to my being hired by a national CPA firm at age twenty-nine. Once again, Spirit's message to me, while I was cutting meat in a Safeway many months before, that I should transfer to the University of Oregon, and learn from one of the best accounting teachers in the country, had awarded big dividends.

After Christmas, I visited my parents, who lived in Gresham, Oregon, a trip that coincided with my interview at a national CPA firm.

Afterwards, I knew, without a doubt, that I wanted to work for such a firm. The message from Spirit was that it was like playing baseball in the major leagues, as compared to the minor leagues. The minors being small CPA firms or private businesses. One could have interesting challenges in a small CPA firm, but anyone who works even a few years for a national CPA firm can write his own ticket on what he wants to do for his future. Pay for work at a national firm paid substantially less than at a private company but, within a few years, one could often earn more than double the income of an accountant in a private business.

I graduated in March 1960, we moved to S.E. Alder Street in Portland, and on April 1, I began work in the Portland office of Touche Ross, a national CPA firm which employed thirty-five accountants, plus administrative staff.

First Day of Work in a National Accounting Firm

They hired six new CPAs simultaneously and each would earn four hundred dollars a month. (This was half as much as I had earned as a head meat-cutter for Safeway, four years before.) That first year, I began to get offers from other firms. One of my colleagues, Bob Collins, in his first year of work for one of their clients, was offered six hundred dollars a month, the second year, eight hundred dollars a month, and the third year, one thousand dollars a month. Eventually, Bob accepted a position with a company on the "big board" of the stock exchange, where he became chief accountant, sales manager, comptroller and, finally, president of the company, all by the age of thirty-two!

It was obvious to me that Spirit had carefully mapped out my accounting education in multiple unusual ways, and dead-ends had brought bountiful results. Clearly, after graduation from high school, my life had been orchestrated meticulously, so that I would graduate in eleven years, in a manner that could only be described as divine timing. The divine message that I received at 9:00 PM, while I worked in the meat department at Safeway in Vermont Hills, near Portland, Oregon, changed the direction in my accounting career from business college to the challenge "head-on" at the University of Oregon and it had paid huge rewards. Thanks, Spirit.

We had been committed to the Emerald Baptist Church in Eugene, and we were disappointed to leave its congregation and all that it represented. I told Ruth that if our move did not please us, we could always return to Eugene and play accounting "in the minors." That spring, we moved into a little house on SE Alder Street in Portland, where we began a long relationship with the family next door, which exists to this day.

I had yet to pass my CPA exam and I was eager to put that behind me. In order to pass it, I knew that I would need intense preparation and that necessitated peace and quiet. I did not have a private place in which to study at home, where the sounds of Catherine's cheerful play were a distraction. So, that spring, I purchased eight sheets of plywood and built myself a box, 8 x 8 x 8, around a window in the garage. I cut out a little door and I went into this tiny cubicle each morning, or whenever I had a spare moment, and studied for the exam. It was difficult to leave my family and study there, but it was a divinely inspired solution. In November, I passed the CPA exam, the first of my University of Oregon class to do so.

The exam, which occupied a half-day plus two full days, was easier than I had expected, largely because I had been taught by the master, Dr. Johnson. Although I did not realize the concept at the time, Dr. Johnson was a very right-brained person, who taught us how to solve problems that we had never encountered before. To pass the exam, this had been critical. For example, about a fifth of the CPA exam was on law. I had taken only one law course, and that had been in my first term at the University of Oregon, so, in that area, I was relatively weak. But, I passed the law section because, overall, it was really designed to measure one's skill at solving problems that had not been met before, and that was my greatest strength, expanded by my tutors.

Working for the national CPA firm was a fantastic experience. I worked with companies all over the country and one of my biggest clients was a lumber retailer, Feddes-Moore, which had nineteen stores across the country. That meant that I had to do corporate tax returns in nineteen different states, which was very useful in later years, when I worked for Christmas tree growers all over the United States. I still do tax returns for people in different states, but it is a lot easier now, as tax software is readily available.

The national CPA firm had as clients some of the largest timber businesses in the Pacific Northwest. I discovered that a great many timber properties had Jewish owners, whose ancestors had come from Germany as Oregon was being settled. As I worked with those firms, I developed tremendous respect for their method of doing business. They taught me that it is not working hard that counts on the bottom line profit of the business, it is working smart. In order to keep costs down, and to maximize profits, these Jewish business owners always found ingenious ways to work efficiently.

One of my more challenging jobs was to do the accounting for a client in Cottage Grove, who had sold a lumber mill to Crown Zellerbach, and with the profits, built a motel, which created jobs for the community. I also did the personal tax returns for Les Schwab, who had only twelve locations at that time. One year, I did the tax returns for one of the wealthiest men in Oregon, at that time, who owned huge timber holdings. Touche Ross saved him from bankruptcy more than once. It was fascinating to see how he conducted business, focusing on how to deliver more product for less money.

What I did not like about the big CPA firm was the resistance to creativity and left-brained accountants dominance. They operated as they always had and it was virtually impossible to change their system. For example, at that time the tax law allowed a double tax exemption when one became sixty-five. I was doing tax returns for people I had never met, so, each time I did one, I had to ask, "Is this person sixty-five or older?" In a group meeting, I suggested that the birth date be written on every file's front and I was told, "That is not the way we have been doing it."

That was left-brained thinking, which convinced me that I should leave the national firm, along with its pecking order of people above me, who were more interested in the domination of accountants below them than they were to operating as a team, which would maximize profits for everyone. In the Army, I had experiences with some people who went "drunk" with power, who abused their subordinates and who showed no mercy - their behavior was regularly irrational. Sometimes, I received the message that Spirit tested people, just to see how they responded to abuse.

After we had lived a year on Alder street, we purchased our first home on NE 115th street in Parkrose, a suburb of Portland, for $7,500. We became real property owners and, with it, an obligation to pay property taxes.

After I had worked at Touche, Ross for three years, an opportunity arose in Corvallis and I saw in it a wonderful way to raise our family in the home of the Oregon State Beavers, a move I had envisioned fourteen years earlier. I did not like the left-brained approach to accounting, which resisted all change and I disliked the pecking order enforced by the kind of rigid thinking that I had experienced in the Army. It amazed me to see people enamored with power in a system that demanded unquestioning respect for authority. Clearly, Spirit had informed me that it was time to move with my accounting career and that my vision had come true. Corvallis has now been our home for the past fifty-one years.

My Angel of Humility
Reminding me to always be in awe of the divine

My Angel of Healing
Helping my body recover quickly

My Angel of Freedom from Fear
Keeping me in the flow, so my faith and confidence protect me in even *the most dangerous situations*

The Angel of My Divine Journey
Seeing to it that the twists and turns of my life always take me in a better direction than I could have anticipated

My Messenger Angel
Giving me divine direction

My Angel of Manifestation
Creating pathways to the places and events I have envisioned

Near-Death Experiences

Near-Death Fishing Fall

In the summer 1953, my brother, Bob, and I climbed over Mt. Defiance, west of Hood River, and fished in Bear Lake. We discovered a large downed Douglas fir tree that provided a good base from which we could cast, and we fished from the downed log successfully for quite awhile, until something went terribly wrong. The bark of the fir tree that I stood on loosened, and my feet flew into the air, as if I had stepped on a banana peel. I fell head-first, straight down, about ten feet, onto volcanic rock. As my brother scrambled to help me, I rolled over, stood up, and realized that I was relatively unscathed. Not only had I not broken my neck, but I did not have any bad cuts. I thanked my Angel of Protection and returned to my fishing.

Near-Death Stove Repair

Soon after moving to Alder Street in Portland, Ruth and I purchased a new washer to help cope with the laundry needs of our growing family. After the appliance repairman installed it, I asked him if he could fix the electric clock on our stove. To do so, he removed the metal plate at the back of the stove and replaced the fuse. In a rush to his next appointment, he asked me to reattach the metal plate. As I lifted the metal plate, I accidentally touched it to a live 220-volt wire. Sparks and metal shards exploded throughout the kitchen, sprayed Ruth and seven-month-old Cathy, and the metal plate melted in my hands. Amazingly, I was not shocked or burned, nor were Ruth and Cathy. Lesson learned: before working on it, always unplug an appliance, and turn off the breaker!

Second Near-Death on a Bicycle

In June, 1992, I had a bizarre near-death accident at the hands of a six-year-old. Ruth and I were visiting friends, who lived in a fifth wheeler at an RV park on the Oregon Coast. I decided to ride a bicycle with their grandchildren. As I cycled down a steep dirt path, their six-year-old grandson took a side path and crashed his bicycle broadside into my right calf. My bike stopped abruptly and the right handlebar jabbed into my sternum. Because I had gripped the bike's handlebars, I was propelled into a somersault over its front and I landed with the back of my neck on a hard pan concrete-like surface, where I could easily have broken my neck. Instead, my worst injuries were a sizeable blood clot on the side of my leg and excruciating pain in my ribcage, every time I took a breath. Fortunately, when we returned to the fifth wheeler, my host placed a package of frozen peas on my leg, which eased the pain. Ruth drove us home, because to turn the steering wheel caused me excruciating chest pain. Once again, what could have been a fatal accident was just another bump on the road of life. Thanks, Guardian Angel.

Vignettes

Great-Aunt Catherine

My grandmother Simpson was on her deathbed when I received my military orders. Her sister, Catherine, a lively redhead who lived in Los Angeles, came to Hood River to assist in the funeral arrangements. She took charge of the entire situation and, in the process, radiated love and peace to everyone.

Two weeks after my grandmother's death, I began basic training at Camp Roberts, halfway between San Francisco and Los Angeles. Over the next four months, I often used my thirty-six hour passes to visit great-aunt Catherine and her husband, Fredrick Mason. I left the base at noon on a Saturday, hitchhiked to Los Angeles and then hitchhiked back to Camp Roberts on Sunday afternoon. It was about a five hundred miles roundtrip; a long way to go on a thirty-six hour pass! The hitchhiking went quickly. When you were in uniform, almost any driver would give you a ride.

Catherine and Fredrick were exclusive realtors for movie stars and they took me to see some very famous people's homes, including those of Robert Cummings and Clark Gable. The Cummings' home had a cloverleaf-shaped swimming pool, a guest house, and a full bar for guests, but neither of the Cummings drank alcohol, although they provided it to their guests.

Wayne Stays Stateside

Eight years before my basic training injury, my brother, Wayne, in a very similar way, missed being shipped out for World War II combat. He had trained as a Navy Corpsman and his unit went into Iwo Jima with the Marines. Wayne was struck with rheumatic fever on the eve of their departure for the Pacific and he was hospitalized for three weeks. His unit suffered ninety-eight percent casualties and, when my brother was sent to Seattle, after his hospitalization, he assisted with autopsies on some of his friends who had died at Iwo Jima.

Wayne Bowlby

Ruth's Family Ties

Ruth's Aunt Nora died in 1963 and in 1964, her maternal grandparents died. After their deaths, Ruth and I often visited her mother's brothers' families in St. Helens, Oregon, and Spokane, Washington.

On her father's side, Ruth always kept in touch with her uncle, Carl, her father's half-brother. His family are wheat farmers in Prosser, Washington and we have maintained close relations with them. Ruth and I visited them last summer, on a trip we took with Cathy, Bruce and his three daughters.

Baby Boom Repeated

In the summer 1959, my parents saw the arrival of four grandchildren in less than five months: Karen, Wayne's daughter; Robby, Nancy's son; Patrick, Lillian's son; and then Catherine Irene, our first child.

Similar events happened for my grandmother Simpson the year that I was born. Three of my mother's sisters were pregnant at the same time as my mother, and within eight months they all gave birth. My grandmother Simpson was thrilled! She adored her grandchildren, as did my mother.

Part 3: Growing Family and Business

Corvallis, Oregon Becomes Our Home

Our second child, Barbara Lynn, was born March 16, 1962, while we lived in Portland. In our happiness and gratitude for her birth, it seemed fitting that she had arrived on the date of that most fundamental Bible verse, John 3:16, "For God so loved the world that he gave his one and only Son, that whoever believes in him shall not perish but have eternal life."

I have always felt that being a mother is the most important job for any woman. Ruth was an exceptionally good mother (and still is!). She gave each of our children the nurture, discipline and individual encouragement that enabled them to become strong and successful. A full-time devoted homemaker, she was always there for them, ready to listen and share what was important. She may now have some regrets that she missed out on college and a career, but, at the time, she knew that she was exactly where she needed to be.

With two daughters under the age of four and dreams of more children, the priority for our next home was a family-friendly community. As Ruth and I discussed options, I remembered a message that I had received fourteen years before.

When I was a junior in high school in Hood River, some friends and I drove to Eugene to check out the University of Oregon. As we approached Corvallis, I suggested that we stop and look quickly around. Our detour took less than ten minutes, but a message came to me from Spirit that this was the place where I was to settle down and raise a family. Fourteen years later, the divine manifestation became true, as we have resided in Corvallis for nearly fifty-two years.

Our family moved to Corvallis on Thanksgiving Day, 1962, we purchased our first Thanksgiving meal at a deli downtown, and ate as we sat on the boxes ready to be unpacked in our new home.

Angels guided us to our first Corvallis home. We discovered that there were seven new homes at the end of Thirty-Fifth Street near

Grant, on a cul-de-sac. The homes were unsold after six months on the market and we wished to buy one, but until we sold our home in Parkrose, we did not have enough money for a down payment.

We talked the builder into a one-year lease option: we offered to pay $135 dollars per month, thirty-five of which would go toward the principal, if we decided to buy the home for thirteen thousand dollars within one year. The builder accepted our offer, and a year later we exercised our option and became the owners of a new 910 square foot home with three bedrooms.

It was a wonderful neighborhood, as the other homes sold quickly, mainly to buyers with young families and the cul-de-sac was perfect for the children's play. Bruce was born November 10, 1964, at the Bess Kaiser Hospital in Portland, as Ruth and I were not impressed with the birthing facilities in Corvallis. Additionally, our family medical insurance was with Kaiser Hospital at a cost of thirty-eight dollars a month.

Ruth's Doctor Cohen, at Bess Kaiser Hospital, had delivered Barbara, and he utilized hypnosis in his deliveries. During Barbara's birth, he advised Ruth to focus on the most beautiful view that she had ever seen, which was Lake Louise in Banff. She gave birth with minimal anesthetic and pain.

As Bruce's birth date approached, Ruth wanted to have labor induced on November 10, as she was intent on completing her Christmas shopping before the baby's arrival. In Portland, on November 9, we walked what seemed to be many miles, traipsing from store to store, in an effort to find perfect gifts for everyone on her Christmas gift list.

The birth was scheduled for 2:00 PM the following day. Ruth stayed with my parents in east Portland that night and I went back to Corvallis to teach at Oregon State University the next morning. Ruth's labor began about 1:00 AM and, after a hurried trip across Portland to Bess Kaiser Hospital, Ruth called me at 4:00 AM, to tell me that Bruce had been born! I will never forget the joy that I felt as I heard that I had a son. (The walk during Christmas shopping must have hastened the delivery.)

In 1981, we celebrated our twenty-fifth wedding anniversary, in Corvallis, and in 2006, our fiftieth anniversary, with a host of friends and relatives. Nancy Kay, my sister's daughter, spent countless hours and produced a video of our fifty years together, which we still enjoy watching. There were seven of grandfather and grandmother Simpsons' twenty-two grandchildren present; nine grandchildren were deceased.

In 1981, we celebrated my fiftieth birthday at the Elks Club in Corvallis, and we enjoyed the company of many Corvallis friends and relatives. Our son-in-law, Dave Cudo, played his saxophone (in his usual masterful way) for both events, as he has done for all our family celebrations.

My Teaching Dream Comes True

A week after my arrival in Corvallis, Dr. Ed Easton, in charge of hiring in the Business School at Oregon State University, phoned me and said, "We could use another CPA to teach accounting." I responded with, "When do I start?" On January 2, 1963, I taught my first class. How Dr. Easton had gotten my name was a mystery, as he could not remember how he knew that I was in town. My original goal had been to teach at the high school level, but a university was beyond my wildest expectations.

Spirit produced a phone call that shocked me, however, the training that I had received in Leadership School, my four years of public accounting, including the work for a national CPA firm, and my CPA certificate, made me competent enough to teach at Oregon State University.

I had come to Corvallis to work with another accountant and we had agreed upon a certain working arrangement. However, when I commenced work, he changed the whole concept. I told him that I would remain through the tax season, but, that I would then open my own accounting practice. On July 4, 1963, I moved into a rented office space, Ruth and I hung my CPA certificate #1190 upon the wall, declared my independence and I began to build an accounting business from scratch.

I taught four classes at Oregon State University, a full-time teaching load. I loved every minute that I taught new students, who knew very little about business or how to succeed in life.

I had dreamed of teaching ever since I was in Leadership School, where I had taught the finite detail of the hand grenade's killing qualities, as well as its safety features, to army basic trainees, eleven years previously. At the University of Oregon, I learned wonderful teaching techniques from my professors, especially Dr. Charles E. Johnson. There was never a dull moment in his classes because he kept everyone fully engaged. He wrote his students' names on cards, shuffled the cards, and then he drew out a name: "Bowlby: how would you approach this problem?" In my classes, I sometimes used this card trick as a change of pace.

At other times, I called out names at random and presented a problem for them to solve. My students were never bored, as they always knew that they could be called "on the spot" at any time.

I posed students real life situations and they had to think of remedies. When one does tax returns, one sees lots of investment and business mistakes, and I could provide many examples. I did not use clients' real names, but I could demonstrate almost any concept with a real life situation, which assisted them to learn. The students were placed in the shoes of an accountant and then I allowed them to develop solutions.

One example I used highlighted the difficulty of evaluating inventory for a bank loan. The business in question had purchased a railroad. After tearing up the tracks, it had a huge pile of sixteen-foot long rails that it had been trying to sell, unsuccessfully, for twenty years. The business had placed a huge value on the rails, but, if they could not be used as railroad rails, they were good only for scrap at a small amount per pound.

The question was: how does one value the rail inventory when the banker wants a low valuation, and the owner wants a high valuation? How does one determine what something is worth, when no one wants to buy it? In this case, we finally compromised at a price that the bank was willing to accept. Ironically, about a month later, the company found a buyer in South America and it received much more value than we had assigned. This experience teaches a person that the value of anything is worth exactly what someone will pay for it and nobody really knows what something is worth until the item is sold.

More than just learning accounting, my classes learned about life. I related my experiences picking fruit with migrant laborers, gandy-dancing on the railroad, cutting meat, training for the Army, displaying the self-discipline required to climb a mountain, and working with a national CPA firm. Most students were quite sheltered and they did not understand the many complex business and life problems that can arise. My own stories helped to broaden their perspective and opened their minds to new ways of problem-solving.

In one class, I gave a two-person midterm, and I mixed up the students, so that they would not know with whom they would be partnered. They had to arrive at one solution for a shared grade. To enhance their understanding of the problem, tests were open-book and that really pressured the students. They did not want to embarrass their partners so they had to be especially imaginative and learn to give-and-take. In a sense, they taught each other and I believed that tests were an opportunity to learn.

It was not memorization, which has a limited value as far as I am concerned. There were problems that they had never encountered before. Once, I gave a midterm and the Business Dean walked down the hallway. I stood outside the classroom door and, inside, the students talked excitedly and shouted, while they tried to convince one another of a single solution. "What on Earth is going on in there?" he asked me. "I am giving an exam." "You've got to be kidding me!", he said.

The students liked my class and I had high attendance. Most had thought that they would take only a single accounting course, but I convinced many that they should become CPAs. Of my first class of about twenty-two students, almost half became CPAs. My last class was in 1972 and I still meet former students!

I taught at Oregon State University for ten years, while I built my CPA business. I increased my staff, as the steady flow of new clients demanded more and more of my time. Finally, I realized that I did not have time for both business and school so, reluctantly, I resigned from teaching. Often, I became aware that I taught my clients the same issues that I had taught my students on campus and I realized that accounting was really as much a teaching profession as it was accounting. I praise Spirit for my experience at Oregon State University.

The Vision of my CPA Practice

Submission to Spirit for Guidance

Before I began my accounting practice, I was alone as I visited a favorite place, the Breitenbush River on the northern slopes of 10,500 foot Mt. Jefferson. Ever since high school, I have believed that Saint Michael was my Spirit guide and I now consulted him as to whether I should begin my accounting practice, as well as how I should conduct it.

Spirit seemed to have concepts on how I should operate my practice and he sent me many strong messages. The first was that I should commence a CPA practice, and concentrate my energy on being of service to any clients who might request it, whether or not they could pay me; I should not concern myself if they did not.

The second message from Spirit was that I should follow Judge Learned Hand's famous decision in a 1934 court case (GREGORY V HELVERING 69 F.2ND, 809, 810 (2d Cir. 1934) in which he had stated: Anyone may arrange his affairs so that his taxes shall be as low as possible; he is not bound to choose that pattern which best pays the treasury. There is not even a patriotic duty to increase one's taxes. Over and over again the Courts have said that there is nothing sinister in so arranging affairs as to keep taxes as low as possible. Everyone does it, rich and poor alike and all do right, for nobody owes any public duty to pay more than the law demands.

That seemed a good idea, as Spirit had always provided for me in ways far beyond my expectations and which could only be described as divine. I believed that Spirit would always take care of me and I liked the idea of concentrating my energy on helping clients, with no consideration for whether or not they would ever pay for my services.

Therefore, when I commenced my CPA practice, I considered that everyone would be sent divinely by Spirit. As a result, I worked hundreds of hours every year helping people that I knew could never pay, so I never billed them. Spirit provided me with an abundance of clients who could pay, and my collection percentage on what I did bill was nearly one hundred percent.

My practice thrived from the first day that I opened my office, until September 1, 1992, twenty-nine years later, when I sold my CPA business to my employees. Spirit had sent me all the business that I could handle and I increased my accounting staff to a peak of eighteen employees. Clients came in with accounting and tax problems, and no matter how impossible the situation appeared to be, we could always find a way to resolve them. The key was, to look for the simple solution, and be open to the messages from Spirit that would lead me to a satisfactory result.

When I opened my office, I received a beautiful plant from Jim Gathercoal, the architect whose office was next door. The plant was delivered by Sid Jary, the owner of Jary's House of Flowers. After a short discussion, he became my first client in the Corvallis area. The next Christmas, I began a tradition of sending poinsettias to clients and others from Jary's House of Flowers. This gift list grew to about seventy-five; poinsettias were delivered to widows, clients, and almost anyone that I thought needed a lift at Christmas time.

My first client preceded the formation of my CPA firm by over three years. Upon completion of my college studies in March of 1960, we moved to Portland, where I worked for a National CPA firm. I also did accounting for H & H Machine Works at fifteen dollars a month. Amazingly, I am still doing accounting for H & H; fifty-four years later, now owned by Mickey Hillard, the son of one of the founders, Wayne Hillard.

One of the first situations that I encountered in my CPA practice was the loss of my billable time whenever clients came to me with legal problems. I would meet with my clients, and attorneys of their choice, and spend hours discussing a legal issue, but with no solution. I envisioned the meetings as like a cat chasing his tail, with no billable time that I could ever justify.

Finally, I had a difficult legal problem that I decided to discuss with one of the best attorneys in Corvallis. After presenting him with the situation, his comment was, "I do not know how to resolve this issue and neither does any other attorney in town. Locate the largest law firm in Portland and present this issue to them."

I chose Souther, Spaulding, Williamson, and Wyatt, a firm of over one hundred fifty attorneys. I contacted an attorney in the firm, who quickly presented a solution. An agreement was prepared, which I discussed with my client, and the attorney sent a letter of engagement, billed the client directly, and there was no write-off of my time.

Eventually, this firm handled nearly all my legal work, utilizing specialists in all areas of the law, including the setting up of pension plans, estate and will planning, contracts, patents, and the solving of any other legal problems, always considering the tax implications of the agreements that had been prepared. This contrasted with the local attorneys, who generally stated that they wanted nothing to do with the tax law. My thought was that they were saying that they wanted to live, but that they did not want to breathe!

I had several files full of clients' legal matters and this legal business made a very profitable contribution to the success of my CPA firm. I realized that I was as close to practicing law as a person could be without a law license. From a practical viewpoint, the Portland law firm became my "back room" where agreements were prepared, and I presented them to clients with no write-offs of my time.

Thanks, Spirit, for leading me from this loss situation to a profitable one.

Early in my life I had learned many concepts which underlie success. As a child picking beans, I had found that the more focused I was, my mind more cleared to the task, the more productive I could be, and the more productive I was, the more I could earn. The same concepts applied to the accounting business.

I hired people whom I taught to be efficient, how to work smarter rather than harder. My goal was to deliver more product than anyone else, at a reasonable cost.

In exchange for their contribution to the success of my accounting practice, I paid my staff much better than other accounting firms.

Their basic compensation was far above the amount partners earned in many CPA firms. In addition to their salaries, I contributed twenty-five percent of their salaries to a pension plan that was segregated for their retirement and they designated where the money was to be invested. My employees were, in a sense, partners in my business.

One of the insights on life which I had learned over the years was the importance of counseling; discussing whatever problems there were with another. When I interacted with an employee, we solved problems that one of us alone could never solve. It was like exchanging energy: the result was so much greater than the sum of its parts. The women in my office were especially good at this kind of collaboration. I was always pleased when they had an idea before I did, because that told me that they were learning for themselves to "think outside the box."

As a business owner, I was a big believer in delegating responsibility. I reviewed every tax return myself, including every source of information that related to the income tax returns.

My staff was free to manage details of my clients' accounts and to develop relationships with them. Many CPA firms keep their accountants in the "back room," and never allow them to even meet clients, for fear that their employees might steal their clients and use the stolen clients to start their own CPA firms.

I devoted my time to big-picture problem-solving and to supporting my accounting staff. To reach a higher maximum potential, an employee must be responsible. That is the way I was raised, and this concept had expanded when I was in the Army and taught trainees.

My first two CPA jobs helped me to understand that there are two kinds of accountants, left-brained and right-brained. Most left-brained people find it difficult to work with right-brained people, because their methods seem disorganized. Right-brained people have their own prejudices against left-brained people, whose routines may seem plodding and dull, and who are very slow to adapt to a changing world.

I believe that, generally, we are who we are; we usually do not have a choice, but it is important to know what you are looking for in a work environment. I had a right-brained accounting practice, and anyone who came to work for me had to adjust to constant changes, which left-brained people disliked with a passion. I learned that over time it is possible to change a left-brained person into a right-brained way of thinking.

It was not always easy to find accountants who were willing to think "outside the box" and to change as the world changed around them. My first computer usage in 1965 was called an add punch with optic tape.

The accountant number and amount was punched into a full keyboard, and the tape from it was mailed to Portland, where large main frame computers read the tape and converted it to punch cards. These were run though the computer and produced a full set of books and financial statements. In 1969, I was the first CPA west of the Mississippi to use the original Wang computer in accounting, and this computer was less than half the size of other computers on the market. Like my grandfather, I always wanted to be atop the latest innovations!

As computers gradually became more prevalent, I was amazed at how many accountants clung to the traditional methods of pushing pencils to do accounting and tax returns. They relied upon printed tables, pencils and handwritten spreadsheets. In the mid-1970s, I visited a CPA firm in Salem, with the desire to combine our CPA practices, but, they still did all accounting procedures by pencil-pushing and had no computers. I knew that they did not have the right mindset to work with me.

On the other hand, some employees showed immediate promise. One of my favorites was a young woman who came to me in the early 1970s, having just graduated from high school, she applied for a job as front desk secretary. In the course of the interview, I recognized that she was very bright and could go far as a professional accountant. I told her that I wanted her to become a CPA and that I would pay for her tuition while she was working. She told me later that she had almost not taken the job because she had thought that I was crazy!

She had never imagined herself as a highly paid professional and it took a long time for her to overcome her own mental barriers. She eventually commenced classes, graduated from college, and passed the CPA exam when she was forty-four years old, twenty-six years after I had told her to "reach for the stars." After fifteen years in a challenging job at the University of Arizona, she has a very rewarding position in Oregon.

One of my more interesting engagements was when I was hired to do an efficiency analysis for a regional CPA firm. Their CEO asked me to visit three of the company's offices, analyze why they were not profitable, and to measure the dissension in the firms. I reported what he had already suspected: there was a division within the firm between those who wanted computers and those who did not.

The three offices that I visited worked their accountants to death, seventy to eighty hours a week, the result of pencil-pushing. One firm had given away a lot of bookkeeping business, because it was not profitable, a direct result of denying the value of computers, as compared to bookkeeping by hand. Amazingly, the firms had computer software to prepare income tax returns, but, they used them only sparingly, to check what they had done by hand. My grandfather's open-mindedness to change, his arms wide open, was sorely needed to improve the quality of life and the profits of all the firms' participants.

Loving to help people reach their highest potential, I found it easier to teach women than men, because women tend to be much more open-minded. One woman with an accounting degree came to work for me right out of college. For four years I encouraged her, before she finally committed to studying to become a CPA. A year later, she passed the CPA exam.

A business owner's most onerous job is to fire an employee. Fortunately, for several years, whenever it was necessary to dismiss someone, one of my office assistants volunteered for this job.

It is interesting to see how the accounting profession has evolved over the years. When I began as a CPA, the work force was about five percent women and they now make up about fifty-five percent. Women are much more open to change than men, who usually become firm in their ways and reluctant to change.

In 1960, when I commenced work as a CPA in a national CPA firm, I was required to wear a suit and a hat. About fifteen years ago, I attended a tax conference in Medford, where I observed a young CPA with a bare midriff and a ring which hung from her belly button. I decided that some adjustments to change were difficult.

My success was really just the result of my lifelong energy flow. I did not have fear! I always had faith that, to resolve a challenging situation, the right answer would come to me. Fear is an impossible barrier for some people and it becomes a way of life. When one waits to become part of the flow, instead of fearing it, one can overcome many challenges which appear to be impossible.

As a young man, I delivered groceries in frigid Columbia Gorge weather, and it was only my feel for the Earth's energy flow that kept me going at the right speed. I have had the same feeling while skiing, when I sensed my connection to the mountain's energy, skied at just the right speed, and rode with its flow. The bottom line is, have patience to wait for divine timing and wait for divine messages to solve what seems to be an impossible situation.

Income Taxes and Amended Returns

One of the primary goals of my CPA practice was to keep a client's income taxes as low as possible, so long as it was legal, following Judge Learned Hand's famous court decision in 1934. When I interviewed prospective accountants, I told them my game plan about clients' income taxes kept to a minimum and I noted their responses.

Many had already been brainwashed by their college professors into a belief that this was wrong. Their theory was that anyone in business had unlimited deep pockets and it was okay for the government to extract as much money as possible. My theory was that money was more valuable in allowing the business to be successful and that, in the long run, more taxes would be paid. I would leave no stone unturned to avoid income taxes for their unique situation. The wrong answer from numerous potential employees ended with this question.

In the past fifty-four years I have amended hundreds of tax returns, in order to get substantial refunds, when an accountant has, for all kinds of reasons, grossly overstated taxable income. The Internal Revenue Code is so complicated that an accountant must devote time each week to update his knowledge of changes and interpretations that occur daily.

My focus was to find every deduction that my clients could deduct legally, and to teach them to keep records, so that they would not miss tax deductions. People with haphazard ways to do their accounting tend, through these poor systems, to over-report their income and under-deduct their expenses and they end up paying income taxes which they do not owe.

One of my first clients was a woman, recently divorced, and financially distressed, who appeared with two small children and a sticky tax problem. After about eight hours of strenuous work, including negotiations with an arrogant ex-spouse, it was time to present the bill. It should have been several hundred dollars, but, when I considered her state of mind and financial worth, I told her that the charge was ten dollars. She was shocked, as that was far too much to pay! We settled for five dollars and I knew that I had passed Spirit's test.

Many times, the clients who shirked paying their bills, or underpaid us, were not nearly as needy as others. Our largest category of unpaid bills, ironically, was for amended tax returns. I amended clients' income returns that resulted in tax refunds of hundreds, and sometimes, thousands of dollars, plus interest paid by the IRS and the State of Oregon, by finding errors made in the preparation of their tax returns.

The clients could still not bring themselves to pay me, even though my bill was for a very small amount, compared to the refunds they received. Sometimes, I wondered if it was a psychological problem: they did not pay their bills because they could not admit that they had made stupid errors themselves or had hired someone they trusted who had failed them.

Whenever I had a client who was past due in paying my bill, I evaluated whether I should send a mental message for payment. Most often, when I did so, I received a check in a few days. One of my office assistants used to be difficult about our failure to legally pursue clients who had not paid. Calling it "dialing for dollars", she wanted to phone clients and pressure those who were delinquent. I told her that it was not worth the stress and that was not the agreement that I had made with Spirit many years before, when I had commenced my accounting practice.

When I first came to Corvallis, there was a local attorney who charged his clients five dollars a year to prepare their income tax returns. However, he included in their wills a provision to pay him a percentage of their estates when they died. His business plan was to make his clients feel good, by charging them a nominal amount for his services and he planned to "cash in" with excessive fees when they died. His secretary, who was not professionally trained and who generally followed the prior year's tax return as he prepared his client's income taxes, had caused his clients to overpay or underpay their income taxes.

One person, who came to see me after he had gone through this process with the attorney, brought me his three prior years' tax returns to review. At a glance, I could see that there were multiple errors and he had grossly overpaid his income taxes. When I filed amended returns for him, he received over two thousand dollars in tax refunds, plus interest at six percent. I charged him eighty dollars for the time it took to prepare three years of amended tax returns, but he was shocked when he received my bill. He said, "I've been paying just five dollars a year for my tax preparation!" I told him, "It has cost you hundreds of dollars every year, because they did not do it right and you have overpaid your taxes." Somehow, he could not connect between the tax refunds that he received and my eighty-dollar fee. He did not come back the next year for me to prepare his income tax returns.

One of my favorite stories about clients and income tax returns revolves around Frank and Nettie Gathercoal, both in their high nineties, who had immigrated to this country from England. They were extremely proud of their citizenship and they wanted to file their income tax returns promptly. At 9:30 AM on the first business day of each year, they walked from their home to several banks, and had their passbook interest income recorded. They then came directly to my CPA office to have their tax returns prepared.

One year, I took their finished returns to their home for them to sign. Nettie was blind, and the home was dark, but she was in the kitchen preparing dinner. I observed that the red-hot burners reflected the only light in the kitchen. She told me to go upstairs and awaken Frank, who had to sign the returns. I turned on the lights, went upstairs and found Frank asleep. He returned to the kitchen and signed his name. Nettie then asked me to place my fingers on each side of the signature line, where she promptly wrote a beautiful signature! They thanked me profusely for bringing their tax returns to them, which I mailed on the way home. Spirit had taught me how deeply some people appreciated being citizens of the United States of America.

Financing and Avoiding Bankruptcy

Anyone who believes accounting is a dull job could not be farther from the truth. Nothing is routine: it is always a new challenge every day. People arrive with the most amazing stories, and one must use one's creativity to solve what appears to be insurmountable problems and help them get on the right track.

A major part of my accounting practice was the acquisition of money to help my clients finance a business game plan. Each of these ventures was unique and I enjoyed the challenge of finding different ways to accomplish the client's goal. I had a fine reputation with the bankers, and it was fun to package a loan, so that it was beneficial for both the banker and the borrower. Bankers knew that if I were involved, the loan would, most likely, be profitable. I was able to get better terms for the client, based upon the banker's prior experiences with the loans that I had generated for them. One loan only was lost, when a banker released collateral when he should not have. A number of these businesses were on the brink of bankruptcy when they came to me, and we found ways for them to prosper, and sometimes to become millionaires in a few short years. It became apparent that when clients came under my umbrella, and they followed the game plan that we laid out for them, they became prosperous.

The Christmas Tree Connection and the Authoring of the Christmas Tree Manual

My first two accounting employments gave me an excellent foundation in tax accounting for the timber industry and, when I came to Corvallis, I had good references within that community. I had been in Corvallis only a short time when I met Hal Schudel, a pioneer and leader in the field of Christmas tree growing. Hal introduced me to the rapidly expanding Christmas tree business, and in February 1964 he invited me give a talk to the Northwest Ornamental Society. This organization included the Northwest Christmas tree growers.

When I gave my first talk to Christmas Tree Growers at the Memorial Union at Oregon State University, over three hundred people attended. Little did I know that this lecture would launch twenty-eight years of talks to Christmas tree growers, timber growers, and to accountants, and CPAs in twenty-nine states, including the eastern seaboard of the United States. This led to years of challenging engagements in tax matters with the Christmas tree and timber industry.

Once again, Spirit had enabled me to teach thousands of people in faraway communities. I exceeded my expectations in teaching that had begun twelve years before, on a hillside at Camp Roberts, California, when I had taught classes on the potential destruction created by the hand grenade.

In the past, the growing of Christmas trees as a crop and marketing them intensively, was a new idea. Before the early 1960s, most people bought scraggly wild trees cut in the forest, and the business was much like the one my brother, Wayne, and I had commenced as teenagers in 1942, and which we had continued throughout my high school years. When we moved to Corvallis, the Willamette Valley had many Christmas tree plantations and the industry was born. Holiday Tree farms grew to be the largest Christmas tree business in the world, and it sold over a million trees a year. I realized that Holiday Tree Farms' success in business was emulated by many other businesses that came under my divine field of protection. It was as though my success expanded to the many clients I counseled.

In 1971, I assisted Hal Schudel and his partner, Paul Goodmanson, through a major IRS confrontation, which would become a landmark case for Christmas tree growers. The IRS had challenged Hal and Paul's Holiday Tree Farms' tax returns for the years 1967-1969, and it had challenged the tax method which I had used to compute the amount of capital gain. We filed suit against the IRS, but we lost our case in the IRS District Court in Portland. We then appealed the case to the Ninth Circuit Court of Appeals in San Francisco, where we won the case in a two-to-one decision.

This case lasted over seven years, but winning it saved Holiday Tree Farms a fortune in income taxes over the past thirty-seven years and saved millions of dollars in income taxes for the Christmas tree growers throughout the nation. The IRS referred to my Christmas Tree Taxation Manual in their IRS tax brochures and IRS bulletins as the best source for Christmas tree growers to determine how best to compute their capital gain for tax purposes.

Once again, Spirit contributed to our winning the case by the narrowest margin. Our win in the 9th Circuit Court of appeals enabled Holiday Tree Farms and my CPA business to flourish financially.

Losing the case in the District Court had turned out to be a blessing, since, if we had won, we would never have appealed the case to the 9th Circuit court and established a national precedent for all tree growers.

Over the years, this case led to accounting work with dozens of growers across the nation, and expanded my accounting practice beyond expectations. Thanks Spirit, for the two-to-one decision!

In 1980, sixteen years after my first talk to the Northwest Ornamental Society, I spent nine months writing a tax manual on Christmas tree taxation. It became an immensely popular resource for growers around the country as a guide for the computation of the amount of capital gain allowed by law.

At a convention, one grower's wife told me that, after purchasing my book, her husband was so excited about it that he took it on their honeymoon and put it on their night stand.

I became widely known as the national tax expert in Christmas Trees and Timber taxation, resulting in my receiving phone calls from accountants and tree growers all over the country on tree tax situations. I was invited to speak at dozens of conferences, including the Christmas Tree National Convention and numerous other state conventions. Over the next twenty-two years, I gave over 150 talks in twenty-nine states. Ruth joined me on many of these trips, as we always had a booth where I could sell my Christmas Tree Taxation Manuals. I loved the opportunity to teach and to see the country, and these tree talks led Ruth and me to visit all fifty states!

The timing in 1980 could not have been better, as the prime interest rate was increased to cool off inflation to twenty-one percent, and many of the home builders for whom I did accounting work went out of business. My added profits from the production and the sales of my Christmas Tree Taxation Manual, and the new clients that I gained in many states, replaced my lost accounting revenue from home builders.

The Christmas Tree Tax Manual project proved to me, once again, perfect timing and divine inspiration. Sitting in a storage closet in the downstairs of our home, beginning around 4 AM each day, I devoted hundreds of hours to do what no one else has done before or since.

Guided by a message from the Holy Spirit, I demonstrated, by my faith, that the final result would be better than I imagined.

Encounters with the IRS

I looked at the tax code as a big pile of clay: to structure their tax affairs, each person has the opportunity to mold the law as they want to - the Internal Revenue Code is limited only by knowledge of the Code and imagination. But, one has to remain legal. That is what makes tax accounting exciting. Each person in business can arrange his affairs, in any manner, to avoid payment of income taxes, to the maximum amount provided by law. Minimizing income taxes results in more cash remaining to expand the business, to increase inventories, to purchase new equipment and to add new employees, who are essential to businesses' success.

After we won the Hal Schudel tax case in 1977, the IRS audited my personal income tax returns every year for six years in a row. This was in violation of the law, which prohibits repetitive audits when there is no IRS recovery from a previous audit. I considered this inconvenience to be just part of the price for winning the Schudel case.

Most CPAs dislike IRS audits, but for me, it was a game when my clients were audited by the IRS. When IRS agents came to my office, I began the audit doing what I called "riding time." In wrestling, time keepers keep track of the amount of time each person is on top and if one person has more riding time than the other, that one wins the match. That is how I handled my IRS audits. When auditors came to audit, my game plan was to get them to talk about themselves. It is surprising to find how happy they were to be drawn into conversations about themselves!

One IRS agent was very unhappy with his job. He opened his remarks by telling me that he hated his job, but that he was going to "stick it out" for fifteen more years before he retired. He talked about his problems for the entire morning and at noon, he said, "Time to go to lunch!" After lunch, he came back, stayed a half hour, and left. My experience with this IRS agent was a model for all future audits and riding time became the key for a successful audit. There were many issues on the tax returns that might have been disputed, but the IRS agents never found them, because they had run out of time.

Eventually, the IRS Salem district office returned to the IRS regional office in Ogden, Utah all tax returns to be audited that had been prepared by my firm. The IRS in Salem had kept records of how much money they had received from these audits, which was nearly zero, and almost every time the audit resulted in no changes. It became clear to the IRS that auditing my clients was not worth their time, so they finally abandoned their efforts.

After several years with no audits, one of my clients received a notice of an audit, which surprised me. When the auditor arrived, he apologized for wanting to audit one of my clients. He showed me stickers on the file from the two prior years, which showed that Ogden had sent my client's tax returns for audit to Salem two years in a row and Salem had returned the tax returns to Ogden, without auditing them.

When the Salem IRS received audit requests for a third year a row, they were returned to Ogden. However, Salem again received the returns for audit, with Ogden's demand that Salem audit them. The auditor and I had an enjoyable talk, he did a quick once-over of questions, and in less than thirty minutes he left for another audit that might be more fruitful for him. Thanks Spirit!

Over the years, I represented many clients in their battles with the IRS, and I generally managed to come out on top. Sometimes, it was just a matter of putting together a powerful letter, making it clear that the individual had a strong position, and was prepared to defend it. In one case, the IRS had bullied a woman for years and had threatened to put her in prison. I sent them a one-page letter and it ended, just like that.

Some cases were much tougher. A case was referred to me that involved a seventeen-year-old woman, who had gotten in trouble with the IRS when she was an employee in Phoenix, Arizona. The owner of her business had convinced her to "help him out with the IRS" and put part of his business income on her social security number. He had told her that he would pay the taxes for her on his income and then he did not pay them.

The IRS pursued her and would not stop; the IRS agent told her that she had to pay, or go to jail; and that she had no other options. She was so distraught that she attempted suicide and she was placed in an institution for two years. When finally released, she was again pursued by the IRS for taxes due.

When I received her case, I went online, and discovered all kinds of data about the business owner. I built a strong case to prove that she was a victim, that she owed no money to the IRS, and that, in fact, the IRS owed her money from the garnishment of her wages and amounts taken from her bank account. The IRS denied my response, so I researched further, found more documentation that proved her innocence, and wrote another letter to the IRS. A second time, the IRS denied me.

A week later, while skiing at Hoodoo ski bowl, I received a series of messages from Spirit about what I should write in a third letter. At my office again, I prepared a new approach to support my argument and sent it off to the IRS.

This time, my letter was accepted, the young woman was freed from all claims, and she received refunds of the amounts that the IRS had taken from her bank account. I had spent hundreds of hours on the case, all at no charge, but, it was worth it, to free the woman from the unjust charges and the IRS bullies. In my opinion, the messages from Spirit for the third letter were a work of art. (See the letter to the IRS in the appendix.)

The Holy Spirit Sweeps the Country in 1972

In the summer of 1972, I heard from numerous sources that people throughout the United States were having experiences that could be explained only by some super-Spiritual power, which most claimed to be the Holy Spirit. One of the reasons for the Holy Spirit revival was, that evil had increased and a great Spiritual battle was in progress.

I was in my second three-year term as an elder in the Calvin Presbyterian Church, and I was blessed by the Holy Spirit with the most extraordinary experiences of my lifetime summarized as follows:

> ➢ A car salesman called to ask me what I would like, if I could have my choice of everything that I ever wanted in a car, and that led to the Holy Spirit's control of a plan that exceeded my imagination.

98

- ➢ My five-year CPA partnership was dissolved on September 1, a huge blessing, and it turned out be the one day of the year when I had the most financially rewarding experiences. It was the first of many times, in future years, when I would be mightily blessed on September 1.
- ➢ I was in dire need of an exceptional employee, I prayed and, with divine timing, Terry Moss appeared. She came to work on September 1, 1972, and she surpassed my performance expectations.
- ➢ I attended a tax conference in Kansas City, which was filled with the presence of the Holy Spirit, beyond human comprehension.
- ➢ Seemingly, out of thin air, but, clearly the work of the Holy Spirit, Ben came from over three thousand miles away to bring a spiritual revival to Calvin Church.
- ➢ During the Sunday evening services, I was filled with messages in tongues, and I received the baptism of the Holy Spirit, followed by a one-time interpretation of tongues.

My Guardian Angel, Saint Michael, Performs His Divine Magic

The following story covers a ten-hour period when Saint Michael took complete charge of my being and sent message after message to me, which I accepted dutifully.

In October 1972, I attended a national CPA conference in Kansas City, Missouri, attended by about five hundred CPAs from throughout the United States. I noticed a man seated alone, sat down beside him, introduced myself, and his name was Warren Bowlby!

His name was the same as my cousin who lived in Michigan and there were only three other CPAs in the United States with the last name of Bowlby.

With this remarkable coincidence, I felt the presence of the Holy Spirit throughout the three-day conference.

About 4:45 PM, on the last day of the conference, I received a strong message that I should call to see if there was a chance that I could return home that evening, rather than the next morning. I called airline reservations and found that a plane was leaving at 6:30 PM, but the plane was full. The agent said, "Wait: we just had a cancellation." I reserved the seat and headed for my hotel, a few blocks away, to check out.

Four people were in the hotel check-out line when I arrived. However, the first person in line asked if I would like to check out first. The room clerk waived my room fee for the late check-out, I cleared my room and headed for my rental car.

The traffic in downtown Kansas City was bumper-to-bumper in the 5:00 PM traffic. However, as I drove through the downtown area, every light was green and I proceeded nonstop across the Missouri River to the industrial area. Thousands of factory workers were leaving from work and there were dozens of stoplights at every intersection for several miles. As I drove on, every light turned green and, as I arrived, every crosswalk was clear of pedestrians.

Finally, I arrived at the Kansas City Airport, a distance of about twenty-one miles, having never stopped from the time I had left the hotel! When I lined up to return my car, three people were ahead of me. Again, the first person in line allowed me to go first. I checked in the car and then discovered a shuttle driver with a full load awaited to take me to the airport.

I raced into the airport and ran several hundred yards to the plane's departure gate. I arrived at 6:30 PM, as they were closing the door to the airplane's walkway.

Everyone was seated on the plane and I took the only empty seat. I wondered if I would be served dinner. As soon as we were at cruising altitude, I was served a very nice dinner. Thanks, Spirit.

Switching planes in Denver, I boarded a nearly empty DC-10. As we ascended through the fog from the Denver airport, a white cross danced in the misty clouds and, before my eyes, it increased and decreased in size. Finally, the clouds departed and a large cross appeared on the mountain by Denver. To me, this was a sign that Saint Michael watched over me.

Arriving in Portland, the moon was setting in the west. As I drove across North Portland through the St. John's District, I approached over thirty green lights. I drove to St. Helens in order to surprise Ruth, who was staying with her aunt and uncle.

As I entered Scappoose, six miles from my destination, I braked as I entered the town, only to see a blue light flashed by the local patrolman. He had stopped me, he said, in order to tell me that, as I had entered the city, I was driving five miles over the speed limit. However, he did not give me a ticket.

The message that I received, after my safe arrival at nearly midnight, was that there is no such thing as luck or coincidences and no limitations on the power of Saint Michael to watch over me.

The House on Hillcrest

While I built my career, Ruth was on the home front raising our three children. I had wonderful times with my children on the weekends, but, during the week, Ruth helped them with their school assignments, took care of them when they were sick, drove them to their various activities, kept the household clean and well-organized, and prepared a well-rounded dinner every night. She was a superb cook, who used fresh ingredients and, sometimes, fruits and vegetables that she had canned herself. Our children still say how grateful they are for the wonderful meals Ruth prepared, and now the grandchildren are the benefactors of her cooking.

Ruth and I agreed that the most important time to connect with your children is when they first arrive home from school. They burst through the door, and in those first five minutes they have so much to tell. Then, it is all over and they go on to other things. Being there when they come home from school is critically important. Ruth was always there for our children, and they are a testament to her good listening skills and quiet dependability.

In June 1965, our friends, who lived on 14th street in Corvallis, were moving out of state, and we were to tell them goodbye. As we were leaving their house, the husband suggested that we buy their home, which had not sold after several months on the real estate market. Ruth and I walked around the house and, in thirty minutes, we decided to buy it. Definitely, it was a Spirit-guided decision and, as it turned out, a very wise one, as we lived there for eleven years, until Spirit guided us to another location.

We were very happy in our home on 14th Street, where we had discovered the world's best neighbors. There were many children in the neighborhood, and all the adults watched over everyone else's. We got permits from the city and blocked off the street for block parties, a big hit with the children. Forty-nine years later, a nucleus of the women who call themselves "the 14th street gang" still get together to talk over old and new times.

Another fact that weighed heavily in our decision to buy the home was that Calvin Church was only a block away.

Ruth was very active in Calvin Church. She kept our children involved throughout their childhood. For many years I was the church Treasurer and took the offerings to the bank each Sunday.

Upon our arrival in Corvallis, we attended church at First Presbyterian downtown, but we soon transferred to Calvin Presbyterian, a block away from our home on 14th Street. We were active members of that church for forty-eight years, both of us as deacons and elders. We enjoyed many great relationships with the members, who were like family to us.

I served two three-year terms as an elder in the early 1970s. During that time, the church planned an expansion and I served on the building committee. We had about half the money needed, so we tried to do anything we could to keep down the costs. One morning, I opened the paper and read that Willamina Brickyards was going out of business. I called one of the church members, she drove to the brick yards, and bought a big pile of bricks at a terrific discount. It turned out to be exactly the number needed to add the wing onto the church. As it was with my clients, so it was with my church: good things happened when I was involved.

In 2009, we moved to a home in Stoneybrook, a retirement community.

The one drawback with our new location was that it was only a fifteen-minute drive to Calvin Church, but it was like running a gauntlet, with bicyclists darting in and out of our path. The thirty-minute round trip created too much stress on Sunday mornings. Ruth and I searched for another church nearby and we were pleased to find the Suburban Christian Church, four minutes away from our home.

Steve Lee, the senior minister, delivers terrific sermons and I have always found his message to be a perfect fit for whatever I have thought about during the week.

My Angel of Education sometimes spends months teaching me about a subject, and then Steve will preach about that very same theme, as if he were divinely guided. He is a dynamic speaker, with a gift for adapting the lessons of the Bible for everyday life.

A Fire at Calvin Church

At home on 14th street, I received a divine message that allowed me to save Calvin Church from serious fire damage. While eating lunch at home one day, I caught a glimpse of smoke rising less than one hundred away yards, in the direction of Calvin Church. I sent Ruth to get a better glimpse of what was burning, as my first thought was that it was a brush fire. I received a message from Spirit that the church was on fire. The next message that came quickly was that I should grab a garden hose to take with me to the fire. I ran to the front yard, grabbed the garden hose, and headed straight through my neighbor's hedge row, crashed through the shrubbery wall and past my neighbor, who was sunbathing, Arriving at the church, I found the whole south side ablaze, for about forty feet, together with bushes along the wall.

I assumed that some students from a nearby junior high had smoked in the bushes, and left a burning cigarette. Across the street at Garfield Grade School, the children screamed and jumped up and down. Seeing a hose bib about six feet from the fire, I hooked up my hose, raced down the wall, and sprayed water onto the flames.

The fire was completely out by the time the fire truck arrived. Had I arrived a few minutes later, the fire would have reached the asphalt roof, and the entire church would have been involved. This episode reminded me of the days when I had fought numerous grass fires with my older brother, Wayne. Once again, I had obeyed the messages from Spirit, raced to a fire that I could not see, brought a hose, and found a water bib a few feet from the fire. I was enabled only by the divine timing of my Angel of Quick Response, and the training that I had received while in the Army.

Bicycling on 14th Street

On 14th Street, our children had bicycles, and we often rode around the neighborhood. Sometimes, I took our eighteen-pound dog, Lucy, with me. One day, while I rode down the street as fast as I could, Lucy swerved suddenly, in front of me, and my bicycle stopped, as if I had smashed into a brick wall. I was thrown over the handle bars, nearly struck my head, and missed the concrete curb by inches. Fortunately, I suffered only a broken bone in my wrist, which healed on its own, without surgery.

The Building of Our Home on Hillcrest Drive

In 1975, divine Providence changed our lives again. The series of coincidences which led us to build our home on Hillcrest Drive in 1976 truly amazes.

One day in 1972, I received a cold call from a car salesman, who said, "If you could get anything you wanted in a new car, what would you ask for?" I told him that I was not looking for a new car, that I was very happy with the one I had. He persisted, and I told him that I would prefer a three-seat station wagon, so that our son, Bruce, could be in the back seat, our daughters could have their own seat, and that many other features were desired. Six months later, I got a call from the salesman: "I have your car. Why don't you just come down and look at it?" I told him that I was not interested.

Hillcrest Home, Corvallis, OR, Planned and Built by Vernon and Ruth in 1976

More than a year later, on April 16, I took the children for our traditional end-of-tax-season drive. As we drove around the curve on Hillcrest, I noticed a for-sale sign, partly hidden in the blackberry bushes, six feet tall, which covered the entire half- acre lot. It struck me that the lot had possibilities, so, I stopped to get the realtor's phone number. The property was so dense with brambles that I did not try to walk on it. When I called the realtor, he said that the listing had expired years before, and that the lot was now owned by the Signer Motors car dealership.

I knew Don Signer, the son of Signer Motors' owner, because we used to have seats next to his parents at Oregon State University basketball games. I did not have cash to buy the lot, but, I had an old house that I had taken in trade for seven thousand dollars, and I proposed to trade the lot for the house, plus four thousand dollars cash to me. Don counter-proposed: he would take the house in trade for the lot, plus giving me a new car that they had not been able to sell. It was the very same automobile that the salesman had tried to sell me! And so, I got the car that I had "ordered" eighteen months previously, along with the lot, and at the same time I was rid of that old house!

Clearly, the entire event was the work of Spirit, as I had no idea when I ordered the car and acquired the home, that one day I would trade the house for the new car of my dreams, and a lot that would have a view of my beloved Mt. Hood, from over a hundred miles away. It was one of the very few lots in Corvallis that had such a view of Mt. Hood. Could this have been what Spirit had in mind for me when I first drove through Corvallis twenty years before, in 1948? Had he planted the seed in my mind, that I should reside in Corvallis, now nearing fifty-two years, raise my family, and spend the remainder of my life there?

Once the lot exchange closed, the first order of business was to "skin" the blackberry vines from the lot, in order to see what we had purchased. We owned the lot for six months before we realized that we could see Mt. Hood, the tip of Mt. Jefferson, the Three Sisters, Mt. Washington, Skinner's Butte in Eugene, and the entire Cascade Range to the east!

It was a tricky property to build on, rising fifty feet from front to back, which is probably why it had not sold for so long. We did not like some key components of the plans that we had had drawn, which necessitated us driving into a garage one level below the main floor. We knew that we did not want to carry groceries upstairs every day. Instead, we designed the driveway to curve up and around the lot. We could then park on the kitchen level.

When the basement was dug, we found that a shelf of solid rock was right below it. If we had wanted to dig deeper, we would have had to pay for its removal. Our excellent builder placed river rock under the house, so that water coming down the hill could flow under our home. It also served us well when we had an Earthquake in Corvallis. Our daughter, who lived near Hewlett Packard at the time, was shaken out of bed, but, we did not feel a thing, as the gravel and the solid rock had absorbed the Earthquake's rumbles.

Planting grapes is one of the first things that I have done after moving into any home that we have ever owned. It is a small tribute to my dad, who always planted a garden as soon as he moved into a new home. At the Hillcrest house, we canned about fifty quarts of grape juice and grape jelly every year.

When my mother was seventy years old, she came to Corvallis with my father to help us move from 14th Street to the Hillcrest home. We planned to pack for the move, and then move the next day. However, my mother was eager to begin the move, and she suggested that we hire the truck and begin the move that day, to which I agreed. Moving to a new home was one of my mother's favorite things to do, since she liked the idea that we were transitioning to a better place, and she wanted to experience the joy of helping us move. We owned a heavy Magnavox stereo, one of our first big purchases, and my mother bent down to lift it, saying, "Let's get going: grab the other end of this!" She lifted her end of the several hundred pound stereo, and expected me to pick up the other end, which I did, and I was shocked at the weight that she had lifted with ease.

Spirit had led us to the lot where we built our first home, and we lived there for nearly thirty years, during which time our three children graduated from high school, and grandchildren grew up and loved the home as their own. We loved to watch the incredible dawns over the entire Cascade Range for about 120 miles. It was a somewhat sad day when we moved to a beautiful 4,200 sq. ft. home on Buttercup Drive, in the Timberhill Subdivision of Corvallis.

Our Buttercup Drive home in Timberhill subdivision of Corvallis, OR

Our only reason for selling the lot was because, at some time, every family member had fallen, due to the steepness of the lot. Ruth and I feared that one of us might take a serious fall, as we reached the age when a fall was more likely.

Near-Death by Boulder

When we excavated for the Hillcrest house, there was one big boulder on our property, which we rolled down to the front yard to become part of the landscaping. On December 9, 1990, I was atop a twelve-foot ladder, trimming branches from a tree, when the ladder tipped and my feet flew up over my head. I fell headfirst onto the boulder, hit my right cheekbone, which broke in ten places, crushing into my eye-socket and jawbone, and the roots of two molars were forced into my sinus area. The pain was excruciating, but, I had fallen on the only bumper on my head, my cheek bone, which had protected me from a severe concussion, a broken neck, or death. After two and a half hours of surgery by a plastic surgeon and an oral surgeon, the bones were reset, and my jaw was wired closed. I expected plastic surgery in six months, but, within four months, there was no sign that the fall had ever happened, and it left no scars.

Family Time

I have loved golf since I was thirteen, when my grandfather Simpson introduced me to the game, at the 5/9 hole miniature golf course around his home. During the years that we were raising a family, I found that golf consumed too much time, and I had to defer the pleasure. I could not feel comfortable on Saturdays at the golf course, when three children were at home who loved to be with me. Weekends were for family drives, camping, and fishing, and to create special memories, I often took just one child for a trip.

Barbara was the one who always wanted to go for rides on Saturday, before Bruce was old enough to travel. When she was four or five, before seatbelts, she used to stand behind me in the car, and put her arms around my neck. We would spend the day driving around the countryside, travelling towards the coast, or visiting Valsetz, a little lumber company town that has long since been leveled. Other times, we would go to the mountains for a little fishing.

When she was young, Barbara was a night owl. There was a time when we first moved to Corvallis when I taught Oregon State University evening classes, and I returned home after 10:00 P.M. Barbara waited for me, standing up in her crib in the dark. I would pick her up, we would go into the kitchen for a beer, a tiny glass for her, and the rest for me. We talked, and then I put her into bed. That is such a sweet memory for me.

Barbara was naturally smart, and I have always felt that, for her, the school system had disappointed. She was one of the top math students in junior high, completing most of her high school required classes by the end of her sophomore year. It was difficult to motivate her academically, since she had mentally completed high school so quickly. After high school, she spent one term in college, and for a short time she worked for me in my CPA office. She then spent eleven years at Hewlett Packard, working her way up very quickly, until she was ready to start her own business. Everything always came easily to her, and she could accomplish anything that she wanted.

Barbara and her husband, Steve, have two children, Kimberly and Andrew. Kimberly graduated from Azusa Pacific University, near Pasadena, California, with bachelor's degrees in Psychology and Music. At the Newmark Theater in Portland, Oregon, Kimberley has performed as Eponine in Les Miserables. She currently pursues a professional career, studying at the American Musical and Dramatic Academy in New York, City. Andrew graduated from Oregon State University, and he currently pursues a master's degree in Education.

Any endeavor that challenged Catherine was met with boundless energy and enthusiasm. At age twelve, she travelled with me to San Francisco, and she was the perfect companion in the big city. Catherine was always very mature for her age. As a child, she had a strong personality and was a very hard worker, which paid dividends for her as she made her way through school and college. She earned a Master's Degree of Education In Curriculum and Instructional Leadership, and was halfway to a Ph.D. degree when, due to budget cuts, her program closed.

Catherine became a teacher, and I would be surprised if a better one could be found. She demanded total discipline, and the children responded well. When they walked into her classroom, they knew that they had to be ready to learn. She taught them a quick transition between play time and learning time. If any children came in from the playground and made a racket, they had to leave, and come in again quietly. She taught them social responsibility: each person pays the price when another person creates a problem.

Catherine and her husband, David, have one daughter, Jennifer, who graduated from Western Oregon University with a Bachelor of Arts degree in Interdisciplinary Studies.

Jennifer competed In dressage, and she performed outstandingly on her Friesian horse, Westley. She won numerous national titles, including the 2005 Presidents Trophy for Friesians in North America, and she was the winner of dressage's highest point total among all FHANA horses in North America. Jennifer and her husband are the parents of our first great-grandson, Adam, born in May 2014.

Jennifer Wins Region 6, Jr. Young Rider Title in 2005

Bruce and I took some wonderful trips together, including camping and fishing in the Steens Mountains with my nephews, Mike and Patrick Magee. When there, you can drive all the way up to the top of the mountain at ten thousand five hundred feet, and you can also see the Alvord Desert about six thousand feet below. The Steens Mountains were created by an Earth upheaval about twenty-five miles long and thirty miles wide. The wildlife preserves in that area give hunters and fishermen an incredible place in which to appreciate the gifts of nature.

Bruce was an incredibly hard worker, and he managed to achieve A's and B's all through high school. He ran cross- country at Crescent Valley, and he won the most inspirational runner award two years in a row. For his undergraduate degree, he enrolled at George Fox University, then transferred to Pacific University and Western Oregon University, and finally, he completed his degree at Oregon State University, maintaining a high grade point average throughout. Bruce completed his Master's Degree in Communicative Disorders at the University of Wisconsin-Madison in three semesters instead of four. Bruce has extraordinary compassion. After starting his career as a speech language pathologist in Melbourne, Florida, he moved to Oregon, and was employed by a community reentry program for adults who experience traumatic brain injuries. For over ten years, Bruce has provided speech therapy services in skilled nursing facilities in Oregon.

It is interesting to see that Bruce has followed in the footsteps of his great-grandfather, Frank Simpson, who pursued healing to his last job as an ambulance driver assistant, as well as his uncle, Wayne Bowlby, who was a Navy Corpsman during World War Two, and me, his father, in the healing arts.

Bruce, and his wife, Edith, have three daughters, Elise, Angie, and Danielle. Elise is in her third year at Oregon State University, pursuing a degree in Occupational Therapy. Her sister, Angie, joins her in the fall, as a freshman. Danielle is a sophomore to-be at Crescent Valley High School, and she has been selected for the varsity volleyball squad.

All our children are very affectionate, and they have passed that trait on to their own children. Every time our grandchildren come into our house, they give us hugs. That is how I grew up: I never came into my mother's presence without hugging her.

Throughout our years rearing children, Ruth was the heart of our family, keeping us organized, well taken care of, and extremely well fed. In addition to managing our daily routines, she coordinated weekends and vacations, and brought the extended family together for Thanksgiving and Christmas. When my parents were alive, she invited them to join us, along with my sister's family, and anyone else who could come. Those big family gatherings were just like the ones at my grandparents' house as I grew up, when all the cousins had fun together. There is something really special about family bonds, and I am appreciative that my children experience many joyful family times.

Besides being a wonderful mother, Ruth has always been a wise home economist. She is a dedicated coupon clipper, and she has set all kinds of money-saving records at Safeway. I read that frugality is the number one quality millionaires look for in a wife, and Ruth fills that role perfectly. Both Ruth and I were raised in households where money was what you earned, and we know how to stretch a dollar to the maximum degree.

We have been blessed with two outstanding sons-in-law, first, Steve Wilson, and then Dave Cudo. Our daughter-in-law, Edith, has produced three beautiful, talented daughters. As a result of Edith's devotion to her daughters, and her having taught them to enjoy life to its fullest, we have received extraordinary joy from these relationships.

Dave Cudo is generous with his time, plays his saxophone at all family occasions, and makes each event a memorable occasion. He shares his music with the community, as he plays inspirational music for weddings, funerals, and other events. In December 1997, Dave, being the world-class saxophone player that he is, was invited to play for Christmas parties in the White House, the result of Catherine's having sent a CD of his music to the White House for its perusal. Dave played for the staff and security people, and Dave, Catherine and Jennifer were given a private tour and had their picture taken with Buddy, the white house dog, much to Jenny's delight.

I have had a very close relationship with my sister Lillian's children, especially her sons, Pat and Mike. The boys were twelve and twenty when their father died of a heart attack. Mentoring these boys has been a rewarding experience, and both have graduated from college and grown into remarkable men. Lillian's daughters, Debbie and Nancy live in Corvallis and Nancy has contributed many hours towards the production of this book.

Near-Death from a Falling Tree

Lillian's sons loved camping in the Steens Mountains with my son, Bruce. In July 1988, Pat joined Bruce and me for a trip in our camper. We left Corvallis in a wind storm, and were only ten miles from town, when a four-foot thick oak tree, which must have been over one hundred years old, crashed across the entire highway, less than one hundred feet in front of us. When we approached the tree, we found that there was an arched driveway, which would allow us to drive around the blocked highway. Not only did we miss being crushed to death when the tree fell, but, we were provided with a safe passageway in which to continue our expedition, with no loss of time. Thanks, Spirit.

Manifesting a Pair of Needle-nose Pliers

In June 1997, I was invited by my nephews, Mike and Pat, to fish at Detroit Lake. When we were in the center of the lake, Pat attached his sinkers to his fishing line with a pair of needle-nosed pliers. As I watched him, I thought to myself, "Why don't I have a pair of those in my own fishing basket?"

Three days later, I was in Sisters, Oregon, with my son, Bruce, and his family. We had heard that the fishing was fine at Three Creeks Lake, and we stopped at the store to get Bruce a fishing license. There was a bit of a wait while the cashier showed a fellow ahead of us how to bend his hooks, so that the fish would not escape. Another reason that I needed a pair of needle-nosed pliers! Bruce was in a hurry to get back to the family, as his daughters waited in the car, and so, I delayed buying the pliers.

The next morning, Bruce and I drove the sixteen miles to Three Creeks Lake, and spent two fruitless hours fishing. We headed back toward Sisters, and drove into one of the many side roads to fish in the creek. We parked and began to fish downstream.

I found a large pool with a swift current, reached into my bag to pull out some sinkers, and wished, once again, that I had a pair of needle-nosed pliers. As I brought my hand up to place the sinkers on the line, my hand brushed a small pine tree limb. My eyes were drawn to it, and I saw, balanced on the limb, a small pair of needle-nosed pliers, apparently placed there by some fisherman months or years before. I wondered how many other fishermen had fished from this same spot, without discovering the pliers. If Bruce had come to this spot, instead of me, would he have found them? What if we had taken a different road? Would I have found a pair of pliers in a different spot? The question became: did I create my own reality, or was it God's timing transmitted through an Angel?

The Most Terrifying Seconds of My Lifetime!

The following story relates the most terrifying thirty seconds of my life, when any second could have been my last!

In March 1975, on Friday before spring break, I received tax information from Clip, one of the long-term clients of my CPA firm in Corvallis.

Next morning, our family and several other families from 14th street, departed for the Whistler ski area, about five hundred miles north of Corvallis, where we settled into our motels for a good night's sleep before the much anticipated ski slopes of Whistler Mountain, seventy miles north of Vancouver, B. C.

To get to the ski area, we boarded a gondola, which lifted us about two thousand five hundred vertical feet to the ski runs, all of which were above that elevation, and where there was fresh snow.

After many runs that Sunday morning, I went to the lodge for lunch. The dining area was literally wall-to-wall with people. I managed to get through the food line and looked for a place to sit down. After several minutes, I saw an open spot for one person about thirty feet away. Hurrying across the crowded room, I sat down, and was startled to see, sitting across from me, Clip, the person whose tax information I had received on Friday afternoon in Corvallis. Neither of us knew that the other was going to travel five hundred miles to ski at Whistler Mountain. Clip was as surprised as I, and we marveled at the impossibility of such a meeting. The message that I received from Spirit was, that this was the forerunner of a very special event about to take place.

Later that day, I was about to retire from skiing, when I noticed a trail that looked interesting. I started on the trail, and suddenly realized that the trail dropped below the 2,500 foot elevation. The slope was pure ice and very steep. I commenced my descent at a terrific rate of speed, and I had no chance to stop on the icy slope. At this speed, any attempt to stop would have sent me into the trees, and sure death.

The slope carried me to the left, and I headed straight towards a three-foot thick Douglas fir tree. Barely able to maneuver away from the tree, I missed it by less than three feet. As I skied past, I was airborne for about fifty feet, the first time that I have ever been airborne on skis. As I landed on pure ice, it was a miracle that I was able to keep my balance.

While I was airborne, the thought flashed through my mind that this was no place for the faint of heart. I continued my terrifying descent, and I tried to keep on the trail, with no idea about what the next slope might bring.

About a hundred yards ahead, I noticed a trail that joined with the trail that I was on. Slowly, I maneuvered my skis to head up the trail coming down the mountain.

Finally, after going uphill for at least one hundred feet, I stopped abruptly, lost my balance quickly, and fell backwards down the slope. The steepness of the slope on slippery ice sent me down the slope on my back, my head leading the charge down the hill. Utilizing all my strength, I threw my legs into the air and was able, finally, to turn on my side. I then rolled over several times before I was finally able to stop my fall. I lay spread-eagled on the ice, afraid to move for fear that I would begin another slide. Finally, I removed my skis and was able to crawl off the trail and drag my skis downhill, cross-country through the icy forest to the bottom of the mountain, with numerous short slides into branches and trees along the way. This happening was twenty-six years before I began to ski with a helmet, which would probably not have saved me, for, if I had fallen along the trail, the rest of my body would have been smashed by countless trees.

Coincidentally, friends who had come to Whistler with me were riding the gondola to night ski, they had watched part of my descent, and they were astonished that I had skied that area on purpose, and that I had not fallen down.

The message that I received from Spirit was that He had arranged the coincidence of my meeting with Clip, the prelude of another instance of Spirit placing me in a near- death experience, where any second I could have met a tree and died. As usual, my faith and my lack of fear, allowed me another escape from the grim reaper, with only a few minor scratches to show for it . My angels watched over me again!

Annual Ski Trip to Mt. Hood Meadows

Each year, for my skiing event, I have skied at Mt. Hood Meadows on the southeast slopes of Mt Hood. In March 2001, aged seventy, my opening run was on the Texas chair, on the highest slope of the ski area. I prayed for all my high school classmates who have died, and gave thanks that I am alive to enjoy one of my life-time sports.

After making a lot of runs from top to bottom, I was about to leave for home when the message came to me that I should make one more run, so, I took a four- seat chair lift with another fellow about my age. We rode in silence, and in the last thirty seconds he asked me why I was not wearing a helmet. I told him that I usually did not fall down during the entire ski season. His response was, that it took only one out-of-control snowboarder, and I would be vulnerable. (His prophecy held true, as in the following years, two men who were not wearing helmets were hit by snowboarders and died.)

That sounded like a message from an Angel, and when I returned home, I noticed that Anderson's Sporting Goods Store was having a closing sale. For sixty dollars, I purchased a helmet marked two hundred dollars, and I immediately thanked my Angel of Abundance for the unexpected discount.

From that time on, I wore the helmet each time I skied, and I bought helmets for my granddaughters, and told them, "No ski helmet-no ticket." They understood grandfather completely.

On April 16, 2003, two years later, I had survived another tax season, and was headed to Mt. Hood Meadows for my annual ski trip. By 1:00 P.M., I had made ten runs without falling down, and I proceeded to the lunch area. Depositing my skis in a storage facility about one hundred feet from the lodge, I walked across a concrete roof that had wires in the roof to melt the snow. Apparently, the heating had failed, and the roof was sheer ice on concrete, in spots covered with light snow.

A few feet from the door to the lodge, my feet flew suddenly skyward, and I lunged backwards, landing on my left hip. My head was propelled backward, and with a terrific force I smashed the back of my head on the ice and concrete. Many people rushed over to me, and as they had seen the ice explode into the air when my head hit the concrete, they expected that I would be injured severely. For about twenty seconds, I was stunned, and then I realized that I was okay, as I had worn my helmet. The man on the lift, two years previously, will never know that he saved my life. My Guardian Angel must have placed him there for my last run, and he must have believed that it was his last opportunity to advise me to wear a helmet. Had I not accepted his advice, I most likely would have died.

The next day, April 17, 2003, Dr. Atkins of Atkins' diet fame, died after slipping on an icy sidewalk in New York City. It is interesting that he was born in Columbus, Ohio, where my great grandfather, C.C. Piatt, was born, and that Dr. Atkins was six months older than me.

The message from Spirit was clear, that I had dodged another bullet, and I could easily have died like Dr.Atkins, in the wink of an eye. But, Spirit was not finished with me yet. I praised the Lord that my experience of near-death at Mt. Hood Meadows was guided by my Guardian Angel in an Angelic manner, and that I was not hurt in the dramatic fall on the back of my head.

The Travel Years

When Ruth and I married, she had never been south of Portland. We have now traveled to about forty countries and all fifty states. Ruth began traveling with me to tax conferences, and while we toured the United States and I gave talks about Christmas tree taxation, she sold tax manuals. We always enjoyed each trip, no matter where we were.

Ruth and I were blessed to have three journeys to Europe with Doug and Betty Thompson. Doug planned all the trips of three weeks each, and he made all the reservations for us, including the route, lodging, and restaurants. He rented a car, and drove us through France, Spain, Portugal, Austria, Switzerland, Italy, and Germany. We could not have asked for better travel companions. A divine gift, for certain.

Manifestation

Some of our trips were manifestations of dreams that I had dreamt early in my life. When I was in grade school, I had loved the picture of the Chinese working in their rice fields, and I loved learning about the Civil War, and manifested that I would travel to both places some day.

I loved to study maps, and to think about what the battles of the Civil War must have been like. I envisioned that I would travel to China, and that I would visit the American Civil War battlefields. I did both, in an unplanned manner. My Christmas Tree Taxation Manual brought me invitations to speak in a number of key Civil War states, and I took full advantage of those trips to tour the historic sites and my friend Hoover's wife planned the trip for us to China without our knowledge.

Sense of Direction

I have always had a good feel for direction, even in a place where I have never been. I seem to have a sixth sense of a city's layout, and without a map I am able to find my way. This was especially apparent during the 1980s and 90s, when we traveled around the country, and I gave talks on Christmas tree taxation.

Once, Ruth and I drove a rental car from the airport to our bed- and-breakfast in Springfield, Massachusetts. It rained hard, and we passed numerous exits for the city. I suddenly received a message that I should take the next turnoff. Ruth was quite skeptical, and she wanted me to stop and get a map. But, I continued to drive to a crossroads, where I received a message that I should go up the hill. A half-mile later, a car drove in front of us, and I received another message that I should follow that car. We continued for another half-mile, before I turned onto the road that matched the address of our B & B. The car we followed stopped in front of that exact address, and the driver turned out to be the husband of our hostess. Again, my Angel of Guidance had aided us.

Japan, Hong Kong and China

In 1936, I attended public school kindergarten in a home near Park Street Grade School, where I first met Hoover Lee. I was seated by Hoover, and we became fast friends. I was impressed with his straight black hair and his beautiful "tan." Our friendship continued through two years at Coe Primary School, and when we entered the third grade in Park Street school, we asked to sit together. Miss Andrews agreed to this immediately. I observed that this did not happen when other kids requested to sit together, and I wondered why.

Each year thereafter, our request to sit together was granted. In the sixth grade, Mrs. Clark announced that we were going to study China, and a wonderful picture book on China was distributed. I remember that I gazed at that book, with pictures of the oxen working in the rice patties, and envisioned the day when I would visit that remarkable land.

In 1943, Kimmie, twelve years old, was also in the sixth grade. She had been born and raised in Tokyo, nearly five thousand miles across the Pacific Ocean. Shortly thereafter, American B-29 bombers had made thousands of bombing raids over Japan, and destroyed their cities from the air.

Who could have foreseen that Hoover would one day marry Kimmie? Or, that one day, Hoover would own many restaurants, including the HO-TI, which became the hottest nightspot in Portland, Oregon? Years later, Hoover co-partnered with his brother, Fred, to own many restaurants together. I became their financial advisor, and for many years thereafter, I did their tax and accounting work.

A month after my son, Bruce, graduated from high school in 1983, I received an unexpected call from Hoover's wife, Kimmie, who owned a travel agency. As she was going to visit her mother in Japan, she suggested that Ruth and I fly to Tokyo, and she would show us about.

Without knowing if we were interested in such a trip, Kimmie planned for us to spend five days in Tokyo, and six days in Hong Kong and China. Ruth and I seized upon this opportunity, and as his graduation gift from high school our son Bruce joined us. It was an incredible trip. Kimmie met us at the airport as planned; however, she suffered from an inflamed tooth, and was unable to give us the tour that she had planned; but, she did give us tips on places to see. Bruce and I puzzled out the subway system, and we traveled many miles underground.

Our stay in Hong Kong convinced me that it is the most exciting city in the world, and I still remember the thrill of seeing the harbor, with its junks, cruise ships, and other ships of all sizes, maneuvering through choppy waters.

During the trip to China, we watched water buffalo till the rice patties, as I had observed in the book on China forty years previously. At that time, agriculture employed nearly nine-hundred million of China's one billion people, in order to produce food as it was done four thousand years ago. We ate fabulous Chinese meals, and enjoyed every day of our trip. Since 1983, China has moved to capitalism, and the country has flourished beyond all expectations.

My Angel of Abundance aided us again on the plane ride home from Hong Kong, as I was moved from business class to first class.

It never ceases to amaze me, that a twelve- year- old grade school boy could manifest a trip to China, and that his best friend's wife, who had grown up in Japan at the same time, would become the key person to the complete my manifestation.

Spirit had fulfilled my forty-year dream of traveling to China, and to boot, had exceeded all my expectations by sending me to Tokyo and Hong Kong.

It is my belief, that this series of events demonstrates the unlimited power of the Holy Spirit, and that everyone can access this power.

My favorite memory of Hoover is that of our senior year in high school, when we played football against Camas, Washington. Hoover was a guard, and I was a linebacker. Camas had the ball on our thirty-yard line, and someone smashed me from behind and flattened me to the turf. As I staggered to my feet, the Camas quarterback was, apparently, trying to "ground the ball," as no receivers were open, and the ball struck me squarely in my stomach. I never saw the ball, but, from my pain response, I grabbed my stomach and caught it. Stunned, I stood with the ball in my hands, and Hoover yelled, "Run Bowlby run." I ran, following Hoover to the right sidelines, while Hoover ran protection for me, and I knocked down would-be tacklers with reckless abandon. Finally, I was forced out of bounds on the ten-yard line. Hoover had run interference for me seventy yards down the field.

Many years later I "ran interference" for Hoover, spending thirty years advising him in the constant complex battles he fought in the business world.

The last time I saw Hoover was when I visited him in a retirement facility in Beaverton, Oregon. When it was time to leave, I shook hands with him, and he did not want to release my hand, and so, we stood, holding hands for over ten minutes. He died a few days later. We had had a fruitful life together, from the time we met in kindergarten some seventy years before.

Hawaiian Island Miracle

In 1974, I took my family, for the first time, to the Hawaiian Islands, where I was to attend a CPA conference. Cathy was fourteen, Barbara was twelve, and Bruce was nine. The Holy Spirit came with us and revealed his divine presence in a most unusual way. We had a guided pre-tour of all of the major islands, with Maui the first stop. When we disembarked from the plane, the wind blew strongly as we observed the many fish ponds. Suddenly, Barbara realized that she had lost a contact from her eye, and after a frantic search, we could not find it. Barbara would have to wear glasses for the rest of the trip.

The next day, Ruth and I sat by the pool, and the children swam with a group on the beach, about a hundred yards away. Cathy ran to tell us that Barbara had lost her glasses in the surf, and that she was quite unhappy with her limited vision. I walked to the beach, and asked where she had lost her glasses. No one knew where they had been lost. As I looked up and down the beach for about a half mile in either direction, I observed that the sand was of a heavy, granular, orange color. about two to three feet of sand came to us, and a ten-foot rise came with every wave. I spotted a group scuba diving, and asked them if they could help find her glasses. Their response was that they had lost a foot-fin the prior day, and had spent hours looking for it, without success.

I began to walk up the beach, and I requested Spirit's guidance as to how I might find the glasses in the pounding surf. Spirit guided me into the ocean, and neck-deep in the water, I observed a huge wave coming at us. At that very moment, I noticed several inches of a dark object, about six feet further in the ocean. Instantly, I dove for the item, and I seemed unable to reach it, but, I made a final lunge, and grasped the object.

The big wave had picked me up and dropped me on my knees onto the beach, about fifteen feet away. When my eyes opened, I realized that I had Barbara's glasses! When we told our tour guide that story, he said that I was surely a kahuna, which is the Hawaiian word for priest. Clearly, Spirit had saved Barbara's vision for the rest of the trip! Forty years later, Barbara's glasses would still be buried in the sand on Maui, if the Holy Spirit, working through me, had not intervened.

Hyeres France-Lucky Angel of Abundance

Some amazing things happened in the course of our trips with Doug and Betty Thompson. My Angel of Abundance often traveled with me, and that was never clearer than during a trip to southern France. We were staying overnight in Hyeres, and as I rise early, usually at 5:00 A.M., or 6:00 A.M., I typically walk around to see the city. On that particular morning, I walked several miles, knowing that I could find my way back through the winding streets. I came upon a beautiful lighted building, with lots of cars around it. I was curious as to what went on there, and I was amazed to find inside a gorgeous casino, in full swing, at 6:00 A.M.

It was full of smoke, and there were more than five hundred people there, all busy at card tables and slot machines. I wandered about, and found several slot machines not in use. I had three five-franc coins in my pocket, worth about one dollar each. When I inserted one into the machine, I heard Bangety Dee Bang Bang, and a huge stream of francs poured out. Wow! I inserted my second coin, and again, another flood of money came out, adding to the big pile already accumulated. I looked around, but, no one was paying attention. I felt as if I were robbing the place!

I spotted a stack of big buckets across the room. Should I leave my pile of francs and get some buckets? I risked it, and when I returned, the coins were still there, and they filled two buckets! Meanwhile, a five-franc piece was still in my pocket, and I inserted it into the machine. A third time, Bangety Dee Bang Bang, and I filled another bucket, hauled the three buckets to the cashier, and exchanged the francs for eight hundred dollars. Clearly, my Angel of Abundance had led me divinely to that machine, and also managed three wins in a row for me. Dinner that night was on me!

Bicentennial Trip in 1976

In May 1976, the entire family spent three weeks on a Bicentennial tour of the primary cities in Virginia, plus Washington, D.C., New York City, Boston, and Philadelphia.

Bicentennial Trip in 1976

Mt Vesuvius and Pompeii

I had an extraordinary experience of an entirely different kind in Pompeii, the Italian city which was buried by an eruption of Mt. Vesuvius in 79 A.D. As soon as I entered the grounds of the excavation, a fiery pain began on my back. It felt as if hot volcanic coals were piled upon me. We remained there for two hours, and I could barely walk because of the pain. I thought that I was going to die! The minute we were away from the grounds, the pain stopped. I had to be receiving the same fire that the people had received from the volcanic hot ash over nineteen hundred years previously.

Tanzania and Kenya Trip

Ruth and I travelled with Corvallis friends to Africa where we toured Tanzania and Kenya. It was an unforgettable experience to see the Serengeti National Park, and to observe cheetahs, and a couple of million other animals. It was a spectacular trip, like a chapter out of the Peoples of the World course that I had taken in college. We observed how the Maassai people lived in a compound with a twelve-foot high fence of sticks all the way around it to keep out the lions.

Their homes were low mud huts, about ten feet long and five feet high, and rose from the ground like a mound. The Maasai are tall people, six feet or more, including the women, who performed a spectacular dance for us. The people earn money from the cattle they raise. The most gorgeous cattle that we had ever seen. They never eat the cattle; they drain small quantities of blood from them, and mix it with flour to make bread.

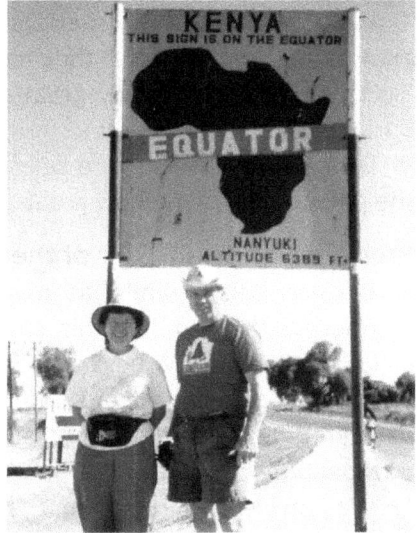

Ruth and Vernon

We stayed in the beautiful lodges built by the British many years ago, which included a lodge on the edge of the volcanic Ngorongoro Park Crater. Twelve miles across and at a two thousand foot elevation, the volcanic crater is now the home of over 25,000 animals. When the top 18,000 feet of the mountain exploded, ash, rock, and cinders fell as far away as India. It makes Washington's Mount St. Helen's explosion look like a small puff!

Roots Trip to Cooperstown North Dakota

In August 1986, I was a speaker at the National Christmas Tree Growers' annual convention in Minneapolis, Minnesota. I also sold my Christmas Tree Taxation manuals while there. The following day, we drove to Cooperstown, North Dakota to locate my great-grandparents' 640-acre farm near Cooperstown, North Dakota they homesteaded in 1881. This is where my grandfather built a home and where my mother and her three sisters were born.

We planned to arrive in time for a Sunday morning church service.

After driving by four churches, we selected one, walked in, and sat down. The minister asked us why we were there, and I told him that we were looking for my great-grandfather Piatt's homestead. The woman next to us said, "I own it," but, she could not take us to the farm that day. A couple on our other side said, "We'll take you to the farm." We accepted, and enjoyed our visit to the original homestead and the barns built in 1881.

In Cooperstown, we visited the historic Piatt home built by my great-grandfather in 1905, after they had sold their farm to their son, Chester Piatt. We also visited my great-grandfather's grave, with two infants buried beside him.

Divine timing must have selected the church where we could meet the person who owned my great-grandparents' farm. Thanks, Spirit.

Presbyterian Choir Tour of the British Isles

In June 1994, while at my dentist's office, Dr. Jerry Bowman mentioned that, in July, his choir planned to tour the British Isles, including England, Wales, and Scotland. Two additional people were needed to complete the bus. Ruth and I thought that it might be the trip of a lifetime, and we immediately accepted. Spirit had arranged an unexpected trip for us.

We arrived at Heathrow airport, and were then bussed to Stonehenge, which I had always wanted to see. That night, July 4th, we arrived at Ruthin Castle, where we were met by a large American flag. Ruth recalled that in 1960, my mother had given us eight cups with a picture of Ruthin Castle and Ruth's name on them.

Our trip included a stopover at St. Andrews, where the choir sang, and where we were guests for dinner at church members' homes.

With free time the following morning, I arose early and went to the famous St. Andrews golf course, where I was lucky enough to get a tee time with a golfer from Michigan and a member of the club. The round was more spectacular than I had expected, but, I avoided the ten-foot deep bunkers. Afterwards, the club member treated us to lunch and drinks, as we sat at a table overlooking the 18th green. Thanks, Spirit, for an unplanned memorable occasion.

We also visited York, where in 306 A.D., after his father's death, the Emperor Constantine was crowned by the Roman garrison.

It was a wonderful trip, and I filmed the choir as it sang in cathedrals and other places.

Presbyterian Choir Tour of England

Baltic Capitals Cruise

Ruth and I embarked a Baltic Capitals Cruise departing from England to the sixty-one mile Kiel Canal in Northern Germany that was opened in 1895. As we passed through the canal, every car stopped and waved to the passengers on the ten-story cruise ship, which must have been an awesome sight to see such a huge ship passing through the farmland. We shared a remarkable moment, as we sat in the lounge, a hundred feet above the farmland, as a setting sun showered sunlight across the bow of the ship.

We visited Berlin, Copenhagen, Oslo, Stockholm, Helsinki, and St. Petersburg, where we visited the Hermitage Museum. Thirty days before we toured the museum, Russia commenced a display of the art collected at the end of World War II, works which the Nazis had stolen from the Jews and kept hidden for fifty years.

Tour to Ireland

We flew to Dublin, Ireland, and took the train to Belfast in Northern Ireland, where our Bed and Breakfast host, Lynn Nigel, gave us a personal tour, on the way to our night's lodging, and then took us to see the Giant Causeway. We then traveled by bus around the island, where we joined a Tauck tour group in Limerick, went to the five- star Dromoland Castle, and had a fabulous tour to Dublin.

The Giant Causeway in Ireland

Other Trips

Ruth and I have traveled to Spain, Portugal, Greece, France, England, Germany, Italy, Scotland, Wales, Switzerland, Austria, Israel, Turkey, and other Middle-Eastern countries.

These trips have given me a deeper understanding of the world. As a child, I had seldom left the Hood River Valley, and I was fifteen before I visited the Oregon coast. Not travelers, our family listened to radio broadcasts and read *The Grit* newspaper. My brother, Bob, and I pored over our world map and imagined what it would be like to visit places whose names we could not pronounce. Who would have guessed that one day we would visit the foreign countries we had dreamt of, eat their food and meet their citizens? It is truly amazing that we were able to visit the number of places that we had dreamed of.

Stories of my Auto Guardian Angel, Saint Michael

In sixty-six years of driving, I have averaged at least fifteen thousand miles a year, totaling about a million miles, with never an accident. However, it has become abundantly clear that my Auto Guardian Angel, Saint Michael, has saved me countless times, as illustrated in the following stories.

Near-Death on Ice

In December 1960, Ruth, Cathy, and I left our Portland home, and were en route to Goldendale to spend Christmas with her grandparents. The highway was a little icy, so, I had crept along the freeway at about twenty-five miles per hour. I rounded a curve several miles past Mosier, and I was suddenly driving on glare ice. I quickly realized that I had no traction at all, we drove into a long downward straightaway about ¾ mile ahead, and the car increased its speed at an alarming rate. At the bottom of the hill were two cars already crashed into the rocks at the bottom of the grade, and a state patrol officer's car with flashing lights was parked there.

When I was within a hundred yards of the cars, the state patrolman with a flare crept slowly to the middle of the highway, directly in my path. By that time, we traveled close to sixty miles per hour, and still we gained speed. I knew that I could not avoid him, and that braking would spin me out of control. Most likely, I would crash into the disabled cars and the people standing outside their vehicles. I sped past the cars, and the patrolman slid out of the way, with only a second or two to spare! We rounded the corner and slowed gradually, as the highway was on the level and slightly uphill. What a ride! My Guardian Angel, Saint Michael, gave us clear passage, and saved the patrol officer and other people standing by the road.

My Gas Tank Angel

In 1970, our family took a trip through the southwest in our new 1970 Buick station wagon, which I thought had a twenty gallon gas tank, as had my previous automobile. Ruth always keeps a close eye on our gas gauge, and as we approached Las Vegas, she began to worry that we were going to run out of gas. I wanted to fill up when we got to the city. It was 115 degrees outside, three children were in the car, and it would have been unpleasant to run out of gas in that heat. To placate Ruth, I drove to a remote gas station, which I had spotted on a hill about a mile off the freeway, and I filled the tank with 17.4 gallons. Later that same year, I ran out of gas at the top of a bridge in Seattle, and I had coasted down the hill to the gas pumps at a station below the bridge. When I filled the tank near Las Vegas, I realized that the tank had been within .1 of a gallon of being empty Ruth was right: without adding gasoline, we would never have made it to Las Vegas! Once again, I obeyed the message from Spirit and, along with Ruth's urging, I filled the tank just in time.

My Gas Tank Angel looked out for me again one hot summer day when we had all three children with us. As I drove west on highway I-84 east of The Dalles, a tire blew out at the point of an off-ramp. There was a tree-lined park at the bottom of the ramp, and I was able to drive into the shade. Ruth and the children played in the park, while I changed the tire under the shade of the trees. With divine timing, my Gas Tank Angel had placed me exactly at the ramp when the tire blew, and I was able to replace the tire in a cool, peaceful setting, instead of on the sweltering highway.

Another close call was when I drove with Ruth and our three children on I-5, south of Salem, in a very heavy rain storm. I believed that I had plenty of gas to drive to Albany, about ten miles away. Suddenly, there was a "ping" noise that I had never heard before, and in an instant, I received the message that I was out of gas, and that there was a ramp that led to a gas station. With the last ounce of energy, I coasted right beside the gas pump. (I do not consider arriving at a gas pump with an empty tank-running out of gas.)

Once again, my Gas Tank Angel had saved me while I drove on a rain drenched highway. So far in fifty-eight years of marriage, I have never run out of gas as my Gas Tank Angel has never failed me. It is like Jesus, who will never fail you when you commit to divine guidance.

Near-Death by a Rolling Tire

In October, 1972, I received a message that I should write my life's story, but, I was so busy with my accounting practice and family that I could not imagine how I was to make time for such a huge undertaking. I pondered this one day as I drove south on Interstate 5, and approached the Santiam overpass near Albany, Oregon. Suddenly a large tire and rim rolled off the overpass, and bounced about twenty feet directly in front of my car. Traffic was traveling at about sixty miles per hour at the time. The tire bounded across the center median, rolled across the three lanes of northbound traffic, and continued up the hill to the top of the overpass. Miraculously, it did not cause a single accident.

Since then, I have tried to understand how a tire could fall from an eastbound car, cross three lanes of westbound traffic, jump a four-foot bridge railing, and still have momentum to cross the freeway, and roll back up to the overpass. There seems to be no Earthly explanation. I believed the message to be that to write my life story should become a top priority, because my life might end at any moment. I isolated myself for three days and, with the help of my secretary, Rebecca Friesen, I completed the first draft in August 1997.

Hoodoo Whiteout

While returning home from skiing at Mt. Bachelor in 1973, I had worn my brown sunglasses, as it was sunny in Bend. When I arrived at the top of the hill, past Suttle Lake, the weather turned very suddenly into a snow whiteout, with terrific winds for the two miles in front of the Hoodoo ski area. Ruth asked me how I could see where I was going, as I weaved by over fifty cars stopped on the highway, and many were involved in minor accidents. At first, I could not understand her concern, as I could see for over a hundred feet. Finally, I lowered my glasses, and I could not see past the front of the car! I realized then that the brown sun glasses had eliminated one hundred percent of the glare. I tested another pair of dark glasses, and I could not see past the car's hood. I passed all the stalled cars, and looked for someone who needed help, but, I saw no one in trouble, and I finally got past the whiteout. I drove alone on the highway, as no other drivers could see past the front of their cars. Spirit had come to my assistance when I had donned the brown glasses, and He had guided me to safety through a frightening storm. Thanks, Saint Michael.

Near-Death from a Texas Longhorn and a Large Deer

I had a very strange near-death experience in 1977 near Rooster Rock on the Columbia River Highway. Driving late at night, suddenly out of the fog, I came upon an enormous Texas Longhorn walking up the highway in my lane. I swerved to the right, and narrowly missed the horns of the bull, then barely regained control of my car in time to miss the concrete highway barrier by inches. Amazingly, it was in almost the same spot where, years before, while driving about sixty miles per hour, at night in the fog, a deer had suddenly appeared right in front of my car, and had then vanished before my eyes.

Near-Death from a Rain Deluge

In May 1978, Ruth, Bruce and I were on a trip to Hood River at 9:00 P.M. We had just turned from I-5 to I-205, and were driving east, when a rain deluge struck. A dark cloud appeared, it became inky dark, over one-half inch of rain covered my windshield, and completely obliterated my vision. It was impossible to see the lights of our car on the roadway.

Fresh in my mind was the story of a car that had stopped in a thick fog which covered the highway, and had been hit by a truck that crushed the car's occupants. I peered into the dark, and drove for ten miles at fifteen miles per hour on the somewhat wavy highway. More than an inch of water on the highway made steering difficult. Finally, the deluge stopped as we approached Oregon City. We had not observed a single vehicle for the entire ten miles. I can only believe that Saint Michael had led me through the rain-soaked highway, in much the same way He had on a prior occasion, when I had driven through a total whiteout with my load of Christmas trees.

Near-Death on Highway 97

The tax season of 1991 ended on April 15 with a sixteen-hour work day marathon, followed by an employees' retirement party that evening. The next day, Ruth and I slept in, and then drove to Black Butte Ranch, where we had a leisurely lunch. After lunch, we headed to our vacation home in Sunriver. As we rounded Lava Butte, fifteen miles south of Bend, less than two miles from the Sunriver-Cottonwood entrance to Sunriver, Ruth and I were having a brisk conversation. Seconds later, we both fell asleep, with the car on cruise-control at fifty-five miles per hour. My head bumped on the steering wheel when I suddenly awoke 1.2 miles later, as we headed off the roadway. I pulled the steering wheel to the left, and brought the car back onto the highway. The two northbound lanes were bumper- to- bumper with cars and trucks. Had our car drifted to the left, instead of to the right, we would surely have had a head-on collision. Spirit watched over me, even when I was asleep, and while driving a car at fifty-five miles per hour.

The next day, I went back to the same place to reenact the incident. In the same 1.2 miles, I had to brake three times for cars that were not traveling the speed limit. This was the first of three near-death experiences that I had on Highway 97 over the next five months.

In another incident, Ruth and I were headed south on Highway 97, where Highway 197 forks to the west across the highway. As we approached the turnoff, a carload of people, driving about seventy-five miles per hour, careened directly at us, while trying to make their turn to the west. I swerved to the left, into the northbound lane, and missed their car by inches.

Several months later, I drove north on Highway 97, and came to the Crooked River Bridge, which spans a gorge three hundred feet deep. As I approached the bridge, I noticed a pickup truck, loaded with firewood, coming from the north, moving fast and entering the bridge. I received a message to exit the highway as quickly and as far off the highway as possible, and I did so, about fifty feet from the bridge. The truck proceeded right down the middle of the bridge, and then veered to my side of the highway, missing my parked car by a couple of feet. Once again, I had obeyed the messages from Spirit and extended my life.

Miracle on the Road to Prineville

In July 1992, I spent a week in the Wallowa Mountains with three friends, Emery "Red" Bedea, Gene Bench, and Fritz Barsch. As I drove home, about 9:00 P.M., we were about thirty miles east of Prineville, in heavy summer traffic. I rounded a curve, and narrowly missed a large flat rock, about a foot thick, on the yellow center line. As I continued to drive, my brain raced with the knowledge of how close we had come to an accident. The next drivers might not be so lucky; they might hit the rock, veer off the cliff, and be killed. Suddenly, I received a message that I should turn around, and remove the rock from the highway. At that instant, a pull-out appeared on the left side of the highway, so, I turned the car around, and drove back to move the rock.

The thought raced through my mind that this would risk my life, and the lives of my three friends, in order to protect people whom I would never know. That thought was quickly discounted, as I parked our car on the highway shoulder near the boulder. Three senior citizens, aged sixty-one, sixty-seven, and seventy-two, got out of the car, leaving the fourth asleep in the car, and hurried to the center line. Our first attempt to push the rock was completely fruitless, and It was as if the rock were bolted to the highway.

My friends had scurried back to the car, when I received another message, "Vern, go back and remove the rock." I coaxed my friends, and we tried again to push the rock. This time, however, it was as if the rock had become weightless as a marshmallow. Without employing any physical strength, we pushed the rock from the highway. It felt as if we had tapped into an energy source that flowed through us, and was unlimited in scope and power.

Safely in the car, we talked excitedly. What had happened? It seemed miraculous in two ways: first, on our second attempt to move the boulder, we discovered that the rock had become weightless, whereas, previously it had been immovable. The second was that not a single vehicle had come down the highway, from either direction, during the entire eight-minute incident. And then the traffic flowed steadily again.

In retrospect, I have developed the following explanation for this event:

> ➤ First, I had received the message to move the rock, and I had requested that a higher power provide the needed energy.
> ➤ Second, the predominant motive was one of unconditional love: to sacrifice oneself for unknown persons.
> ➤ Third, my will/ego had been surrendered to Saint Michael, who has the power to suspend gravity.
> ➤ Fourth, I had obeyed Saint Michael's messages as they came to me, and I had not hesitated to respond to His request.

For years after the boulder episode, Red and Gene never passed up an opportunity to talk about the amazing miracles that had occurred on the highway to Prineville. It may have been the most remarkable thing that either of them had ever experienced. Gene has since died, but, I recently wrote an account of the incident, and had it signed by Gene's wife, Ila. Of the many miraculous events in my life, this one is outstanding, because my friends shared directly in the experience.

More Experiences with Weightlessness

Two years after the boulder encounter on the road to Prineville, I had a similar experience with two large railroad ties, each of which weighed several hundred pounds. I had pried the ties out of the bank in my front yard, straight into my pickup truck. I planned to haul the ties to my farm, where I could burn them. Upon my arrival at the farm, I parked the pickup on a hill, in order to make it easier to unload them, but, when I tried to push them out, they would not budge. Then I remembered the weightless boulder experience on the road to Prineville, and I requested that I be given that same power to move the railroad ties. Instantly, the ties became weightless, and with no physical strength, I was able to push them out of the bed of the truck.

Six months later, I found myself in another struggle with a heavy object. For Calvin Church, I had harvested a twelve-foot Christmas tree, which weighed over two hundred pounds. I parked my pickup beside the rain-soaked tree, and tried to lift the heavy tree into the pickup bed, but, I could raise it only to chest height. I stopped struggling, and requested that divine energy be given me, so that I could hoist the tree into the pickup bed. On my next try, the tree became weightless, and without any physical strength, I was able to lift it.

In March 1999, nearly seven years after the first divine experience of an object becoming weightless, I purchased some plants for the Bowlby Building. I drove into the parking lot behind the building, and I noticed immediately that someone had driven over a concrete parking bumper that weighed over two hundred pounds, and had pulled it over the top of a rebar, leaving a dangerous steel rod sticking straight out of the blacktop. I reached down, to get an idea as to the weight of the concrete bumper, and I realized that there was no way that I could move it any direction. As I thought of how I was to lift the bumper over the four-inch steel rod, I decided to plant the flowers, and then to see if Spirit would give me an insight on how I might resolve the problem.

As I dug in the dirt to plant the flowers, Spirit gave me the message that, when I had finished planting, I was to try again. I went back to the parking area, reached down with my fingers on each side of the bumper, and found the bumper weightless!

Once again, I lifted without physical strength, and I dropped the bumper over the rebar, praising Spirit for such a simple answer to what had seemed to be an impossible task. It would have cost several hundred dollars to have brought a bobcat and a crew to move the bumper. Curiosity then got the better of me, and I requested an explanation from Spirit as to how objects become weightless. Several nights later, I went to sleep with that thought on my mind. Shortly thereafter, I received an answer – my requests had accessed heaven through Saint Michael, and in heaven there is no gravity. Awake, I wrote down the answer, so that overnight I would not forget it. The answer was that, with my requests, I had accessed heaven through Saint Michael, and in heaven there is no gravity.

These experiences made me wonder about some of the other mysteries of the universe, such as how the pyramids were built, and how the statues were erected on Easter Island. I wonder if the Egyptians knew the secret of suspending gravity? That could explain how they had managed to move stones, weighing many tons, in an area where there were no trees to use for rolling them. If one wonders how the rock at the entrance to Jesus' tomb was moved, perhaps the women moved it, enabled by the Holy Spirit. I fully believe that, by their surrender to a higher power, in a Spirit of unconditional love and sacrifice, they may have found the same unlimited power that I had.

Near-Death on the Road in Ohio

Ruth and I have always had great travel experiences, but, sometimes things go even more smoothly than usual. That was the case on our "roots" road trip to Ohio in June 2012. We must have had an angelic tour guide, because, at every step, happenings were better than we had anticipated.

Our only disappointment was in the rented car, a new one, but it did not function properly. When I pressed the gas pedal, sometimes nothing happened: It might start, and then die. Other times, when I pressed the gas pedal, it moved forward with a jerk. We almost returned the car, but, we decided that it would, most likely, improve after being driven awhile; but, it did not.

When we were outside the big cities in Ohio, we discovered that we were in the boondocks, as time seemed to bypass the countryside. Compared to Oregon, the roads were narrow and in poor condition. As I drove on a back road, a stop sign was obscured by foliage. I passed the stop sign and drove right through the intersection, finding myself in the middle of it as a speeding truck drove directly at us. Where had the truck come from? I had not seen it at all. The truck whizzed past us and missed us by a split second. It almost felt as if the truck had driven right through us. In that terrifying situation, the car performed perfectly, without a trace of its usual fitful behavior. Thanks again, my Guardian Angel Michael.

Near-Death by Drugged Crazed Driver

I celebrated the last day of my eighty-second year by skiing off the top of 9,100 foot Mt. Bachelor with my son, Bruce, and his three daughters. Driving home, I was about to turn onto Camp Polk road, two miles from our home in Sisters, Oregon, when a blue Porsche drove by us at over one hundred miles per hour, and missed us by a few feet. Had the car hit us, we most surely would have died!

The Porsche swerved back into our lane, and then back into the approaching lane, barely missed two cars head on, and swerved again into our lane. The driver drove around the corner in a cloud of dust, spun in a counterclockwise circle, and hit a fifteen-inch tree, which sent it into the driver's door and then sliced down a couple of eight-to-10 inch trees. The driver was still conscious after the wreck! A helicopter arrived shortly thereafter and took him to the hospital. Our Guardian Angel, Saint Michael, had watched over our entire family and, once more, protected us from harm!

Searching the internet, we found that the driver was an executive in a large company, who, two years earlier, had cashed in over two million dollars of stock. He had recovered from his accident, but before his trial, he had been released with no charges, as he claimed to have been on medication. We wondered whether the verdict would have been the same had he killed all five of us, and if he hadn't money in the bank?

Travel and Mental Health Observations

To travel is the best way to strengthen a marriage. It does not have to be a big trip, just a day or two out of town, at least monthly. To change one's environment, where one sleeps, where one eats, enhances the flow of energy and refreshes one's mind so that it can make decisions. Fishing, for instance, teaches patience and is similar to meditation.

Mental healing is very different from physical healing. One occurs when one is awake, not when one is asleep. When one rests one's body in sleep, one's physical being rebuilds its cellular structure. Mental rest happens only when one is awake in a new and different environment. Physical presence has to change. Camping affords mental rest because of its many challenges: sleeping in a sleeping bag, cooking over a fire or camp stove, eating on a stump or bench, being part of the environment, instead of being at home. It gives one an entirely different outlook. However, it does not take a trip into the wilderness to revive mental powers. For example, I find that I am energized by attendance at a tax conference in a different city, where suddenly, my thoughts fire into new directions. Outside normal routines, my mind rests and deep thoughts result as former barriers are extinguished.

Golfing with Angels

Of all the angels who watch over me, my Golf Angel is one of my favorites. He loves to participate in my golf game, and enables me to make incredible shots, and to win matches against far better golfers. My Golf Angel makes the shots in divine timing, as do all angels. I am always amazed and thrilled, and I am okay when my Golf Angel utilizes me with angelic discretion.

Several years ago, my Golf Angel was with me at a three-day member/guest tournament at the Corvallis Country Club. As part of the Saturday night festivities, after a three-day putting contest, one person qualified to win five thousand dollars, if he could make a one hundred-foot putt on the 18th green. After dinner, most of the tournament's participants and their spouses had gathered around the green to watch the potential five thousand dollar putt. A stiff wind, probably thirty miles per hour, blew across the green, and the hole was at the bottom of the downhill green.

The eventual winner putted and his stroke stopped with his ball a foot from the hole. Given the conditions, it was a great shot. Several minutes after the five thousand dollar failed putt, one of the golfers in my foursome, who was not my partner, and whom I had never met previously said, "Vernon, you can make that putt!" I took it as a message from Spirit, so I asked the fellow who had attempted the putt if I could borrow his putter and give it a try, and he agreed.

Vernon's Two old Hickory Putters in Use for Over 25 Years

One hundred people stood around the green as I putted the ball. I felt as if someone else controlled me, and moved my arms, as I stroked the ball way to the right into the crosswind. I thought, "Oh, what a horrid shot," and I could scarcely watch as the ball rolled way to the right and down the green. The ball appeared to head at least ten feet right of the hole, but, the wind guided the ball slowly to the left, and into the cup! When one considers all the possibilities of making that putt, there is no other explanation for my success, other than divine intervention.

Who won the golf putting contest, and graciously loaned his golf ball and putter to me?

What if the person whom I had never met before had not suggested that I try the putt? If I had not agreed to accept the message to putt the ball? If the wind had gusted a little differently? If the crowd had left the green after the first attempt, who would have witnessed the putt? If the golfer who attempted the putt had left the green?

Over my twenty-six years of golf competition, I never cease to be amazed when my Golf Angel enables me to hit a spectacular shot. What an Angel to have on your side just when you need one, which has been my life's experience!

Sometimes, I am able to manifest energy for other people's success on the golf course. About ten years ago, Ruth and I had an amazing experience when we were playing golf in Florence. It was a slanted green, and when Ruth chipped to the green, the ball traveled at least ten feet past the hole. As it rolled, I yelled, "Stop: roll backwards!" And the ball rolled back about a foot. I yelled, "Roll again, keep rolling!" This time, the ball rolled about fifteen inches. Six times I said this, and inch by inch, the ball rolled all the way back, until it fell into the hole. Our fellow golfer could not believe his eyes.

In August 1996, while playing in the Oregon Seniors Tournament at Waverly Country Club in Portland, I received the message that I should pray for my opponent to hit good shots. Without fail, before he stroked the ball, I prayed silently that he would have a good shot. I like to win, and at first, this strategy seemed to be counter to my best interests. But, as the game continued, and our scores stayed close, I realized that I was experiencing a different kind of pleasure: not the usual competitive thrill, but, the joy of sharing in someone else's happiness. I won the match by a few strokes, but, it seems that my prayers for my opponent had relieved some of the pressure of the game, and it had worked in my favor after all.

I had my first hole-in-one when I was seventy-four years old and had played golf for sixty-two years. By that time, I had played golf for sixty-two years. I played with Spike Gathercoal, one of my best golfing buddies, two or three rounds a week, over the course of twenty years. We could have gone back and forth across the country in all the time we spent together in a golf cart! As we golfed, we talked, talked, and talked. Spike was a great philosopher, who had written nine books on teaching methods and psychology. He continued to teach at Lewis and Clark College until he died, aged eighty.

When we played that morning, Spike said, "This is the day you should make a hole-in-one." I thought, "That is a great idea. I am all for it." I walked into the clubhouse and told the boy, "Get me a cart that will help me make a hole-in-one." He picked cart number 11, and it happened to be November 11, the most energetically powerful day of the year. (That is when the World War I armistice was signed, at 11:00 A.M. on the eleventh month and on the eleventh day in 1918.)

Hole # 11 is 190 yards uphill, and there was sleet. Hitting the ball, I could not see the elevated green. Arriving at the green, we found a groundskeeper sitting on a tractor above the green, who said, "One of you guys is going to be really happy." His name was Masters, and he signed my card to confirm that he had seen the ball roll into the hole.

My second hole-in-one came at the very same hole on August 22, 2007, just twenty days after I had surgery on my arm to remove my second LMS cancer, and my arm was still bandaged! Spike Gathercoal was lucky as well. He had a hole-in-one on #11 in March 1980, one of nine in his golfing career.

Mountain Homes

As our children grew up, one of our favorite winter activities was skiing. We started them early: Cathy at ten, Barbara at eight, and Bruce at five. We first took them to Hoodoo Ski Bowl in 1968, and once they had learned to ski, they advanced to Mt. Bachelor, where we usually stayed at the Entrada Lodge, southwest of Bend.

In 1981, Ruth and I purchased a home in the Mountain View Lodge area of Sunriver. The house had a great view of Mt. Bachelor, and it was located on the lodge's 14th and 15th fairways. The children were older by this time: Cathy and Barbara had graduated from high school, but, they still loved our ski trips. When both daughters married skiers, their husbands joined us. Bruce married in 1991, and his wife, Edith, soon learned to ski. Over the years, I taught all six grandchildren to ski. I skied the face of Mt. Bachelor with Bruce and his three daughters to celebrate my eighty-second birthday, and Edith provided a cake in the lodge to complete the celebration.

For ten years, the Sunriver home worked well for us; however, as I drove home towards Sisters, Oregon for twenty years, and viewed the panorama of the Cascades Mountains, I envisioned a place where we could view all the mountains.

In June 1991, I manifested that long-held vision. On the way home from the Mountain View Lodge, I received a powerful message, what I would call a golden message, to stop at a realtor's office in Sisters and engage one to find us our dream lot.

The realtor took us to the first phase of the Rim at Aspen Lakes, a development of two-acre lots going north to south, on a rim overlooking Whycus Creek, five miles east of Sisters. The lots shared 138 acres of dedicated open space, and they had an uninterrupted view of all the mountains: MaCarthur Ridge, Broken Top, the Three Sisters, Millikan Crater, Black Crater, Belknap Crater, Mt. Washington, Three-Fingered Jack, Black Butte, and Mt. Jefferson.

Red-tailed hawks and turkey buzzards rode the heat currents which flowed over the rim, and the land seemed to be a bird paradise, the air thick with birds who flew everywhere, including mountain bluebirds, western bluebirds, California quail, and grosbeaks. The view from the rim also provided an open view to Whycus Creek, across the meadow to the rim on the other side.

What really assured me that I was in the right place was the pine tree in the center of the lot on the edge of the rim. For me, this pine tree somehow represented the spirit of my older brother, Wayne, who had died in 1985, six years before. It was as if Wayne were there, and viewing the mountains through eternity.

I recalled that in 1936, when I was five years old, Wayne had taken my sister, Lillian, and me to see the first colored movie, *The Trail of the Lonesome Pine.* The pine tree became my brother, Wayne, and he approved of my wish to purchase the lot.

As I viewed the mountains, I knew that I had never felt such extreme euphoria flow up from the Earth through my body, as it had that day. I felt attuned to all the energy it held, and all that had occurred on that location over eons of natural isolation. Surely, this was a place of miracles. We would be the first non-natives to live there, and I was deeply grateful for the privilege.

Once we had purchased the lot near Sisters, we needed to sell our condo in Sunriver. The message came to me that we should list it for $119,500. None of the condos in the development had ever sold for more than $99,000, and Ruth was concerned that we would not receive that price, but, my message from Spirit was that we could.

On the way to meet with a realtor and list our Sunriver property, Ruth and I stopped at a restaurant in Black Butte for lunch. The waitress, making small-talk, told us about a development nearby, which required $500,000 to build a home on a lot. With that knowledge, the message came to me to add $10,000 to the sales price of our Sunriver condo. We listed the home for $129,500, and within days we received two cash offers. A waitress had given me a $10,000 tip! It must have been divine timing that caused us to meet her in the restaurant that day, and I had obeyed the message from Spirit to raise our asking price.

Ruth and I purchased the property and began to plan our home. One early morning in September, before construction began, I stopped to visit the lot. As I stood under the lonesome pine, and looked out at the rain clouds that engulfed the entire Cascade mountain range, I felt an intense desire to see Mt. Washington. As a feeling of elation surged through my body, I stared out at the place where the mountain should be, and slowly, the clouds began to part, revealing the snow-peaked Mt. Washington. Behind the mountain the sky was a deep blue color, and a full silvery moon shone directly over the peak of the mountain. I watched as the moon set, the clouds closed in and shrouded the mountain.

Home in Sisters, Oregon, Planned and Built by Ruth and Vern. 1972

The question was: how was this event orchestrated? How could I desire to see Mt. Washington when the entire Cascade Range was obscured by rain clouds? Did the power of the Holy Spirit flow through me? Was my brother's (Wayne) spirit involved? Was there a message not yet interpreted? Was this the weather that my friends call "Bowlby weather", the sun which always shines brightly when we travel with them?

In our twenty-two years on the Rim, we have had many incredible experiences. Once, while I used binoculars to observe the face of North Sister, an avalanche began. I called to Ruth to come watch it and, for several minutes, we saw the rumbling snow cascade three thousand feet down the mountain.

Another time, we watched a severe lightning and thunderstorm approach from the south. Lightning struck a tree less than a third of a mile away, and the tree exploded into flames. My granddaughter, Jenny, rushed to curl up in my lap, which she felt was the safest place in the house.

One of the most wondrous occurrences that I have witnessed on the rim was a ceremony performed by a magpie, a robin, and a rabbit. Through my binoculars, I first observed the robin chase the magpie, back and forth, from one side of the rim to the other. (I assumed that the magpie had eaten the robin's eggs, and that the robin was exerting his wrath on the magpie.)

Finally, the magpie and the robin landed in the lonesome pine tree, directly off our deck. The magpie flew to the left side of the deck, and landed near a small tree. A rabbit ran from under the deck to join the magpie, and stood up on its hind legs. The robin then flew down, and the three danced a jig. Ruth and I watched the performance, and after pondering the entire event, we agreed that we had seen something beyond human comprehension.

Later, I asked Spirit for an interpretation of what we had observed, and the answer was, that there are some events that humans will never understand. We just had to maintain faith.

On July 4, 2014, my nephew, Pat Magee, while he observed the dawn at our Sisters home, wrote the following song.

Mountain in the Distance

Like a dream they seem so far
There to teach you who you are
Step by step, the closer you get
Before you know it, larger than life,
Standing before you, in all its glory
The mountain that is your life story.

Beauty in the eye of the beholder
Reaching for stars makes us bolder
The mountain in the distance is the way
Doesn't matter what others say.

A billion years to create this moment
Standing still before my eyes
Yet ever changing, ever moving
The beauty I now realize
Is blessing this chance
This spec in time
This story unfolding
This truth beholding
The glory of the mountain in the distance

By Pat Magee   July 4ᵗʰ, 2014

Land and Trees

I invested in the 320 acre Timberhill addition in north Corvallis with the Brandis family and eventually traded/sold my Interest for Jack Brandis Jr's interest in the 480 acre timber plantation near Wren which gave me 100% ownership of the timber plantation.

Helped by four other people, two women and two men in their early twenties, we clear-cut one forty-acre tract and planted it with thirty thousand timber trees.

The first thinning was done fifteen years later, and it more than paid for the cost of planting the trees. Gradually, the trees became a forest, and a sanctuary for elk and other animals.

My son-in-law, Steve, planted eighty thousand Christmas trees on the property, and we purchased a new mobile home and placed it on a choice building site. Several years later, just after the first harvest, Steve and Barbara decided to move to Sisters and open a retail store.

From the time of my earliest endeavor with my brother, Wayne, when I was twelve years old, Spirit must have wanted me to experience, and to expand my knowledge, of the Christmas tree business. With the help of a great team of Hispanic workers, I commenced harvesting the trees. Some trees were harvested by helicopter; however, most of the work involved using a pickup truck with a trailer to haul the trees across muddy fields to the loading site. Marketing of the trees, and the collection of money for the trees sold, was still another new experience.

My angels help me, but, sometimes, their help comes in the form of a test. A typical example is that of my Angel of Overabundance. Like my Angel of Abundance, this angel brings wealth into my life, but, in ways that are often repetitive. For instance, when I go into a store to purchase something, the cashier often gives me back too much change, or undercharges me for what I buy. Ruth has long since learned to watch my transactions, and she makes certain that I am charged the full price, and that I return excess money to the cashier, which I always do.

My Angel of Overabundance worked overtime when I was a timber plantation owner. I wanted to cut some trees near the highway, but, the State of Oregon would not give me a permit to cut them within a certain distance of the highway. The setback was much larger than I had thought was necessary, and I was disappointed to learn that I would not be able to harvest several thousand dollars worth of trees.

One day, an out-of-state driver drove by my timber site in a two hundred thousand dollar RV. Right beside my property, the RV caught fire, which spread to my land and burned into the trees. The fire department arrived and put out the fire before it killed the trees, so they maintained their value as timber.

However, the burned trees represented a potential road hazard, and I was required to cut them down to prevent them from falling on the highway. The insurance company paid me ten thousand dollars for the damage to my trees, and I received the full price for the timber. While I appreciated the outcome, I felt sorry that the man's RV had gone up in flames, although it had allowed me to harvest my trees. My Angel of Overabundance seems to have had no limits when it comes to blessing me in unusual circumstances.

I learned a lot about the Christmas tree business first- hand. The most harrowing experience of my Christmas tree involvement happened in a most unusual way, and it could easily be considered another near- death experience of my life. I had an order to deliver several hundred trees to the J C Market in Newport, Oregon, about fifty miles away on the Oregon coast. With the help of the work crew, we loaded the pickup and a large trailer with the trees. As we finished work that night, I went home ready to move the trees to Newport in the morning.

The weather was cloudy and dark as I arrived at the farm at 6:00 A.M. As I drove down the driveway, with no sign of bad weather, I expected an easy drive to Newport. Suddenly, three miles from the farm, light snow flurries began and in a couple of minutes the weather turned into a raging winter storm complete with strong winds and a total whiteout. I could barely see past the front of the pickup, as I drove down the hill, knowing that, if I stopped, I could easily be run into by someone who could not see me in the storm. It was like driving in an open field as the landscape before me blended together and was nothing but blowing white. My headlights barely penetrated the darkness, and combined with the snow, it was nearly impossible to see anything.

The message from Spirit was that I should drive on, that I would be cared for, and for the next five miles my navigator was Spirit. Suddenly I drove on blacktop, the snow ceased, and the rest of the trip was uneventful.

I equate the experience of going through the many storms of life not knowing what the outcome might be with the need to have faith. That I should trust my Guardian Angel Saint Michael to watch over me, no matter how grim life appeared to be, and most likely I would have a better result than I could ever envision.

Realistically, I could have driven those loaded trees off the road, with the trees and trailer going helter-skelter in every direction, and I could have frozen to death beside the road in many places. Thanks, Spirit!

Managing that timberland was one of the major highlights of my life. I would have been happy to keep the property, but Ruth convinced me that I should sell the farm for the sake of our estate and I agreed. From my accounting experiences, I had experienced many situations where siblings wanted to kill each other over a legacy. The children were tied together like Siamese twins, each with a different lifestyle and ideas as to what should be done with jointly inherited property.

I sold the tree farm to Starker Forests who will be excellent stewards of the land; cutting, replanting and managing the timber as a long-term crop. Interestingly, both Bond and Bart Starker, the managers of Starker Forests, were my accounting students when I taught at Oregon State University thirty years before.

Timber is one of the greatest investments that anyone can ever make. In Oregon, Douglas fir timber generally grows five to six percent a year no matter what the stock market does. The bigger the trees, the more they grow exponentially, so the value of the investment increases at an increasing rate.

Investments

Six Rabbits

When I was eight years old, my first investment was the purchase of three pairs of rabbits for six dollars which I had earned picking beans, strawberries and cherries.

The rabbits were aged two, four and six months. My dad helped me to build pens and I was solely responsible for their care and food.

I was very excited when the mother began collecting rabbit hair for the nest where the first babies were to be born.

After a diet of chicken for the past four years, rabbit now became our meat of choice. We soon had more than we could eat, and sold or traded live rabbits for fruit.

I think that it would be fair to say that my original six dollar investment earned me more than a one thousand percent return on my investment! I had recognized immediately that more money could be earned selling product than selling my labor, and so I became a free enterprise capitalist at an early age.

Gas Money for Wayne's Two Seat Auto with Rumble Seats

Wayne and I began our Christmas tree business when I was eleven, and he knew that I had cash, so each time that we harvested trees from the National Forest, we filled his car's gas tank and split the cost, as we split the profits, fifty-fifty.

Throughout my high school years, we harvested about fifty trees the first year, and over a hundred trees every year thereafter. We made a very tidy profit, as our only cost was gasoline. By the time I graduated from high school, I had amassed the sum of thirteen hundred dollars, including the $18.75 war bonds, which I had purchased at the Victory Center in Hood River, where rallies were held to sell government bonds. These bonds matured for $25.00 and the other money was invested in postal savings at the local post office.

The Purchase of my First Adding Machine

I opened my CPA firm in July 1963, and Ruth and I financed a loan of three hundred dollars with Citizens Bank in order to purchase a three hundred seventy-five dollar Odhner adding machine. At least twenty times during the loan preparation the banker called us a debtor. Each time was like a knife in Ruth's heart, and to this day incurring a debt is a nightmare for her.

In order to get the loan for the adding machine, I had to prepare a net worth statement, which Ruth typed up for me. Our total net worth came to two thousand dollars. Ruth felt that I had stretched the value, and that the banker might deny the loan, based upon his determination of the two thousand dollar net worth.

Each time he called us a debtor was like a knife in Ruth's heart, and to this day, she has never recovered from that experience. Any debt is a nightmare for Ruth.

Every investment that I made from that time forward was a traumatic experience for her, as I borrowed money for many investments.

The Construction of the Bowlby Building

In February 1964, as I worked late in my office, out of the corner of my eye I saw a movement, then, a long tail which protruded from behind a bookcase: a rat!

I grabbed a broom, and chased the rat out the front door of my office. The rat bounded down about twenty stairs, turned a corner, and ran into an empty office under construction. I followed, with my trusty broom, and arrived just in time to see the rat plunge into a toilet bowl, down the drain, and into the sewer.

That night, the experience of the rat in my office was going through my mind, and I received the message from Spirit that it was time to find another office.

The next day, on the way to work, I observed a realtor pounding a For Sale sign on an old house at the corner of 5th and Van Buren. Instantly, the message came to me that it would be an excellent location for an office building. As I arrived at my office, I met Jim Gathercoal, an architect, whose office was next to mine, and I told him what I envisioned.

Bowlby Building Built in 1965

Jim suggested that I immediately secure a one thousand dollar option to buy the lot for one year, which I did. The next day, Jim presented me with a color sketch of the Bowlby Building, which we built over the next eight months. I moved into my CPA office, October 15, 1965.

As people pass the Bowlby Building on 5th Street, no one could ever guess that my Angel of Abundance had used a rat to inspire me to build the Bowlby Building.

The first hurdle was, to change the zoning from residential to a downtown central business zone. The property zoning on three sides of the intersection was already a central business zone, so it appeared that it would be a breeze to change the zoning. However, a member of the planning commission, who owned a downtown office building, opposed the zone change.

The planning commission gave us a highway commercial zoning that required large setbacks, which would not allow us to have enough parking to make our investment successful. The next day after receiving this setback requirement, I suggested to Jim that we raise the building and have parking underneath. Jim said that should be no problem, and he redesigned the building.

What appeared to be a fatal zoning requirement turned out to be a blessing in disguise, as the underground parking made the project far more successful.

In order to get the loan to build the Bowlby Building, I had to have signed leases for the building totaling seventy-five percent of the rental square footage. After hundreds of hours dealing with possible tenants, I convinced prospective tenants that they could become owners if they would sign the leases, and be responsible for a percentage of the loan, which was $150,000 dollars at six percent interest, over twenty years of payments.

Less than two years after I had borrowed three hundred dollars for an adding machine, I was able to borrow the full cost of the office building with the tenants' guarantees!

The investors invested one hundred dollars or so each, and I was the largest investor at two hundred dollars. The insurance company's loan covered all the costs of acquiring the property and the building cost of one hundred ten thousand dollars.

Over the following years, I purchased all of the other seven investors' interests, with significant gains to them. Part of their gain was because I paid them the fair market value of the property, which included my own time planning the building development. The insurance company had placed a value of fifteen thousand dollars on the property that I had never charged for originally. For an investment of forty-seven dollars, I paid one investor ten thousand dollars.

The Lavender Window

The day that the wrecking crew came to raze the old house, built in 1870, on the lot that I had bought for the Bowlby Building, I happened to notice a window over the front door that had been bleached lavender by the sun for over ninety-five years. A divine message came to me that I should save that window for a future purpose. The workmen removed the window carefully, and I took it home and placed it in my garage. Amazingly, it was never broken over the next eleven years that we lived on 14th street. When I purchased the lot on Hillcrest Drive in order to build a new home, the message came to me that the lavender window should be placed on the south side of the house, so that the color purple, my daughter's favorite, would cascade into her bedroom.

Over time, I have learned patience, as divine purpose may take years to come to fruition.

Ruth lost sleep worrying about the insurance loan, as she remembered being called a debtor when we purchased my first adding machine, and she disliked having any debt.

Purchasing the other investors' interests was another debt, but, twenty years flew by quickly, and the building became clear of debt. I sold it nearly forty-two years later. One of the major reasons that I was able to get the loan, after being in business for only eighteen months, was that I was empowered by having CPA after my name. The title CPA carried with it an intrinsic borrowing power, which was a major asset in my portfolio.

Ruth's Uncle Ed's prophecy, which he had written in the front of the Bible Ruth had given me as a wedding gift, came true: the value of a good name is worth more than silver and gold. I have always felt that my Angel of Abundance was the invisible key participant in the acquisition of my building and its financial success.

The Purchase of a 485 Acre Timber Plantation in 1967

Originally, there were four investors in the purchase of the timber plantation property, but, the same manifest destiny occurred as it had with the Bowlby Building. Eventually, I purchased the three other interests at a substantial gain to my fellow investors.

I planted about sixty thousand timber trees on the property. In addition, eighty thousand Christmas trees would be planted and harvested. I felt honored that Spirit had awarded me the stewardship of this property for thirty-six years before it was sold.

The Purchase of 14 Rental Homes in 1986

To purchase these properties, I requested a loan of more than $400,000 from Citizens Bank, which was granted in less than a week.

This was the bank from which I had borrowed three hundred dollars twenty-three years previously, and had been called a debtor many times. However, this time I was not called a debtor!

The Purchase of the Benton County Bank Stock

Thirty years later, Spirit presented me with an opportunity to learn the banking business, as one of the seven bank board members.

In high school, I had once thought that a banking career might be interesting, and I had applied for a job at a local bank, but, I was not selected.

In spring 1977, I received a phone call from an employee of a local bank, who asked if I would be interested in assisting to select a board of directors for the new bank, to be called the Benton County Bank. I selected three clients and an attorney friend to become board members, and we met every month for fifteen years. In many of those years, I served on the finance committee, and I learned about the loan business from a lender's viewpoint. It was a wonderful education, and Spirit came through once again with a plan that was far beyond my expectations.

The Purchase of the 320 Acre Timber hill Addition to Corvallis

I became a ten percent owner in the development, and sold/traded my interest in the development for the last ownership in my timber plantation.

The Bowlby Family Legacy

Both Ruth and I strove to be strong models for our children, guiding them to make wise choices on the path of life. None of our children (and none of our grandchildren) has ever smoked or ingested drugs. We are a loving family, close and supportive of one another. Ruth talks to each of our children at least once a day. The grandchildren stop by on a regular basis, and we have been a kind of refuge for them. I think that it has made them strong, and I marvel at the amazing persons they are becoming.

I have always worked well under pressure, and that characteristic has been passed down through the generations.

My grandfather, who climbed mountains into his sixties, taught us that the tougher it gets, the tougher you work. Recently, my son's children climbed Black Butte with their parents and me.

Edith wanting to stop before the top, but Danielle could not agree, and said that she would drag her mother to the top if she had to! Edith made it to the top, and was pleased that she had persevered.

If there is one message that I have tried to pass on to my children and grandchildren, it is the advice my mother gave me: one can do anything one wants to do; one just has to set one's mind to the task at hand.

We have inspired our grandchildren to graduate from college: three have graduated; one is in graduate school, one is   a junior at Oregon State University;   and another will be a freshman at that university next fall.

As I have told them, their paths in life are completely up to them, but, it requires sacrifice and discipline to pave the way. They understand that a successful future begins with a good education, and that they will acquire it only by studying and "keeping their nose to the grindstone." I like to tell them stories about the things that I had envisioned as child, and the ways in which I manifested my visions decades later. Everything comes with prayer, patience, hard work, and faith.

One of Vernon's Favorite Stories: Forty Dollars Well Invested

Sometimes, I receive messages from my Angel of Generosity, who reminds me that giving is one of the most joyous acts that anyone can experience. That is how I interpret what happened to me one afternoon at the Truax gas station on 9th Street in Corvallis, many years ago.

The station was empty as I arrived, and I asked the attendant to fill my gas tank. As I got out of the car to wash the windows, a mother, with three small children, in a dented 1970s-vintage car, drove in. Seconds later, another well-worn car, with another harried mother of three, drove in. I heard both women ask the attendant for five dollars worth of gasoline less than three gallons at the time.

Instantly, I received the message that I should slip two twenty dollar bills to the attendant, and tell him to add that much to each of the women's gas tanks. With a smile, he took the twenties, added the gas, and collected their five dollar bills.

Both drivers left without another word to the attendant. I will always wonder what they thought of their good fortune. Did they think that the attendant had made a mistake? Did they think about telling him? Did they think that they had received a blessing from above? Did they feel guilty? Did they feel happy with their good fortune?

I will never know, but, I do know that it was the best forty dollars that I have ever invested, because it brought me such great pleasure. I had submitted myself to a message from my Angel of Generosity, which I believe encourages more divine messages and Earthly abundance. The Truax station has long since been razed, and a parking lot is now where the station once was. My investment in giving the forty dollars still pays dividends every time I pass that spot. That experience confirmed my philosophy: that the only true value of money is in the joy that money brings.

My Angel of Challenge
Keeping the inspiration and excitement in my work life.

My Angel of Freedom from Anger
Reminding me that it's not worth getting stressed about small irritations.

My Angel of Divine Timing
Creating the most amazing juxtapositions of people and events.

My Angel of Generosity
Reminding me that it's better to give than to receive.

My Angel of Plentiful Clients
Bringing me an abundance of interesting, challenging CPA Clients.

My Golf Angel
Giving me an edge over my worthy opponents on the golf course.

My Angel of Gravity Suspension
Teaching me that with faith and love, anything is possible.

My Weather Angel
Giving me breaks in the weather to make the most of family outings.

My Angel of Abundance
Assuring that my financial transactions come out for the best.

My Angel of Divine Descendents
Giving me the most wonderful gift of all, children and grandchildren who strive to live a good life and help others.

Part 4: Health and Healing

In the summer of 1972, as I began my second three-year term as an elder in the Calvin Presbyterian Church, I read in the Bible at 1 Corinthians 12:14 about the nine powerful gifts of the Holy Spirit mentioned by Paul in Chapter 12:

> ➢ The ability to give wise advice — wisdom 12/14 and Acts 2:38
>
> ➢ The special talent of teaching — knowledge
>
> ➢ The giving of special faith to another — faith
>
> ➢ The power to heal the sick — gift of healing — relief of pain and suffering
>
> ➢ The power to perform miracles — working of miracles
>
> ➢ The power to prophesy — foresee the future
>
> ➢ The power to know whether evil spirits are speaking or whether it is the spirit of God — discerning of spirits
>
> ➢ The power to speak in languages never learned — different kinds of tongues
>
> ➢ The power to interpret the languages — interpretation of different tongues

The reading of the gifts of the Holy Spirit was very exciting to me. I felt a powerful surge of energy that touched every cell in my body, and my soul ascended to a higher level. It was as if I were lifted by Spirit to receive personal messages from Spirit, and I began to converse daily with God. This was like a silent prayer, and I received answers to my prayers silently.

Of these nine gifts, the one that most excited me was the gift of healing. How could any gift from Spirit be more rewarding to one's soul than to assist someone to heal, and to be relieved from pain and suffering? The message came to me that all the gifts from Spirit were dispensed at the discretion of Spirit, in what is known as divine timing. I prayed silently to Spirit that someday, determined by Spirit, I would receive that divine gift! I envisioned myself working in a healing center that would use the ancient powers of healing, rather than modern medicine.

It would be another eighteen years before I recognized that the gift of healing had been bestowed upon me. This was before I had learned anything about Eastern medicine and energy healing, as it had been practiced for thousands of years. I received the message of the power that God has given us all to heal ourselves from within.

My Awakening as a Healer

The Holy Spirit Comes to Me

My life as a healer began in the fall, 1972, when I attended a service at Calvin Presbyterian Church. Ben, the minister, was an engineer, who had left North Carolina, after he had received a divine message to inspire a spiritual awakening in Corvallis.

Ben began the Sunday evening praise service with instruction from the Bible and spiritual songs. He then requested the presence of the Holy Spirit, and told us that someone would receive a message in tongues. Shortly after he said that, I received a long, strong message in a foreign tongue, which repeated itself three times. It was as if I were plugged into earphones, but, instead of coming from the outside, the message exploded through my entire body! I did not speak in tongues, but, the high-pitched message permeated into every cell.

That message, from Spirit, was that my internal prayers were far more powerful than any verbalized prayer. This was evident when I became filled with the Holy Spirit, but, I did not speak in tongues.

The next Sunday, an identical thing happened. Ben announced that someone was receiving a message in tongues, and I heard the strong message, again in a foreign tongue, repeating in my body three times, this time in a different tongue.

The third Sunday, I received the message in a strong clear voice, three times: *WON-MON-NEE-TAH*. The fourth Sunday, during the praise service, as we were singing the song Hallelujah, the words came forth from my mouth as *WON-MON-NEE-TAH*. I had received the interpretation in tongues of the word "Hallelujah," which means, "Praise ye the Lord."

I believe that you can be filled with the Holy Spirit in multiple ways, at different levels. Receiving a message in tongues is the highest level, because it is a direct communication from God, not heard by the ears, but silently, an unspoken one inside the body.

The message came to me that the Holy Spirit determines who, and when, a person is blessed with a message in tongues, and it can only be described as divine timing. My receiving these messages in tongues opened up a whole new line of direct, silent communication with the Holy Spirit, including divine golden messages.

Although I had only spoken once while singing in tongues, I had clearly been filled with the Holy Spirit. The message I received from my experience with Ben, that internal prayers were stronger than verbal ones, reinforced what I have always done: prayed silently, and my communications with the Holy Spirit continue to occur on a deep internal level.

Several years later, I read in a book on The Holy Spirit by a minister that indeed some people receive only messages in tongues and do not speak in tongues and receiving the message in tongues without speaking was a higher level of communication with Spirit.

Early Experiences in Self-Healing

My first experience of healing from within occurred in the summer of 1972, as my partner and I dissolved our CPA partnership. The stress was starting to build, so I paid a visit to my doctor. When my blood pressure registered 145/110, the doctor prescribed pills to lower it. After taking the first pill, I felt so dizzy that I could scarcely stand up. I knew that I needed a different solution. I requested a divine lowering of my blood pressure, and did not take any more pills. A month later, when I returned to the doctor, I learned that my blood pressure had returned to normal, 120/70. In the succeeding forty-one years, it has remained in a normal range.

About a year later, I had a strange, very brief, experience with depression. Driving home for lunch, I suddenly felt as if the weight of the world were on my shoulders. It was a physical sensation, as if I were being crushed downward. This overwhelming feeling lasted about seven minutes. Finally, the thought came to me that I should be extremely grateful for having received the sensation of depression, knowing how others felt when they were depressed. Years later, I realized what had happened: I had blessed the depression, so it had left. The message came that depression is the presence of an evil spirit – It was cast out of me as I blessed the depression, because it could not stand the presence of divine energy.

The next two decades were filled with amazing experiences and insights. I felt the incredible presence of the Holy Spirit, with a heightened awareness of the divine messages that flowed my way more and more frequently. Sometimes, I would receive repeated messages on the same subject, over the course of several months. Often, these cycles began in January of the New Year.

My next opportunity to self-heal was at 6:00 A.M. on Thursday, January 25, 1990. I ran up my steep driveway with the morning paper, and I experienced a sharp pain in the back of my right leg. My first impression was that I had been shot by a shot gun! As I whirled around, my second thought was that I had been hit by a brick. I then realized that no one was there. In running up the steep driveway, I had torn my Achilles tendon entirely from the muscle, nearly all the way to my knee. I lost all control over my foot and toes, and had to hobble up the rest of the driveway on one foot and two hands.

Ruth took me to the emergency room, where I was told that I had ripped my right Achilles tendon apart, where it attaches the full length of my calf muscle. He said that there was nothing medical science could do: I would have to stay in bed most of the time, let it heal on its own, get up only for therapy, and be on crutches for six to eight months. If I used my leg too soon, it would take up to a year to heal. I should make an appointment with an orthopedic doctor for Friday afternoon. That night I awoke at 2:00 A.M., with my left calf in excruciating pain. For about thirty minutes, I felt as though my leg were being ripped with knives. The pain then went away. With hindsight, the pain in my left calf muscle was the preliminary divine healing of the right calf muscle that had been torn apart.

The following day, the orthopedist told me that my injury would take at least six months to heal, with a lot of therapy and bed rest. At that time, my CPA firm had about eighteen people on staff, and tax season was about to begin. After we returned home and we ate dinner, I went downstairs on crutches, and sat in my dad's easy chair, and at 6:00 P.M., precisely the time of my birth, I said to spirit, "This is not my style, and I am ready for my calf to heal right now." Instantly, I felt tiny circles of healing about the size of a quarter, as if I were being brushed with a small dry paintbrush. I received the message that, after the first five minutes, when the healing stopped, I would be able to walk. After thirty

154

minutes, I sensed that healing was complete. I received the message that I could now walk without crutches, and I did. The following week, I went without crutches, to the doctor for a checkup, and he was amazed that my leg was healed, and that I could walk without a limp. Over the next six months, as blood came to the surface of my skin, my calf turned all the colors of the rainbow and more.

Thus, I embarked on the path of a healer, without the slightest idea of what it would mean, since that would only be determined by divine timing and divine knowledge. Over the years, I have wondered about the miracle of my Achilles tendon. I have received the message that I was healed in thirty minutes because God made man with the unlimited power to heal himself. The message that I received was that all healing begins within, and the divine energy of the Holy Spirit speeds up the process.

Six Years of Pain

After the experience of repairing my Achilles injury, my mind opened to the infinite possibilities of non-traditional healing, and I began to read on a wide variety of topics related to alternative medicine. This was a very busy time in my career, and my learning was strictly book-focused. I had yet to experience "hands-on healing."

What changed was the result of a serious health issue. In May 1993, I experienced a series of sharp chest pains while walking up the 18th hole of the Corvallis County Club golf course. I finished the hole and went straight to my doctor. He did a stress test in his office, and when the pain returned in three minutes, he called St. Vincent's Hospital and scheduled an angiogram for the next day with Doctor Sutherland. The angiogram procedure entails inserting a wire into a blood vessel in the lower groin, and following the vessel up to the heart, where a dye is released, to determine the status of the three arteries that circle the heart, and which provide nourishment and oxygen. The patient is fully conscious, and may observe the procedure on a TV screen.

The angiogram determined that my right artery was one hundred percent closed, the left was eighty percent closed, and the third artery was fifty percent closed. I was surprised to learn this about my arteries because, I had spent a full day at the Oregon Heart Center eight months before, and had been told that I was in top shape for my age. It was impossible to know if the right artery had been closed for a month, a year, or ten years. I was informed that over ninety percent of the time, when a heart artery is blocked one hundred percent, a fatal heart attack ensues. It was a close brush with death when my right artery closed, without my even knowing it!

When I asked Dr. Sutherland if a bypass was needed to correct the blocked artery, he said that it would not be necessary, because my heart had performed its own bypass. I had never heard of the body creating its own bypass. The doctor explained that, as the right artery closed, new tiny collateral arteries had grown around my heart, rejoining the right artery after the point where the artery was clogged. The left artery that was eighty percent closed had sent a message -- in the form of pain -- that it had more work than it could manage.

The doctor explained that he needed to do an angioplasty, which involved expanding a balloon inside the artery to squeeze the plaque open, and to allow greater blood flow. He inflated the balloon, and closed the blood flow entirely, which resulted in excruciating pain — every cell in my body screamed for oxygen! For two minutes, I experienced severe pain, with the intensity of a major heart attack. When the doctor finished, he told me that the procedure had increased the blood flow from twenty to fifty percent, and that he would have to apply the balloon a second time. The whole process was repeated, and once again, I felt my body explode in pain. This time, five seconds into the pain, a nurse came from behind, placed her hand on my forehead, and the pain stopped immediately. About five seconds before the finish, she removed her hand, and the extreme pain returned. The second balloon trick increased the blood flow to seventy percent. I was shocked that her touch had stopped the pain completely. With hindsight, I really do not know for sure if there was a nurse, as I never saw her, or I if the pain had been cancelled by an angel.

I played golf a week later, and the next week I ran a stress test that indicated I was in peak condition. About two days after the angioplasty, I developed a raging facial pain in my inflamed sinuses, bands of pain raced around my head, and a roaring in my ears made me totally deaf. My sinuses felt as if they were on fire, and in the back of both eyes I felt a piercing sharp pain. I often had throbbing toothaches in entire banks of teeth simultaneously.

The pain seemed to come and go, concentrated in one place or another. My pain was so intense that the pain brought me to my knees. Sometimes, a particularly strong smell, such as fertilizer, or a cough or sneeze, triggered the pain. The smell of cigarette smoke was especially painful. While a on a trip to South Carolina, where it seemed that everyone smoked, as I packed to leave, the pain commenced, and I dropped to the floor, on my knees, my head on the bed, not knowing whether I could make it to the plane to fly home.

Pain medicine was totally ineffective. An MRI showed nothing amiss. My doctor had no idea what to do for me, other than medicine that did not work. That is when Spirit commenced my healing journey. I now realize that, most likely, my sinuses had been severely sensitized by the coal smoke, forty years before, when I was in Officers' Candidate School at Fort Benning, Georgia for sixteen weeks, and the medications during the angioplasty had triggered a violent reaction that would continue for six years.

The first significant pain relief came after I played golf with a friend at Rock Creek in Portland. The golf course had just been fertilized, and the fumes triggered my facial pain in all its fury. As we finished the 18th hole, my friend noticed tears in my eyes, and asked why I was crying. I told him about my facial condition, he used his cell phone to call his masseuse, who said that she had a cancellation for that evening. What divine timing!

I was buried underneath four inches of blankets, she placed her hands over me, and the pain ceased immediately, just as had happened when the nurse had touched my forehead during the angioplasty! Two hours into the session, I felt the release of a big blob of black energy the size of a football. It started in my groin, and slowly moved upward through my body, and out of my head. The message that I received was that a demon had been cast out of me! The facial pain did not return for about three weeks.

Next, I received a session utilizing therapeutic touch. The pain relief lasted for over a week. When I realized the power of the technique, I decided to learn that method myself.

My first class in therapeutic touch was at Springfield General Hospital. My classmates for my very first energy-healing lesson were thirty hospital nurses from all over the west. One technique we learned involved movement of the hands over the body, in order to detect energy blockages. I immediately felt a blast of cold air emanate from the body of the person on whom I practiced. The instructor explained that it was a blockage that needed energy balancing, and the person confirmed that she frequently suffered pain in that area.

And so began a period of intensive learning; I took classes in a variety of energy-healing techniques, including Therapeutic Touch, Reiki, Qigong, Etheric Healing, reconnection healing, and Chinese healing. I began to accumulate a library, with hundreds of books on alternative approaches to health and healing. The Holy Spirit began to send me people to heal, and I drove hundreds of miles, with my portable table, and treated people in their homes or hotel rooms. Patients came to me for healing from all over the United States, including Alaska.

The end of my six years of pain came with the death of an extraordinary woman, whom I had helped with financial as well as health issues. She came to my CPA firm after she divorced her husband and was awarded his business.

I taught her the fundamentals of her business, and she became very successful.

Ten years later, in January 1999, she developed a disease which caused her lungs to solidify. I gave her several sessions in the Providence Hospital in Portland, for which she was very grateful. On April 3, I visited her in the hospital, and she said, "I'm so glad to see you. My feet are so cold and I want to feel my feet warm one more time before I die." I put my hands on her feet, and immediately felt a cold shock in my wrists, elbows, and shoulders, all the way through my nerve centers. It took about seven or eight minutes before her feet were warm.

She died the next day, April 4, at about 4:44 P.M., and my six years of pain ceased at that time. This was at the same time that people around the world were praying for world peace.

Learning to Use My Healing Energy

In February 1995, I was in the middle of a tennis game, when I moved to my left and heard a pop so loud that it sounded as though it had come from outside the court. Suddenly, my foot would not work, as it was completely numb. My left Achilles tendon, with a portion of my heel bone attached was broken, and the tendon, with the bone, had sprung up my leg. Two and a half hours later, I had surgery to reattach the bone to my heel bone.

The doctor's prognosis was that I would not be able to play golf for at least six months, and could not play tennis for a year. But, I felt healing energy race up and down my leg, and I knew that it would heal much faster than the doctor's prognosis. When the cast was removed on the ninetieth day, my leg had healed, and I played my first round of golf on the one hundredth day.

I took a major step forward in my ascension as a healer in May 1995, in the course of a weekend workshop with a Chinese healer. During the Friday evening session, the energy in the room was extraordinary, stimulated by the healer himself, as well as the hundred or so high-energy people in attendance.

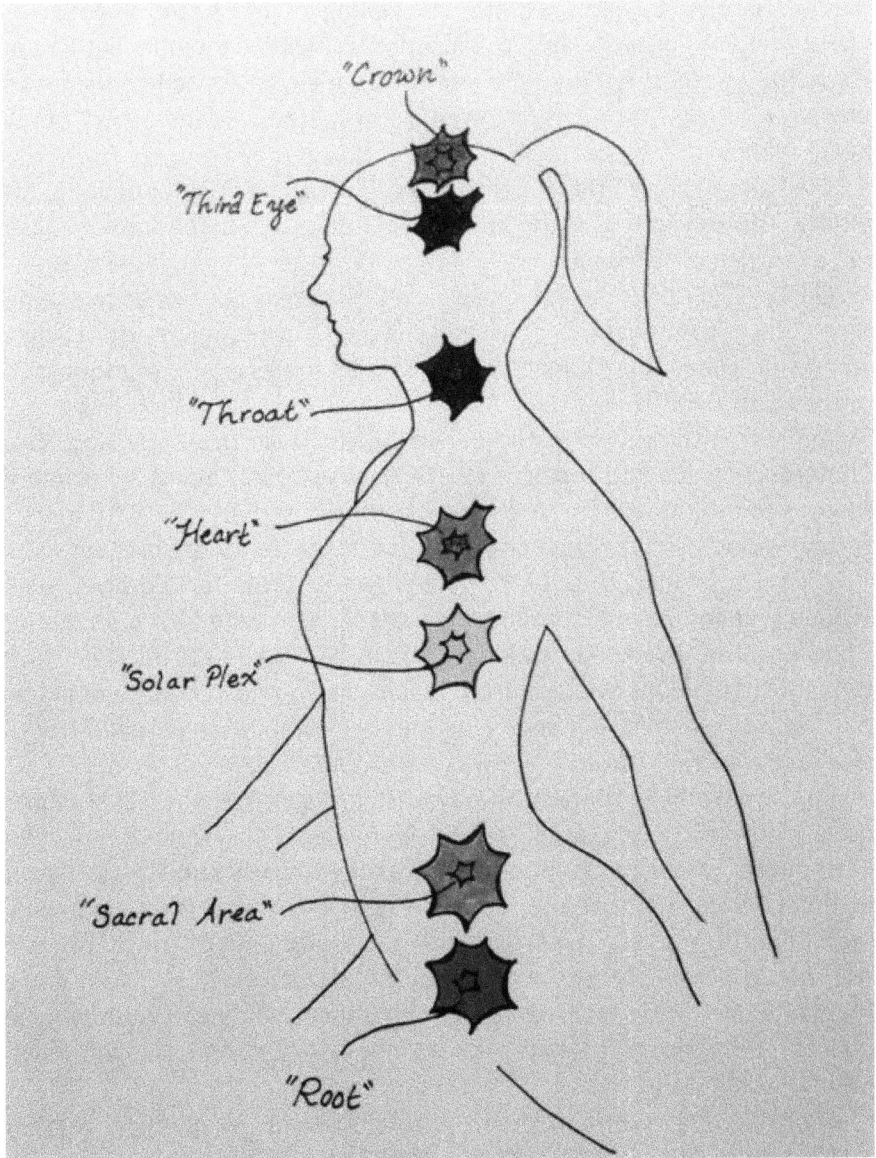

"Crown"

"Third Eye"

"Throat"

"Heart"

"Solar Plex"

"Sacral Area"

"Root"

Drawn by Vernon's granddaughter, Jennifer Cudo Green

The hair on my arms stood straight out, and I became aware of the energy in every hair! Needless to say, I did not know that it was possible to feel the inside of hair, let alone every hair on my forearms.

I still felt strong energy when I went to bed that night, and a few minutes later, I experienced the awakening of my heart chakra. For about thirty minutes, I felt a sensation of whirling white light, and powerful, peaceful energy emanated from a circle about five inches in diameter, four inches deep centered over my sternum, the center of my heart chakra.

Over the next six Friday nights, my other six chakras opened, one at a time. The awakening of the crown chakra was the most dramatic, as I felt every cell in my brain.

On the 7th Friday, the sub-chakras in both knees opened at the same time. Since the awakening of my chakras, they open automatically whenever I have any thought of healing, as the energy commences in my hands and feet.

Another inspirational gathering of healers was the Body and Soul Conference which I attended in Seattle in May 1996. One of my primary reasons to attend was to experience the positive energy flow that I was certain would be there, as many high- energy healers were present.

After I arrived and settled into my hotel, I took a two-hour walk around Pioneer Square in downtown Seattle. As I waited for a pizza that I had ordered, my knees suddenly began to shake and buckle. I first thought that I might be weak from having walked on so much concrete, but, when I looked up and saw the restaurant's chandeliers were swinging wildly, I realized that I was it was an Earthquake.

That weekend I experienced powerful energy from each of the four basic elements: Earth, air, fire, and water. Earth, of course, was the Earthquake, which at Magnitude 5.6 was the biggest to hit Washington in thirty years. Air was the conference, where were learning a new method of breathing. Fire was the devastating blaze at a historic warehouse across the street from my hotel, its flames shooting more than one hundred feet above the ten-story building. Water was a peaceful three-hour boat ride with my nephew, Pat, on Lake Union and Lake Washington.

I felt that four-element theme throughout the weekend in Seattle, and it seemed to dovetail with my own sense of energy balance. The conference lasted four days, and many of the presentations were organized around four critical theories or methods. The energy at the conference exceeded my expectations, generated by the more than one thousand women and about one hundred men in attendance.

The Bowlby Building Healing Center

I built the Bowlby Building in 1965, and started practicing there as a CPA on October 15, 1965, continuing until my employees took over my practice on September 1, 1992.

In October 2006, I opened the garage door to a room in the parking area under the building, where over forty-one years of building remodeling debris had accumulated. The 16x16-foot room was stuffed to the ceiling. A divine golden message came to me that I should clean out the debris, and convert the space into a healing center.

The remodeling project flew swiftly into completion in less than a month. The healing space allowed me to be available instantly, whenever Spirit sent me someone to heal.

Two women decorated the place, and they selected items to create a sense of healing. People commented that they began to heal as soon as they opened the door. Eventually, the space included gifts from many people who had healed there, and they wanted to express their appreciation, since I did not accept money. The walls were covered with inspiring images. Many people said how surprised and delighted they were to open the door from the parking area, and to walk into that healing space.

Over the next seven years, hundreds of people from the eastern seaboard to Alaska found relief from pain and illness, at no charge, in a former storage room. It was with considerable sadness that I closed my healing space on June 30, 2013, in order to devote more time to writing my book. My former landlord now offers me space rent free to do healings as long as he does not rent the space.

Anatomy of the Spirit by Caroline Myss

In October 1996, I was in Portland on business. As I left my client, she told me that Caroline Myss was reviewing her newest book, *Anatomy of the Spirit* at the Women's Building. Her subject was energy medicine, and it sounded interesting, so I purchased her book and spent the afternoon reading it.

As a result of her lecture that night, my budding knowledge of energy healing was greatly increased. It was a marvel that in such a short time she could cover so many different areas of healing. At the time, when it came to healing, I thought that she must be the most informed person on the planet.

Myss autographed my book and I was elated over my new knowledge. Over the years I purchased every book, audiotape and video that she produced.

Nineteen years after hearing her lecture, I believe that her knowledge has come from Spirit, and that she connects directly with God.

To me, the most powerful statement in Caroline's book was the following: "We contain the scripture. We contain Divinity. We are Divinity. We are the church, the synagogue, the ashram. We need but close our eyes and feel the energy of the sacraments, the sefirot, the chakras, as the origin of our power—as the energy that fuels our biology. Ironically, once we realize the stuff of which we are made, we have no choice but to live a spiritual life."

Fundamentals

My healing practice constantly evolves as I learn new techniques, and receive information on how the body heals. There are two fundamental rules which have never changed.

The first is that I do not advertise, or otherwise seek out clients. People are sent to me, sometimes, by others who have experienced my services, and sometimes by divine Providence.

The second is that I never charge for my sessions. I have discovered that the universe rewards me with abundance, in ways that I would never dream of. I consider the healing energy dispensed through me as a gift from the Holy Spirit, and I am merely a conduit for the flow of divine energy.

People are always surprised, and sometimes resistant to the idea that my services are provided free of charge. One fellow in Portland was so determined to give me one hundred dollars that I finally told him, "Give a contribution to Salvation Army instead." He looked at me as though I was kidding, but, a few days later, he sent me a copy of his check to the Salvation Army, and that helped him to heal.

Patients have found their way to me from every corner of the United States, including Florida, New York, Alaska, Washington, D.C., California, Washington, Idaho, and many points in between. I just wait for the Holy Spirit to send me people, and the flow is constant. I would be happy if I could do healing all day long, and nothing else, as it is the most rewarding experience of my life.

Quadruple Bypass

On February 9, 2008, nearly fifteen years after my painful angioplasty, my heart health hit a new crisis point. Through an amazing chain of divinely timed events, I am alive today, thanks to the divine messages that guided me, and the angels, in the form of humans, that were spiritually guided to keep me alive.

February 7, 2008, I had an errand to do eight miles north of Corvallis, where one of my tax clients had tax paperwork for me. Instead of taking my car, as I normally would, I decided to drive my pickup truck.

When I reached Highland Drive, I received the message that I should stop at Rite-Aid, and get some water-absorbing pellets for my camper, which I had stored in my client's garage. Had I not made that decision, I would have been near Crescent Valley High School when a tire on my pickup exploded, and I would have used my phone to call AAA. Instead, after visiting Rite-Aid, I was driving on Highway 99, a quarter mile past the entrance to Good Samaritan Hospital, when the tire blew.

For some unknown reason, my cell phone would not work, so, I decided to walk to the Les Schwab tire store that I had passed a mile before. In the first fifty feet, I developed a burning pain in the center of my chest. About halfway to Schwab, the pain stopped, and within a couple of hours, I was back on the road to visit my client.

On the way home, I received the message to stop by my primary physician's office, as I needed to schedule an annual physical with Dr. Mark Rampton, who has given Ruth and me superior medical care for decades.

While I was making the appointment, I casually mentioned to May, the receptionist, that I had had a pain that morning. As I was about to leave, May suggested that a nurse should check my heart, and I agreed.

The nurse could not detect anything wrong, but, she suggested that I be checked by Dr. Thomson, whom I had never met. He did not detect a problem either, but, he had me take an enzyme test before he sent me home, and said that he would call me that evening, if anything was amiss.

I was not called that night, and on Friday morning, I gave healing sessions to six people for four hours. Around noon, the doctor called and said that he wanted me to check into the hospital for an angiogram that afternoon. The enzyme test had shown that I was only one point over the normal range, but, he wanted the angiogram that would eliminate any doubts.

The angiogram was commenced at 6:00 P.M., and Dr. Thomson told me that I had a critically ill heart. Both my left arteries were over ninety percent closed, and the right artery had closed before 1993. Preparations were made for a quadruple bypass the next morning.

Balloons were inserted into my chest and attached to a pump to keep my heart functioning until morning. The surgery began Saturday at 7:30 A.M., and was finished by 11:00 A.M. I awoke from the sedation around 5:30 P.M. and was ready for discharge just seventy hours later! While I was in the hospital, a nurse looked at my chart and commented that I must not be through with my mission on the planet. Had only one artery shut down, she said, I would probably have died.

Looking back on the chain of events that led me to the doctor's office that day, it is clear that divine timing saved my life. I had planned to spend the weekend in Sisters, possibly skiing. The choice to drive the truck, the blown-out tire, the cell phone that would not work temporarily, the pain I experienced walking to the tire store . . . all of these were orchestrated to get me to the hospital for a badly needed repair.

Not to be overlooked were the team of people involved who each could have been the one who perpetuated my life. First, May, the receptionist, who had suggested that I see a nurse. Second, the nurse who had suggested that I see a doctor. Third, Dr. Thomson, who had a "hunch" that I should have an immediate angiogram. Fourth, the doctor who performed the angiogram, and who placed the pumps that kept my heart functioning, and who had placed my name at the top of the bypass list for surgery the next morning. Fifth, Dr. Taylor, who performed superb surgery on me.

And last, but not least, were the angels in the extreme recovery room, who radiated love upon me, to ensure my continued existence on Earth. All in all, it was a command performance by my Guardian Angel Saint Michael!

The Eel and the Shoulder

A few years ago, I watched a TV program about the Amazon eel. This amazing creature can grow up to nine feet long, and it has the power to ignite its own "batteries," creating a chain reaction generating up to six hundred volts of electricity. The eel can kill an alligator with this self-generated power!

This supports my longstanding belief that humans, like Amazon eels, can generate power from within to heal themselves. God gave us seven main chakra centers, and many sub-chakras, which we empower through prayer to send out healing energy. Our chakras can ignite others' chakras, generating healing cells in both the giver and the receiver. Everyone has this power, so long as they believe.

Toward the end of 2011, I began to experience severe pain in my left shoulder joint. When my doctor examined me, he was puzzled by the feel of my shoulder area, which is chunky, as if it were filled with many disconnected bones, instead of a smooth ball and socket. It has been that way since I worked as a gandy dancer, lifting very heavy railroad ties with steel pry bars and swinging a sledge hammer.

The doctor recommended surgery to clip the remains of a tendon that was stuck in the joint, causing the pain. In the course of the surgery, he found that I have no rotator cuffs and I am missing the major tendons that allow a person to raise his arms. He was mystified by the fact that I could use my shoulders completely normally, and had never experienced any pain before this incident. Somehow, my shoulder had repaired itself, creating a system of tiny bones and smaller muscles and tendons that took over the job of the disappearing rotator cuff.

The surgeon predicted a two-week recovery period, and prescribed icing every four hours. Spirit sent my cousin's husband, a semi-retired male nurse, to care for me during those two weeks. However, my shoulder healed quickly, and he went home after four days. By then, I was able to change the ice myself.

When I lay down for the first time ninety-six hours after surgery, I felt a strange sensation centered in the middle of my back, reaching around my body about eight inches below my right breast. It felt as though I had about thirty volts of electricity in constant circulation around my midriff. Suddenly, I felt the energy proceed to my left shoulder joint, where I experienced the sensation of a major healing occurring. This happened again each night for more than a year, as my body created new cells to repair itself.

Interestingly, when I began to have professional rehabilitation, the first procedure was a heating pad applied to my shoulder, projecting thirty volts of electricity into the joint. That feeling was exactly what I had already experienced through my body's own healing system!

This experience led me to wonder whether the Holy Spirit had taken my body to a whole new level, or whether, like the eel, I had learned to ignite my own healing centers. I am in the infancy of learning in my ascension as an enlightened healer. Divine timing will determine my path to better understanding.

The Constantine Connection

One of the mysteries of my life is my connection to Constantine the Great. I was born in Constantine, Michigan in a town of about two thousand people. The town was named for the Emperor Constantine, who ruled the Roman Empire from 306 to 337 A.D.

It is often said that nothing ever happens without a reason. I have read in many books that souls decide when and where they are born. Whether or not this is true is unknown to me. Could it have been that this is where my soul wanted to be born, in the only Constantine in the United States?

In addition to being born in Constantine, over the years I seem to have accumulated numerous other connections with the spirit of Constantine.

Ruth and I have traveled to many places with relevant history to Constantine. In 1995, we toured York, England, where we discovered that, in 306 A.D., the local garrison had crowned Constantine Emperor of the Northern Roman Empire.

We toured Turkey, where Constantine built Constantinople (now Instanbul), and had made it one of the three capitals of the Roman Empire, including Rome and Moscow.

In Rome, we visited the bridge where, after a great victory, Constantine had observed a cross in the sky, and become a Christian. Later, he decreed Christianity the official religion of the Roman Empire, the cross became the icon of the Christian religion.

In Rome, we visited St. Peter's Basilica, where Constantine began to build the Old St. Peter's Basilica in 318-322 A.D., and where, at the Vatican, we admired the statue of Constantine on his horse, eyes raised skyward.

We also visited the Church of the Holy Sepulcher in Jerusalem, where Constantine had built the church on the site of a Roman temple dedicated to Venus, near the place where Christ had been crucified.

In 2002, while shopping in the Lloyd Center Mall in Portland, Oregon, I received the message that I should research my Constantine connection. As I walked into a Barnes and Noble Bookstore, across the room, I noticed a bookshelf, which held one book between two bookends. Immediately, I received the message that this was the book I sought, and indeed, it was *Constantine's Sword the Church and the Jews,* by James Carroll, the winner of the National Book Award.

From that book I learned that Constantine is considered the second most important man in the history of the world. He outlawed slavery and torture; he stopped both human and animal sacrifices to pagan gods. Against overwhelming odds, he changed the religion of the Roman Empire, which for nearly five hundred years had worshipped pagan gods, to a monotheistic culture which accepted Christ as the savior of men. He distributed fifty copies of the Bible throughout the Empire. And he convened the first ecumenical council, the Council of Nicaea, which brought together over six hundred bishops, from around the Roman Empire, and created the Nicene Creed, a statement which unified the beliefs of Christendom, and which is spoken around the world daily.

On the highest hill in Constantinople, the Emperor had built a giant monument in honor of the twelve holy apostles, which also became his final resting place. The Ottoman Turks destroyed the temple in 1453, and built the Mosque of the Conqueror in its place. The Faith Complex was rebuilt in the eighteenth century.

North of Constantinople, now near the town of Isyinye, on a pagan site of healing and medicine and the location of healing waters, Constantine had built the Michaelion Church, which became the model for hundreds of other churches throughout the Empire. Constantine slept there, and reported his vision of an angel, whom he determined to be Saint Michael, and to honor him, the building was converted into a church.

The Christian religion had been outlawed, and anyone caught practicing it was tortured and killed, and his property was confiscated. For over seventy-five years before Constantine, Christian churches had been burned to the ground. In 313 A.D., seven years after he came to power, Constantine issued the Edict of Milan, an agreement that Christians would be treated benevolently, and their confiscated property would be returned.

I continue to seek information about Constantine, and last fall I attended three Oregon State University lecture series given by visiting professors who have focused their lifework on the Emperor Constantine. At the most fundamental level, Constantine and I are linked by the fact that we both surrendered our lives to God for direction and spiritual guidance. Is our common life force, grounded in compassion and empathy, responsible for my path as a healer? Was it just a coincidence that my parents traveled 2,200 miles to Michigan, never intending to live in Constantine, and yet, due to surprising circumstances, I was born there? As I strive to understand my spiritual gifts, and my connection to Constantine, I can only wait with patience for divine answers that may never be given me.

Part 5: Basic Principles of My Healing Practice

When I first began my healing practice in 1994, it was without preconceived notions of what worked, what did not work, and why. I had recognized that through Spirit, that everyone has the power to heal themselves and others, in ways that traditional medicine does not acknowledge. But, I had very little understanding of how it happened, or how I might encourage people to act in ways that would boost their own abilities to heal.

I will always consider myself in the infancy of learning. I thrive on new sources of information and new understandings of the human and spiritual journey. Below, I have described some of the techniques and principles that have come to define my healing practice. I look forward to my continued education with divine patience, because I know that I will receive the information precisely when I need it, as intended by God Almighty.

We all have a mind/body connection that allows us to activate our own immune systems

When your subconscious mind believes that a treatment, pill or vaccine will work, your body will activate and heal itself. Eastern medicine believes that the conscious mind is in the front chakra centers, the subconscious mind is in the back chakra centers, and the subconscious mind controls our actions.

The thymus, master gland to the entire immune system, receives healing messages from the brain and transfers them throughout the body. The thymus gland is "hard-wired" to the brain, and sends healing T cells wherever the body needs them to heal.

Western medicine largely ignores the thymus, focusing on suppressing the body's natural processes, rather than encouraging people to activate their own immune systems. Some anatomy books do not even mention the thymus. It is a battle that has been in progress since 1866, when Mary Baker Eddy spent nine years researching the Bible for healing passages, and wrote *The Science of Mind with Key to the Scriptures*, which promoted self-healing. The Eastern medical establishment has been trying to quash alternative medicine ever since. Healers all over the world continue to flourish, adding countless philosophies and techniques to the array of therapies available to us.

When we take control over our own healing, we become more powerful. The medical establishment encourages people to believe that doctors and medications are the only solution to healing. Everyone has the power to start healing from within. Whenever doctors give me bad news, I immediately do not believe them.

Energy healing creates health through balance

Eastern medicine, as practiced by over half the world's population, balances the flow of energy left to right. The basic tenet is that masculine energy flows on the right side of the body and feminine energy flows on the left. As a person's energy is slowed by stress, chemicals and other factors, an imbalance of energy results in illness and pain.

I have found that people with cancer and other illnesses have almost no energy flow on one side of the body or the other. By working their energy fields back and forth, I can dissipate the blockages and allow them to heal. To begin, I hold their hands and measure mentally how long it takes for their energy to start flowing. For most people it is an average of twenty-thirty seconds. Some people are instantaneous. For people on chemo, it takes at least five minutes. Chemo and radiation are incredibly disruptive to normal body functions, and they create innumerable painful side effects, and seem completely counterintuitive: Instead of heightening the immune system, chemo and radiation close it down. Body- balancing helps bring a cancer-infested body to its normal flow, and corrects the damage incurred by chemo and radiation.

A balanced life, including a spiritual side, is essential for good health. People become overwhelmed and out of kilter when they do not maintain balance in their lives. Work/play, self-care/generosity, practicality/spirituality should be in balance, whereas overemphasis in any one area can create disharmony with the body.

Diet is crucial to the body's wellbeing. By committing to a healthy diet, a person can find balance and send a message to the thymus to create an environment of healing.

Increasing the creation of cells in our bodies helps us heal ourselves and stay strong

Our bodies need to create millions of new cells every day in order for us to have the energy necessary for good health. The creation of new cells allows us to defeat viruses and bacteria and combat stress and other negative forces that are constantly threatening our bodies.

Positive thoughts generate cellular production. Whenever we are feeling good, we are creating cells. Observing any of God's creations -- a flower, trees, the ocean, mountains, a cat or any other beautiful being -- increases positive energy and inspires our bodies to produce cells. Listening to soothing music has the same effect. The practicing of the golden rule, "Do to others as you would have them do to you," is a prime method of speeding up the production of cells.

Negative thoughts slow down cellular production. Every negative thought such as anger, fear, hate, judgment, or refusing to accept God's messages can slow down cellular production and lead to illness. That is why forgiving others is so powerful in healing. In the case of depression, negative thoughts accumulate, cellular production slows down, and it becomes very difficult to escape the trench of despair.

Giving and receiving hugs speeds up the production of cells. I received hugs every day from both my father and my mother, and I was blessed with grandparents who hugged me whenever I came into their presence. I hug my siblings, my children and grandchildren. I have no doubt that when we hug one another, both parties experience increased cellular production. My parents left a family legacy of love and the result is the Bowlby family is a family of love.

Mentally handicapped children are love. Often, mentally handicapped children are bundles of pure love, and inspire divine love in everyone they meet. I have hugged developmentally disabled children many times and felt their unconditional love pouring out at the soul level. They have no mental barriers as they draw and give love freely. My daughter-in-law, Edith, has taught all three of her daughters to participate with disadvantaged children and all three of them have expanded their empathy levels and have been blessed by the experience.

Improving our intake of oxygen creates cells and makes us more radiant. I always focus on the spine in my healing sessions, using massage to release stress from the spinal column and encourage the creation of oxygen. Moving from the bottom up, I work every vertebra, finding blockages where the energy is not flowing due to lack of oxygen. As the oxygen starts flowing, people's faces relax and they look prettier. They often say they feel like they're floating on air, unable to feel the ground. Even their voices change, becoming rich with oxygen.

We should be taught at an early age the God gave us the choice to create cells in our bodies and heal ourselves in the process. The number of choices is infinite as the following summary indicates.

Tell a joke-hug a tree-take a nap-pet a kitten-plant a flower-listen to classical music-forgive someone-go fishing-wash the car-get a pet-watch a fire dance-look at the sky-massage your temples-tell someone you love, I love you-take a swim-look at the clouds roll by-play golf-sing-take a long bath-take a different road to work-daydream-go for a brisk walk-get a massage-hug someone you love-eat breakfast-look at a mountain-quit smoking-look in the distance-plan ahead-take the dog for a walk-walk barefoot on the grass-close your eyes and meditate-run.

All healing must come from within. What energy healers do is speed up the healing through divine energy transferred from the Holy Spirit

We all have the power to heal ourselves, as long as we believe. This is demonstrated by studies of the placebo effect: People who are given a sugar pill but who believe they are taking a product that can heal about thirty percent of the time.

Pain is the body trying to heal itself and should be blessed rather than feared. Pain is the body trying to heal itself; chronic pain occurs when the energy flow is blocked; as the blockage is released, the body finds its natural balance, and the pain is relieved. I have found cold air radiated from a person whose energy flow was blocked. Invariably, the body was unable to heal itself, and pain ensued.

Tumors and other growths are the result of blocked energy. In some cases they are blobs of negative energy that have accumulated. Many times I have been able to reduce these growths substantially with gentle manipulation. Sometimes they disappear entirely, releasing energy to flow naturally.

The body does not heal at a steady pace, but in divine energy rhythm. Most healings occur in three sessions, but, many people find relief in a single session and others require many more. Sometimes my mission is simply to relieve pain, and with others, to provide complete healing. I have learned to divorce myself from the outcome of any individual session, knowing that I am just a vehicle for the work of the Holy Spirit.

Our chakra centers send powerful healing energy throughout our bodies

Our Chi (energy force) has at its center seven major energy centers called chakras, and many sub-chakras that radiate all over the body. In Eastern medicine, the thymus gland is considered the 8th chakra, and it is the most important, as it is the master gland to the entire immune system. Healthy chakras send energy to stimulate our immune system, which is designed to handle all types of foreign invaders to the body.

From my experience over twenty-two years of healing, I have found fewer than five people who have ever heard of the thymus gland, and even if they have, it is unlikely that they know where it is, or what it does! The thymus gland is located just left of the breast bone, close to breast level. When I am healing, I concentrate my energy on awakening the thymus gland, in order to speed up its processes and send healing T cells to wherever they are needed.

The chakras are like batteries for our healing systems. Like batteries, Chakras need to be recharged, and they naturally run down as people age. This deterioration occurs more quickly if the body is slowed down by obesity, stress, the ingesting of chemicals through water and food, and poor diets in general. As the chakras close, we become more vulnerable to the multiple negative entities that are trying to enter, and to control our bodies, which results in an illness. The antidote to recharge the chakras is for the persons to consciously choose to create new cells in their bodies.

Western medicines slow down the chakras and detract from their ability to create healing cells. These medicines generally mask the problems that the patient experiences, and they rarely do anything to heal the body.

When we pray, we fire up our chakra centers. Praying for others fires our immune systems, and results in the creation of healing T cells, which are dispensed from the thymus throughout our bodies, resulting in a speedier healing. Praying is a powerful stimulant to healing, but, it is just one effective tool. We send positive thoughts to one another through our chakra centers. Vibration in the body is the mark of the

173

opening of the chakra centers. It leads to the path of divine ascension, and it is a major step toward surrendering your will to the Holy Spirit.

Energy healing awakens people from the inside out, stimulating their chakras to send healing energy where it's needed. When I am working on someone, I am manifesting the opening of their chakras. I have seen this work in amazing ways. People who have had strokes, or who are comatose, have begun to move, and I realize that this reflects energy coming not from the brain, but, from the energy centers in their chakras' centers.

Each chakra, when it opens, is a distinct color. Blue-green is the color of the thymus gland. The throat chakra is blue, and the heart chakra is green. When the chakras are open, the colors blend like a flower in full bloom. That also describes the radiant look of a person who has just finished a healing session -- fresh as an amazingly beautiful flower. Angels dwell in our chakras, and the angels are the colors of the chakras: the root chakra is red; the sacral chakra is orange; the 3rd solar plexus chakra is yellow; the 6th chakra is indigo and is between the eyes; the 7th chakra is the crown chakra and is violet. I have experienced all the colors of the chakras when I close my eyes and see the brilliant colors of the chakras blend in and out. When I see them, their beauty is beyond my mind's comprehension.

The combination of heat and vibration destroys unhealthy cells and encourages new cell growth

The effect of heating up the body is similar to when fever "breaks" an illness. Research shows that heat can kill cancer cells, but, it does not bother healthy cells. That is because cancer cells are generally weaker than healthy cells. In a healing session, I place my hot hands on the patient's thymus chakra, in order to speed up the function of that gland and to send healing T cells wherever they are needed to destroy cancer cells, and other invaders.

Many cultures have traditionally used heat for healing. Steam baths are an important part of the cultures of the Greeks, Romans, Scandinavians and Turks. Northern Europeans believe in healthful saunas, and Native Americans have a similar tradition with their sweat lodges. My own mother, during the Depression days, used heat to heal many of the medical problems her family experienced. Hot mustard plasters were applied to our necks and chests for respiratory problems, and after water was heated on our wood stove, we were put under tents to breathe the steaming menthol vapors. A standard heal-all was to wrap our bodies in layers of blankets, as our feet soaked in scalding water.

Heat and vibration also help to speed up the body's process of replenishing cells. When I begin a healing session, I generally pile at least three inches of blankets onto the patient, who lies on a heated pad. To create vibration in the body, I use a Chi Machine, which cradles the person's ankles, and moves him side to side at a rate of 140 oscillations per minute. This massages the organs, most importantly, the lungs, which are then stimulated to move the oxygen throughout the body. That is part of the process of getting the body fired up to create cells. More oxygen creates more cells.

Vibrations can occur spontaneously in the course of a healing session. Over the years, I have had many people experience different forms of vibration, as mild as tremors, or as strong as convulsions. This would frighten me, had I not experienced so many variations. Patients generally vibrate for about thirty minutes, which seems to be the magic time necessary for advanced healing. Numerous patients have told me that they had felt incredibly peaceful at the conclusion of the vibration period, and that they are convinced that it played a role in their healing.

Drawing energy from the Earth also enhances healing

The strength of the Earth's energy flowing through me and into my patient's balances their body's right to left. It also brings the function of the thymus gland into harmony, and encourages the creation of cells to heal the body. In a session, I feel this as energy flowing into my feet and legs, out through my hands, and then back into the Earth, like a transfusion traveling both ways.

For the last two years, I have been using a Mediconsult pad under my patients to improve their circulation and oxygen delivery. These pads were built into the suits of astronauts, to duplicate the Earth's energy when they are in space. Recently, I have found that when I stand on a second pad, it substantially increases the energy flow between the patient and me.

Evil, in the form of black energy, depression and illness, can be defeated by divinely inspired healing.

Evil spirits can take hold of a body and wreak havoc. Ellen White, a prolific Adventist writer at the turn of the nineteenth century, said that everyone is subject to a constant barrage of evil messages and divine messages, just as Adam and Eve were in the Garden of Eden. In her book *The Ministry of Healing*, she describes the healings that Jesus performed, starting with the two demoniacs. I have detected this battle between good and evil in everyone that is divinely placed on my table. Sometimes, these demons are cast out during the first session, and other times, it has taken a year or more, and dozens of sessions, to completely eliminate evil from a body.

Evil cannot exist in a body when divine energy is applied. I have heard and felt countless demons leave patients' bodies, and I am convinced that it is the most horrible sound one can experience. These sounds penetrate the cores of one's souls, similar to a nail scratching on metal. I know that divine energy flows through me, and divine energy will always win, as it is more powerful than the devil's energy.

In one healing session, I agreed to work with a woman who thought she was dying, as her lungs filled with fluid, despite many aspirations of fluid by doctors. One of her children stayed with her twenty –four-hours a day, and they expected each hour might be her last. After a period of heat and vibration, I put my hand on her thymus gland, and I could feel a demon rise up against my hand. A horrible sound came from her body, and she asked me if that was a death rattle. Then, we both felt the demon leave her body. After she had turned over on her stomach, I felt negative energy once again in her back. I kept the divine energy flowing, and a second horrible sound came from her back and we both felt the demon leave her body. Within a week, her health returned to normal.

Part of the divine purpose of energy healing is to build up an angelic shield around the body. When I have finished healing sessions, and negative energy has been disbursed, I place my hands above their faces, collect their energy fields, like a magnet from the energy that radiates from their bodies, and bring them out to create a field of protection. The radiating positive energy flow prevents evil from penetrating the bodies' shields. The shield of protection is maintained by positive action, and the creation of cells by choice of the patient.

Self-healing and empathy are at the heart of healing

In order for people to be healed, they have to believe that they can be healed. Because I have experienced tremendous pain, I am deeply sympathetic to those who suffer. Most of the people who come to me are strangers, but, they expect to be healed. My first step is to teach them how to empower themselves so that they can take charge of their own healing, and activate their own immune systems.

Touch is important in healthcare and in daily life because it connects us, reminding us that we're all just flesh and blood. A small but heartfelt gesture, like a pat on the back, or touch on the hand, on someone who is uncomfortable, speaks volumes to them, when finding the right empathetic words is too complex.

Healing and ascension are all about raising the vibrations in our hearts to a higher level. We can do this by praising others, and lifting them in their lives' journeys. Your happiness depends upon the love that you give and receive. Just talking about it is not enough; to be a true Christian, you must live it.

True empathy means giving completely, even to the extent of risking your own life. I have lived through many near-death experiences, and that has helped me to place my life in perspective. After all my second chances, I know that every day is a miracle, and my life's game plan is to strive to give one hundred percent of my energy for the time I am allotted on this Earth. If I ever had the opportunity to sacrifice my life to save another person, I would do so unconditionally. When my friends and I attempted to move the boulder from the middle of Highway 26, I was not the least concerned that we might be killed by a passing vehicle. The need to protect someone whom I will never know is a much stronger force. If I could change places with some child I was healing, I would do so in a second. I am ready to die when my time comes, and I believe that life is not over until God says that it is over.

The following thoughts describe some of the techniques and principles that have come to define my healing practice. I look forward to my continued education with divine patience, and I know that I will receive the information precisely when I need it, as intended by God Almighty.

Healing Thoughts

- ✓ All thoughts are **Energy**
- ✓ When you think you are a victim you have **no** responsibility for your actions which equals victim mentality?
- ✓ We **create evil** when we **accept** negativity
- ✓ We should never allow a negative **thought** to enter our being
- ✓ We have a **choice** - to **reject** or **receive** all negative energy
- ✓ We all have a **choice** to **heal** ourselves, as Mary Baker Eddy determined in 1866, during her nine-year study of how the human body heals according to scripture. This resulted in the publication of Science and Health with Key to the Scriptures.
- ✓ We all make a daily **choice** for our highest good, which results in the healing of our bodies. Imaginary false barriers in the mind prevent us from allowing the God within us to heal ourselves.
- ✓ We must make a conscious **choice** to cast out suffering and anger, and to replace it with Love of one another by not debasing others.
- ✓ **(It is better to give than receive)**
- ✓ We send positive thoughts from our chakra centers to another person's chakra centers
- ✓ Vibration in the body is the sure fire mark of the opening of the chakra centers and leads to the path of Divine Ascension and is a major step to surrender your will to the Holy Spirit
- ✓ When we **pray**- we fire up our chakra centers
- ✓ This in turn fires up our energy centers
- ✓ Which in turn fires up our immune systems
- ✓ Which results in the creation of healing T cells
- ✓ Which results in healing
- ✓ Which results in casting out sin & disease as it loses reality in human consciousness
- ✓ Which results in the Divine influence to heal through the God within us
- ✓ When we accept Divine healing we are harvesting the **fruits** of human faith
- ✓ All thoughts are either **Positive or Negative** - There is **No Neutral**
- ✓ In Life, the first step downward is self-pity!

- ✓ The first step upward is to be kind to someone else without expectation of a return.
- ✓ Angels are available twenty-four hours a day at everybody's **choice** to receive their Divine messages or reject them — all prayer requests are answered by angels, often in disguise, which tests our faith to receive them.
- ✓ Angels dwell in our chakra centers, and the angels are the rainbow colors of the chakra.

Time

On his deathbed, Alexander the Great summoned his generals, and told them his three ultimate wishes: the best doctors should carry his coffin; the wealth he had accumulated (money, gold, precious stones) should be scattered along the way to his burial; and his hands should be left hanging outside the coffin for all to see.

Surprised by these unusual requests, one of his generals asked Alexander to explain. Here is what he said:

"I want the best doctors to carry my coffin to demonstrate that in the face of death; even the best doctors in the world have no power to heal.

I want the road to be covered with my treasure so that everybody sees that the wealth acquired on Earth, stays on Earth.

I want my hands to swing in the wind so that people understand that we come to this world empty-handed and we leave empty-handed after the most precious treasure of all is exhausted --- Time!

Time is our most precious treasure because it is limited. We can produce more wealth, but we cannot produce more time. When we give someone our time, we actually give a portion of our life that we will never take back. Our time is our life!

The best present that you can give your family and friends is your time. May we all have the wisdom to provide time to benefit others, without the expectation of receiving an equal amount of time.

Vernon's comment: May you always think twice before you refuse another's request for your time. You never know what blessing may ensue when you have given someone this gift."

Theories and Evidence - Alpine Healing

Louise was one of my very first clients when I started my CPA practice in 1963. She told me that she had been a German doctor in WWII, and that, after the war in 1946, she worked at a cancer sanitarium in the Bavarian Alps. Each week, the doctors held a roundtable discussion and talked about their cancer cases. One day, a doctor said, "It has occurred to me that we've been studying the wrong people. We have been studying the people who have died instead of the people who have lived. We have many patients who arrive with life-threatening cancer and yet leave here cancer free. We should study the people who heal from cancer to determine if there is a common thread as to why they healed."

The doctors had every patient maintain a daily diary to track their activities, and after two years they concluded that the one thing these people had in common was that they all took long, frequent walks on the forest trails in the Bavarian Alps at 6,000 feet of elevation. The doctors studied the plants and the trees in the area, to discover what might be influencing this trend, but, in the fifteen years that Louise was there, they did not reach firm conclusions. Throughout the study, the doctors encouraged more of their patients to walk in the woods, and the number of people who survived their cancers increased substantially.

This story remained in the cobwebs of my mind for the last fifty years. Over the course of my twenty-four-year healing journey, I have had bits and pieces of insight as to why people may have healed from cancer as a result of walking in the high Bavarian forests sixty-eight years ago. On May 14, 2014, I read an article by Tamara Eberlein, an editor for Bottom Line Publications' *Daily Health News* that explains what Louise was searching for sixty-five years ago.

The article highlighted the research of Mark Hyman, M.D., the founder and director of the Ultra Wellness Center in Lenox, Massachusetts. In Dr. Hyman's book, *The Ultra Mind Solution*, he describes a Japanese study that showed that time spent in a forest or wooded area -- referred to as "forest bathing" in that country -- increased immune function. Stress reduction was one reason, but, in addition, all those trees give off therapeutic airborne chemicals (called phytoncides) that keep plants from rotting, and which have been shown to improve immune function.

Dr. Hyman calls the immune system "an organ of perception," explaining that, "It perceives what is happening in the environment around us, both physical and mental, and responds accordingly." T cells (he calls these white blood cells "the soldiers of the immune system") have receptors for neurotransmitters that are activated, in part, in response to our emotions. Consequently, says Dr. Hyman, "Our thoughts and feelings literally speak to the T cells."

The concept of forest bathing obviously could have been one of the major factors explaining the healing of Louise's patients, who walked in the Bavarian forests. I also support Dr. Hyman's theory that the thoughts and feelings in the human brain control the creation of healing T cells.

A long-term insight that has come to me during my healing journey is that any time a person is feeling good, that person is creating cells at an increased rate. Thus, we all have the power to heal ourselves from any body malady. Here are some other insights that provide additional clues as to why the patients healed after walking in the Bavarian forests:

Einstein advanced the theory in 1905 that the Earth contained an energy field that was connected to all humans. This theory was proved when the first astronaut went into space and she became "spaced out" when she left the Earth's energy field. To counteract this loss of the Earth's energy field, healing pads were created to duplicate the Earth's energy and have been built into the space suits for all subsequent flights.

When the patients walked in the woods, they connected to the Earth's energy field, and balanced their energy left to right, which is one of the basic concepts of Eastern medicine.

Walking at the elevation of 6,000 feet also increased the patient's lung activity, which sends the lungs an increased supply of healing oxygen, which is lethal to cancer cells throughout the body.

In addition, raising the body's temperature speeded up cellular production and destroyed cancer cells, which cannot stand the level of heat as can healthy cells.

DMSO, a product of trees such as Douglas firs, has had incredible success in healing many forms of illness. Those who often use it for minor cuts and burns report that recovery is speedy. Several studies have documented DMSO's effectiveness in treating soft tissue damage, local tissue death, skin ulcers, and burns.

Relative to cancer, several properties of DMSO have gained attention. In one study with rats, DMSO was found to delay the spread of one cancer, and to prolong survival rates with another. In other studies, it has been found to protect non-cancer cells, while increasing the effectiveness of the chemotherapeutic agent. DMSO gives credibility to the power of trees to emanate healing oxygen.

Forest Bathing gains further support as a cure for cancer in an interview with Dr. Melissa Lem, a Toronto family physician:

"Some of the most compelling and biologically relevant evidence comes from Japan, where shinrin-yoku or "forest bathing" has long been recognized as an important part of a healthy lifestyle. A recent study showed that adults who spent three days a week in forests dramatically boosted their levels of cancer-fighting proteins and natural killer cells, and reflected lower stress. Another study demonstrated that young men who sat in the woods, instead of the city, for only fifteen minutes, experienced significant drops in their heart rate and salivary cortisone."

From these insights, it can be concluded that walks in the high altitude forests may be extremely beneficial in improving anyone's health, and may help to cure cancer.

Part 6: Healing Stories

The Healing Session

I was once told by a spiritual reader that my soul was placed on this Earth to have fun, and I am sure that is true. I have fun with everything I do, not just golf and grandchildren, but I enjoy accounting, household chores and especially healing. There is nothing more rewarding than to take someone through a healing session and free that person from pain.

When I perform a healing session, I do so entirely under the direction of the higher power. I pray that the Holy Spirit will guide me to the affected area, that the power of the Holy Spirit will flow through me, and that I will become the conduit of divine healing, bringing peace and relief to whomever the Holy Spirit has brought to me.

I generally perform healing sessions in nearly complete darkness. The patient and I both have our eyes closed through most of the session, which contributes to a sense of spacelessness and frees up the mind for the healing process.

I begin by bringing heat and vibration to the patient's body through the use of blankets and a Chi Machine. My own cellular production speeds up, and the energy flows into my hands to be released as heat. There is so much healing oxygen in my hands that they turn bright red. Then I pray with all my heart to create the flow of unconditional love, and awaken the thymus gland to its healing power. Through my mind, I create a siphon of energy flow from the Earth's core into the patient. The energy starts to surge back to me in a simultaneous exchange.

My body then receives divine energy from the Holy Spirit to such a high degree that I receive jolts in my stomach's chakra. It is like receiving a lightning bolt of divine energy, and each time it is received, my body makes a sharp gasping sound that shakes me to the roots. I become the receptor of divine energy, which flows from me into the patient and fires up her chakras wherever it is needed. This ignites the creation of cells at a terrific rate. Divine energy knows where to go. It moves to wherever there is a blockage, and the person heals as negative energy is cast out.

I use deep tissue massage, with an emphasis on the spinal column, to release toxins from the muscles. Drinking alkaline water before and after the session helps the patient to flush these poisons through the blood stream, and out of the body.

Sometimes, I use a crystal bowl to enhance the healing process. I place the bowl on the patient, and brush the edges of the bowl, which creates a deeply vibrating sound that penetrates every cell in the body, encouraging cell creation. Crystal bowls are forced to the surface from the center of the Earth, and they contain a great deal of energy. When I hold a crystal bowl, it is like a throbbing, living thing, and my energy field explodes as the vibration extends into every cell in my body, as well as into every cell in my patient's body.

Every cell in our bodies is revitalized-"jump started." The bowl I currently use was bequeathed to me from a dear friend, who died of leukemia on Christmas Eve, 2002. It is one of the many tools that have come to me over the years. The crystal bowl is used to enhance a patient's energy flow and speed up the production of cells, as well as to penetrate and dissipate energy blockages throughout the body.

As the patient's chakras fire up, the brain creates healing endorphins that stop pain, and the thymus releases healing T cells to where ever they are needed. No drug produced by any pharmaceutical company can come even remotely close to the power of the Holy Spirit, when a body has healed itself in the way God intended!

I receive incredible bursts of energy as I work, and often I grunt from the intensity explosion of energy that strikes me. The message to me from Spirit is that the blockage in the patient has created an illness or pain, and the patient's body is helpless. It takes an extra amount of energy to break the dam, and to get the body's energy to flow naturally again. When the burst of energy strikes me, it feels as if I have been kicked by a horse in the stomach, and sometimes, from the strength of the explosion, I bend forward at the waist, but, I suffer no pain. I can experience the explosion many times in a two-hour session.

Healing energy works on every ailment and blockage in the body. I have given relief to victims of stroke, shingles, cancer (even inoperable tumors in the brain), leukemia, fibromyalgia, chronic headaches, depression, mental illnesses and other body maladies. All physical deficiencies of the body can be cured by energy healing, when the patient accepts the power of the Holy Spirit.

Most patients reflect on how wonderful they feel after a session on my thermal table. They are amazed at how light their bodies feel, and how free of pain they suddenly are. Amazingly, they look years younger and glow with radiant, positive energy. I consider this transformation the glow of the Holy Spirit. The most common comments, after the sessions is that they do not want to move, because they have never before experienced God's love on such a level. Others say that they feel "born again"!

In the summer 2012, two of my leukemia patients who were in need of increased red blood cells, were having their red cell count tabulated the day before, and the day after, I gave them sessions. The result was that my sessions increased their red cell count by about thirty percent (which was more than the accepted medical procedure of receiving a six- hour blood transfusion.) Medical science has long since known that healing T (thymus) cells are created in the spleen and in the pancreas, that they are raised to "teen age level", and then transferred through the lymphatic system to the thymus gland, where they are raised to maturity, and transferred throughout the body, wherever they are needed. The lymphatic system is where cancer cells can break away from the original primary tumor, and form secondary tumors in organs throughout the body.

I do not have the power to instantly heal anyone. But, everyone who comes to me experiences some level of relief. Sometimes, my mission is to provide a break from crippling pain; other times, I am given the power to remove a life-threatening growth or disease. Whatever healing occurs during a session is determined by a divine power stronger than any human can possess.

Spirit has taught me to divorce myself from the outcome of these healing sessions. My strength comes in surrender to the divine guidance of the Almighty, who has given me the ability to help people along their path to healing.

Two Linked Healings, Five Years Apart

In May 1998, I received a phone call from a Mary whom I had helped with a tax problem many years before. She knew that I was doing energy healing, and she asked if I would come to Portland to do a healing on a friend, Jodi, whose fourteen- year-old daughter was dying of cancer. Mary stated that her friend "would not let her daughter go" despite the fact that doctors predicted that Ann would die in less than a month

Jodi's daughter, Ann, had been diagnosed with cancer in the right knee cap in August 1997. The doctors had replaced the knee cap with a steel plate, and she had been given chemo and radiation for eight months. In April, x-rays revealed that the cancer had spread throughout her right leg, three pear-sized tumors had appeared in her lungs, and numerous other cancers existed throughout her body. Her doctors considered amputating her leg, but, it was decided that the trauma of the surgery might kill her.

I called Jodi, and scheduled sessions a week later for both her and Ann. For the entire week, I agonized over what I could possibly say to a fourteen- year-old who was dying. When I met her, all I could think of was, "Would you like a hug?" Ann's ninety-pound body flew into my arms. In the following months, every session with Ann began and ended with a great hug. She had never met her father, who lived just ten miles away, and she had been deprived of masculine energy.

I gave the mother and daughter back-to-back sessions. Their bodies were both depleted, Ann from repeated chemo sessions, and her mother from blocked energy flow caused by excessive stress. They both twitched and jerked, as their chakra centers were reenergized. When I had finished with Ann, she looked up from the table and said, "I don't want to move." This is a common response from my patients, who have never felt as well as they do after they have experienced the healing power of the Holy Spirit.

I continued to give Ann sessions over the next eighteen months. During those sessions, I prayed and manifested that Ann would heal completely, that she would have a long life, and that one day she would marry and have two daughters, who would emulate her beautiful energy. My vision was of her as a dancer, and that her daughters danced as well.

In October 1999, I scheduled a session with Ann for November 1. Three nights before the session, I dreamed that I floated through a dirt tunnel deep into the Earth. As I moved, light flowed from my head. My mission was to seek out and destroy the darkness of soul-penetrating fear. As I floated through the tunnels, I came upon pockets of inky black darkness, where a battle ensued between my energy, represented by light, and the blackness of evil. Each battle was a struggle to conquer bone-chilling fear, which disintegrated as my light attacked the dark pockets of fear.

This dream was in my mind as I began my session with Ann. I asked her if she had gone trick-or-treating the night before, and she said that she had, but, that it would probably be her last time. Suddenly, I became aware that my positive energy flowed through Ann's veins and arteries, as they sought the chemo and other undesirable elements. An hour into the session, I placed my hands on Ann's back, and I felt a huge surge of negative energy leave her body: a demon being cast out. Instantly, my dream was interpreted: the tunnels were Ann's blood vessels, which needed to be cleansed of the cancerous cells. My energy became the light that would eventually expel the cancer from her body.

Six weeks later, x-rays revealed that the tumors in Ann's lungs had shrunk by half. In October 2000, Ann's doctors told her she was cancer-free!

The message came to me that my hugs were a powerful stimulant to Ann's healing. As a preventative measure, I continued to give her sessions. On May 2, 2001, I received the following email from Ann's mother: "We owe so much to you and your healing gift. You are a major part of Ann's healing. Thank you. We are so amazed at the quick turnaround, and the miracle of the disappearing act of those three tumors in her lungs. Thanks for your love and support."

I continued to use the visualization of my dream in healings with other patients. As I performed each session, I pictured my energy as it flowed through the person's blood vessels, and cleared them of blockages. I thought about Jesus' saying in John 12:35: "The light is among you for a little while longer. Walk while you have the light, lest darkness overtake you. The one who walks in the darkness does not know where he is going. Believe in the light, so that you may become children of light."

In 2009, I attempted to contact Ann's mother, but, the email address was no longer functional. I did not know her last name, so, I had no way to reach her. But, I have continued to send healing energy to Ann for all these years, and I feel strongly connected to her. Spirit tells me that Ann has attained my manifestation of a full happy life.

In June 2003, five years after my first session with Ann, another patient was referred to me with an amazingly similar story. Diane suffered from stress over the death of her fifteen-year-old son eighteen months earlier. He was afflicted with cancer in his right knee cap, which had spread to his lungs and throughout his body. Chemo and radiation worsened his quality of life, and his right leg had been amputated. He died a painful death, and Diane had never recovered.

During our first session, her body was full of blocked energy. I could feel my energy race to each obstruction, dissipate it, and then rush on to the next one. When I had finished, Diane's face wore a radiant smile. After two more sessions, she seemed a changed person. When I touched her, I could feel the energy flow smoothly throughout her body, and she was ready to continue in this life.

The coincidence of two teenagers with cancer in their right knee caps, both of whose mothers were referred to me, defies logic. One lived, one died, and I wish that I could have worked on Diane's son. The thought flows to me that a coincidence is when God acts incognito; to man, it is a miracle.

The day after I gave Diane her third session, her friend's fourteen-year-old son drowned. Diane was equipped with positive energy to guide her friend through her tragedy. Another coincidence, or God's timing?

A Pain-Free Passing

Divine timing brings me healing patients in ways that I can never anticipate. When I played golf at the Black Butte Ranch in Central Oregon, in April 1998, I never imagined that the timing of the Holy Spirit would eventually lead me, three months later, to a session for a dying woman in Portland.

The elevation of the Black Butte Ranch golf course is about 3,000 feet above the elevation of my home in Corvallis, Oregon. Playing golf at that altitude can cause a lack of oxygen in my leg muscles that leads to muscle cramps in the night. To protect against this, I routinely schedule a massage that returns my legs to normal oxygen flow.

After that golf outing, I called my two favorite masseuses, and discovered that neither was in town. I called four more numbers, and got answering machines. Then, I remembered a newspaper ad for a masseuse at Black Butte. I called her number, noticed that her name was Mary, a name that has repeatedly appeared since my healing awakening began. She answered the phone, and had received a cancellation, so, I returned to Black Butte.

Mary gave me a wonderful massage, and I told her about my adventures in energy healing. She asked me to give her a five-minute session before her next appointment. The session triggered an explosion of laughter and jubilation, which is a common response to energy healing.

I was not in contact with Mary again until three months later. On July 27, 1998, she called and asked for my home phone number. Mary wanted me to come to Portland and do a healing on her mother who was ill with pancreatic cancer.

The next day, Sunday, the temperature was over one hundred degrees, as I traveled to Portland to give an energy healing session to a person I had never met. I entered a small air-conditioned room, where seven or eight close friends and relatives were crowded around a raised hospital bed. June was sixty-two years old. She normally weighed 120 pounds, but, she had lost a considerable amount of weight, and her eyes were rolled back into her head, with only her white eyeballs visible.

I placed my hands over June, and discovered that she was extremely hot. Mary told me that her temperature had ranged from 106 to 108 degrees for over two months, and that June was in extreme pain twenty-four hours a day. She was taking morphine, and the doctors had predicted her death around the end of May.

When I placed my hands over June, her body instantly began muscle movement. Her arms, legs, and torso began to twitch. I immediately felt extreme heat radiate up my arms. In a few moments, both June and I sweat profusely. For almost two hours, I prayed for June, as I continued therapeutic touch and Reiki, energy healing methods that I had learned four years earlier. June moaned her approval throughout the session, even though she could not talk. I am sure that we each lost several pounds. I agreed to come back the next day to do another session at noon.

A half an hour after I left, June's temperature was normal, and her pain was gone, never to return!

When I arrived in her room on Monday, I discovered June sitting up! She announced that she was going to have a party that night, and fifty-six friends had been invited to celebrate her life. She thanked me for coming, and told me that I was her angel, Saint Michael, sent to help her to heaven in peace.

Mary told me that the hospice worker was shocked when she had come to visit June in the morning, and had found her sitting in the living room, dressed, and with her hair combed. The hospice worker had never seen June out of her bed in over two months of her care.

As I gave June the second session, I was pleased that she was pain-free. Her body jumped and jerked as her charka energy centers continued to awaken the nerve centers throughout her body. When I finished, June was profuse with her thanks, and asked me to return the next day for a third session.

The next day, June told me that the party had been a smashing success. She was delighted to have had that opportunity to tell her friends goodbye. As I gave her the third session, she emitted moans of pleasure, and she was filled with euphoria when I left. Half an hour later, June went to sleep, and died peacefully. Her daughter called me, and said that the family was overjoyed that their mother had died tranquilly, and pain- free.

A few days later, as I read her obituary in the Oregonian, the message came to me that June and I were in the same flow, and that we were destined to meet at her deathbed. June was born in St. Paul, Minnesota, where my mother was in the first grade. June was married in 1956, the same year that my wife and I were married. Both June and my wife were teenagers when they married.

June's husband had graduated from the University of Washington in 1960, and I had graduated from the University of Oregon that same year. We had both moved to Portland to begin our professional careers. In 1959, we had our first daughters; in 1962, we had our second daughters; in 1964, we had our only sons. June died exactly thirteen years from the day that my brother, Wayne, died of a heart attack.

Ten days after June died, my wife and I were vacationing in northern France. As we approached Mont Saint Michel, out in the English Channel, the weather was overcast and light rain was falling. Suddenly, the rain stopped, and a single ray of sunlight revealed a golden statue atop the abbey. When we entered the abbey, I learned that the statue was Saint Michael, who slew the dragon of death around his feet! The ray that had broken through the clouds was a message from June that she was safely in heaven. I purchased two small statues of Saint Michael to give to her daughters with that message.

From the time that I had first placed my hands over June, I knew that she possessed a beautiful spirit. She was a person that I would love to have known before her illness. The message that I received from Spirit was that I was to divorce myself from the outcome of my healing sessions. My mission was to assist her to heaven in peace and harmony. The power of divine timing has no limits, and once again, demonstrated amazing synchronicity.

The Observation of Katherine's Relief from Pain

In November 2008, Traci, (described as a "cardiac realtor"), Cheri (described as a cardiac nurse), and I gave Katherine, a ninety-year-old woman, a session to relieve her of multiple chronic pains throughout her body. Cindy, Katherine's daughter, witnessed the healing and recorded the messages that she received while watching her mother being relieved from pain.

My observations included this information from the Council of One, and the angels who assisted with this process. I report it as it happened:

"I can see a very Tall Presence behind Vernon as he applies energy techniques from the head of the table. The Presence now becomes one with his energy, thorough his arms, merging with them. I see two Presence on Katherine's right standing next to Traci, one at the end of the table, and another on the left side of the table next to Cheri. These Presences are holding rods of light and are touching them with another instrument – "fine tuning" instruments they tell me – creating vibration frequencies not heard by the human ear drums. They "sound" them in a pattern causing the frequencies that regenerate and stimulate the stem cells awake. The one on the left is putting It's "hand" on the shoulder of the nurse – Yes, I hear, "cardiac nurse – angelic healer of the 6th dimensional energies – the frequencies are directed through her to accustom her to their Presence and assist her in her work"

Optimal energy is flowing through Vernon as spinal cords vibrate to the spiraling adding additional dimension to the Kundalini energy – holographically stimulating pulsating diamond frequencies. There are sparks emitting from the fingertips on Traci's hands – now – stabilizing, integrating, and grounding these frequencies through the body- balancing – integrating – and yes – responsible for the intent anesthesia affect.

A stimulus of plasmatic radionics is flowing through Vernon's crown through the pituitary, pineal and all glandular structures within the human energy system.

Third Eye clearing now taking place – as if a router rooter of high intensity Angelic frequencies are clearing out any debris left in the wake of traditional treatments regarding metals and all metallic substances.

The roots of illumination conduits that ground the God Self through the human self are now freed and are sprouting through the arches of the feet (it looks like roots of pure light) – the healers are assisting the pathway openings – the flow is freely moving and will continue to amplify and magnify and expand at the perfect rate allowed by the participant's (Katherine's) I AM Presence in charge of the distribution and re-distribution of cellular regeneration and New Earth cellular structure.

Above the table, close to the ceiling, in a circle is the Host of Angels – the Angelic Beings who guide each Healer Angel Human present – "Yes" I hear, - They are from a civilization highly evolved and specialized in regeneration to the state of perfection – as the body is meant to exemplify Perfection through human anatomy as well as blissful emotional harmony".

Above the Circle of Angels now I see a Golden Dot perfectly placed in the center. From that Golden Dot I now see spirals like curling ribbons coming down through each angel in the circle, through the guardians, through the Human Earth Angels and now into the body of Katherine, the Magnificent Master Sage of a planet yet to be discovered. She, (called Katherine,) traveled through Universes and Star systems to participate in the New Earth enfoldment. Her (Katherine's) visionary gifts are being bestowed on each healer present today and they will respond with dramatic, expanded Gifts as healers in this New Earth and it will expand beyond - WAY beyond humans.

There are several circles of Beings around the table now... (Concentric circles with the table as the center) – on-lookers from other dimensions, observing, learning from what is happening...multi dimensional, multiracial, multi Universal, multicultural coming together in Oneness each with expertise to bring together for the Whole).

Energy transmutation is taken care of by the Earthly and Etheric Elementals, and the Nature Kingdom is represented in cellular activity – in physicality – as they integrate their intelligence into the cellular activity increasing the momentum to achieve and maintain homeostasis. Balance is achieved through their activity. New brain cells spring forth in response to the diamond spinning while the crystal is dissolving, and once reaching the plasma state, the brain waves will elongate and vibrate at the new frequency needed to maintain this state.

After this healing session, Katherine was pain-free for over two months.

Two Women from Idaho

In March 2010, I was blessed to perform healing sessions for two women from Idaho who were traveling together. Jackie had had excruciating headaches for over a year, and she could find no relief, despite many prescribed medications and consultations with neurologists and other doctors. Candy was in stage 4 cancer, which had commenced in her left breast, and it had metastasized to her lungs and other organs. She was taking a "last trip" to the Oregon coast with her brothers and her mother, when she stopped to visit friends in Corvallis, and these friends referred her to me for a healing session.

I gave each of the women two-hour sessions over a period of three days. With each session, their energy meridians opened to a strong flow of balanced energy.

When I began to work over her, the pain in Jackie's head stopped almost immediately, and she said that a sense of peace surrounded her.

When I did an assessment of Candy, it was very apparent that her left side was almost void of energy flow. In Eastern medicine, this is considered a classic case of unbalanced and blocked energy flow, manifesting itself as cancer. When I explained this to Candy, she remarked that, all her life, she had had numerous medical problems with her left side. I prayed that she would heal, and return to work full time, and I will continue to send long-distance healing energy to her.

I commenced working on Candy, and I felt a slight trickle of energy on her left side. Slowly, the energy flow increased, and by the end of the session, it flowed strongly from side to side.

After Jackie's second session, she called her husband, Logan, to tell him of her relief of pain, and he responded with the following email:

Dear Vernon,

My name is Logan, I am Jackie's husband. I just wanted to take a minute and thank you for what you are doing for her. I spoke to her last night and it was the first time in a very long time that I have spoken to her and her head didn't hurt. She said that she could think clearly and there was no heaviness to her head.

I don't completely understand yet how energy healing works, but I have been doing some research on my own so I can have a better understanding of what it is you do. I am very excited for this and look forward to the day that I can meet you and shake your hand and thank you in person. Thank you again for sharing your amazing talents with my wife. The results of your healing are having a positive effect on Jackie and our entire family.

The top neurologists in the state of Idaho haven't been able to help her, and in only a few sessions with you she is already improving. Words cannot express the gratitude I feel towards you. I hope that you can continue to help those who need it. Logan

A couple of weeks after the ladies had returned to Idaho, I received the following email from Jackie.

Hello Vern,

I just wanted to take a moment to thank you again for seeing me during my visit. I have had very few headaches and they are not nearly as debilitating.

I am not sure if you have heard from Candy yet but she has had the most remarkable transformation! During her last scan since returning home her radiologist called her to inform her that her abdominal masses were all but gone! He actually had thought that he was given the wrong results until he saw the familiar lung scarring. She came to you with her doctors thinking this was finally the end for her and you gave her so much...hope and happiness!

I can't thank you enough for what you have done. Candy and I are already planning our next visit; we are looking at one of the last 3 weekends in May.

I truly hope this email finds you in good health, I heard that you had not been feeling well. I hope that it was not a result of bad energy overload; apparently you took on a whole lot of it between Candy and me.

I hope to hear from you soon.

Very Truly, Jackie

In July 2011, I learned that Candy was still alive, nearly a year and a half after being told that she had but weeks to live! On June 23, 2013, I received the following email from Candy:

I continue to hang in there. It continues to be a roller coaster ride, but God seems to still want me to stay here. Right now, my disease is stable and I am doing well. I had to take some time off last fall because of increased lung disease and it was pretty shaky for a while. I then started a new treatment of a drug that was just approved in June and it turned things around. I went back to work in December and am currently working full time. I continue to feel very blessed.

I will continue to keep Jackie and Candy on my healing energy prayer transmission list for all eternity.

Arrived on the Bus from Berkeley for a Healing

One of the most Spirit- filled healings that I was ever involved in was the message that my special Angel of Education bestowed upon me, and which taught me a meaningful lesson.

In the summer of 2010, I received a phone call from Mary, a long-time energy healer, author, and teacher who lives in Salem, thirty-five miles from Corvallis.

Mary stated that she had Joan, a sixty-year-old woman, come to her on the bus from Berkeley, California, for a healing, and that she had made only limited progress with her. She asked if she might bring Joan to me for a healing.

I asked, "What is her problem?" Mary said that Joan was convinced that, while she attended the University of California in the late 1960's, and while she was sedated during an operation, the CIA had implanted a control device in her, and that they controlled her actions some forty years later!

My first thought was that I could not help her, and I relayed those thoughts to Mary, and she immediately responded, "Vernon, she needs your help."

The message flowed through to me from Spirit that this was an obvious challenge that He would lead me through. I told Mary, "Bring her to my healing space in the parking area under the Bowlby Building, as soon as possible."

An hour later, Mary and Joan appeared at my healing space door, Joan bounding in with the anticipation that I would free her from bondage.

I gave her my customary talk of empowerment to heal herself, and that all healing must begin from within, and that I was only the conduit of energy from the Holy Spirit to "jump start" her on the path of healing.

A little over two hours later, I realized that love poured into Joan had balanced her energy flow, and had transformed her into a different person. She sat up, looking radiant, as she announced that she felt that the weight of the world had been lifted from her shoulders.

Joan asked how much she owed me, and when I told her that she owed nothing but a hug, another sparkle of positive energy flowed from her.

Joan left, after making another appointment for the next morning, just to be sure that the control device that had been in her for so many years was gone.

Later, I found a check for $100 made out to me from Joan. I took the check home, and showed Ruth that I had already removed Joan's signature.

That evening, I received an email that Joan had taken a walk by the Willamette River upon her return to Salem, and that she had determined that she was free from CIA control. She also requested that I cancel the second appointment, and that I hold her check for a week, as she had just realized that she had only about fifty dollars in her bank account. Joan needed part of that money for food on the 550- mile trip back to Berkeley. I told her not to worry, as I did not plan to cash her check. Joan was elated, and thanked me profusely for her healing.

Upon retiring to bed that night, I requested from Spirit what the Divine message was from this unusual healing of Joan. I awoke the next morning with the message that Joan had endorsed hate of the CIA, as had her fellow students, to such a degree that evil spirits had set up "business" within her, and that she was still controlled by hate.

During her session, the power of unconditional Love flowed through me from the Holy Spirit, and cast out the evil of the demon of hate, after enjoying a fruitful claim upon Joan for over forty years!

Vibrational Healing of Adam

During the past twenty-one years that I have been doing healing, it has been very interesting to experience the many different levels of vibration that occur during these sessions. Vibrations can be as small as a slight quivering, to a violent shaking, or, like the following story, a full-blown convulsion.

Adam was referred to me by the daughter of one of my high school classmates from Hood River. Adam was twenty-one- year old senior at Oregon State University, who had been born with a rare cancer that kills about ninety-nine percent of its victims by age six. His life -long vision was that he wanted to graduate from Oregon State University and have a job.

Adam had fought cancer all his life, and when he came to me, his cancer had accelerated, and his death was imminent. About an hour into the session, his body commenced a vibration, somewhat like a convulsion, and I had to restrain myself from calling 911. If I had not been down that path so many times before, I would have frightened myself to death. The message from Spirit was to just stay calm and wait.

What seemed an eternity later, but, in reality, was thirty minutes, the vibration stopped abruptly. Adam remarked that he had gone through various levels of pain, but, that he knew that it was a healing event, and he felt as though the weight of the world had been lifted from his shoulders.

Adam's cancer went into remission, he graduated in the spring, and achieved his lifelong ambition to graduate and find a job. About eighteen months later, his mother called to tell me that he was on his deathbed, and that he wanted me to come to Portland and give him another session. I arrived to give him a session, realized that he was, indeed, dying, and that my mission was to help him to heaven in peace. Adam died a few days later.

I will never forget the panic that I had to overcome to accept the level of violent vibrations necessary to heal his body, but, faith, fortunately, controlled me.

When I met his parents and his sister, I realized how Adam had managed to survive the cancer for so many years: all three radiated unconditional love to a level that I had never experienced.

Chemo Healing

Through a divinely timed encounter with mutual friends in Portland, Debra learned about my healing practice, and she requested my aid to help her survive breast cancer. She was forty-seven years old, and single. She had ignored a lump in her breast, and when she had finally sought medical attention, advanced cancer was in both breasts. Her doctors advised an immediate double mastectomy, but, Debra said that she would rather die. Instead of surgery, she underwent massive doses of chemo and radiation. Three months later, Debra suffered excruciating pain, and slept restlessly twenty-four hours a day. To overcome her pain, she concentrated on painting.

I wondered what the Holy Spirit had in store for me as I carried my table into her apartment. Debra greeted me at the door, and was most appreciative for my coming to help relieve her pain.

I quickly set up my table and Debra settled onto it. But, when I placed my hands over her, she screamed and arose sobbing. I comforted her, and after several minutes, she lay down. This was not what I had in mind: I had come to relieve pain, not to accelerate it.

The phone rang, and it was Debra's mother, who called from Columbus, Ohio, to ask if Debra was all right. She had felt her daughter's pain from 2400 miles away! After Debra assured her mother that she was okay,, we continued the session.

I touched Debra again, and she whimpered in pain. But, I kept my hands on her, and the pain stopped after five minutes. Then, I moved my hands over her in another location, and once again, she arose and screamed in agony. I asked her if we should stop, but, she insisted that we continue. The message that I received was that the chemo was deposited in every cell in her body. Her nerves were sensitive to my energy, resulting in increased pain.

Slowly, I worked on Debra's body, through many cycles of screaming pain and gradual relief. I was sure that at any moment the neighbors would begin pounding on the front door to find out what was happening, but, they never did. As the session went on, Debra learned to overcome the sharp pain, knowing that it would soon dissipate. The hot energy in my hands increased dramatically, probably from the transfer of Debra's painful energy to me.

Three and a half hours later, I had energized her entire body, and the pain was gone. Debra requested that I repeat the process to be sure that I had not missed any sensitive areas. In that last hour, she felt no further pain, and she said that she felt peace, as she had never known it.

After two pain-free weeks, Debra called me, and said that the pain had returned, and she requested another session. This time, she did not scream. Over the next year, I traveled to Portland to give her sessions, and each time, there was a longer pain-free time between sessions. Finally, the phone calls ceased.

I called Debra several months later, to find out how she was, but, her phone was disconnected. When I stopped by her apartment, I learned that she had moved. Once again, I was reminded that I had to divorce myself from the outcome. Whether the person passed on to heaven, or was healed, my mission was to bring peace and pain relief, and then to move on to the next person divinely sent to me by the Holy Spirit.

The flow of people in need of healing continues in endless synchronicity. I never know what the mission, the ailment, or the result will be. I consider this separation from the outcome to be my complete surrender to the Holy Spirit.

In August 2006, I heard from the person who had first placed me in contact with Debra eight years before. She said that Debra's breast cancer had been in remission for several years, but, it had returned with a vengeance earlier that year, and Debra had died August 9, 2006.

Healing in the Sky

In the summer of 1998, I was fully immersed in numerous cases of healing, including helping June to a peaceful ascent to heaven. For many months, Ruth and I had planned a trip to Europe, and we were both excited to go. In the back of my mind, I was hesitant to leave my healing practice, and as we prepared for the trip, I silently prayed for the opportunity to do a healing during the three-week trip. Little did I suspect how quickly Spirit would intervene, and present me with an opportunity?

Six hours into the nine-hour flight to Paris, we had finished our dinners, and most travelers were settled into sleep. Suddenly, a man on the far side of the plane, in the same row that we were in, began to make loud guttural sounds. Passengers squirmed uncomfortably, and became angry, as the sounds were louder and louder. The flight attendants tried to calm him, but, he just got louder.

Sleep was impossible! The plane was a torture chamber.

Thoughts rushed through my mind. Was this the healing experience that I anticipated?

From prior experience, I knew that God was a comedian. I asked myself if this was His way of having a joke at my expense? Or, was it a test of my resolve to carry out the mission of Spirit.

The question was whether I would surrender to this obvious need for healing, or whether I would continue to cower in my seat, and try to ignore the unpleasant circumstances, together with the other 150 passengers. Would I respond to the Holy Spirit's request? Ruth, who had, until now, been less than enthusiastic about my healing experiences, elbowed me in the ribs and said, "Go do it!"

Finally, I arose, made my way to the other side of the plane, and as I walked, I observed the discomfort of my fellow passengers. Not a one slept!

When I arrived at his seat, I found a man with Down syndrome, over six feet tall, and very husky. He looked at me, and snarled in anger. The sounds became louder and even more irritating, as I placed my right hand on his shoulder and my left hand on his wrist.

I dared not speak, as I thought that any sound I made might be interpreted as combative. Closing my eyes, I quieted my mind to let peace and healing energy flow through. I surrendered completely to the Almighty to guide me through this peculiar experience. Through my hands, I felt the forces of evil confront the forces of good within the man's body. I knew that good will always win, so I kept my hands firmly in place.

Over the course of fifteen minutes, the sounds dissipated. Finally, peace came across the man's face, and he was quiet. Without ever having spoken a word, I returned to my seat, and observed that every passenger was asleep, completely drained from the experience. No one said a word to me.

Just before we landed in Paris, two flight attendants brought me the largest bottle of champagne that I had ever seen, and they told me that they had been at a loss as to what to do. They had discussed the matter with the captain, but, he had never dealt with a problem like this one. The rest of the passengers had complained, and it looked as if it were to be three hours of misery. The flight attendants were delighted that I had stepped forward to help them, in what was an otherwise impossible situation.

Over the years, having been involved in hundreds of healings, I have learned to accept whatever the Holy Spirit and the angels send me. I never know what is in store, but, I can proceed with confidence, as I know that God's love always wins over the evil advanced by Satan. I know, too, that I must obey Spirit, no matter the consequences, and I trust that Spirit will carry me through, no matter how far outside the realm of my own understanding I transcend.

Religious Faith Keeps a Patient Away

In October 1999, I attended a conference in Bend, given by Lee Carroll (www.kyron.com), and during the break, I met Laura, a long-time healer from Bend. She asked me to see a healing patient, Zahra, an eighty-two-year-old Jewish woman.

Her niece had driven her from Salem to the healing conference, in the hope that she would find someone who could relieve her of the arthritic pain she had suffered twenty-four hours a day for many years. Medications had provided no relief, and her pain increased daily. Zahra had reached the point of thinking that death was her only option, when she heard of the healing conference. Zahra met Laura during lunch, and decided to entrust herself with a healing session.

Laura asked me to assist in a joint session with Zahra. Whenever two healers work together, the impact is vastly more powerful. Within a few minutes on the table, Zahra said that she was pain-free, and that she felt an amazing peace throughout her body. When we completed the session, she was euphoric, and she was going home to Salem pain-free for the first time in many years.

Two weeks later, Zahra called and asked if I could come to Salem and give her another session, as the pain had returned. When I came to her door with my table the following day, her niece greeted me, delighted that I had come. Once again, the pain was gone in a few minutes, and Zahra expressed her appreciation for the session. She was somewhat upset that I refused gas money, or any other compensation, for my time.

Three weeks later, Zahra's niece called, and said that her aunt suffered again. She offered to bring Zahra to Corvallis for a session, which we scheduled for the next week.

The day before the scheduled session, Zahra called to say that she was not coming. She had talked with her rabbi, and told him how thrilled she was to be pain-free. The rabbi had told her that it was evil for any common person to heal another, and that it must be done in the prescribed Jewish way. So, despite her increased pain, Zahra cancelled her session with me.

About a month later, Zahra's niece called to say that Zahra had died. I felt extremely sad to know that, in her last weeks, she had suffered. But, my mission had been to give her some pain-free days before she died. I had fulfilled what the Holy Spirit had asked of me, and I could only be grateful for the brief role that I had played in Zahra's life.

My experience with Zahra had one very rewarding outcome: Zahra's niece referred her nineteen year-old friend, Sky, to me, which led to a most remarkable healing.

Soon after Zahra passed away, Sky called me to request a session the next day. We spent about an hour in my healing space, and discussed life's journeys before Sky was mentally ready for her healing.

In a healing session, most people's energy begins to flow within fifteen to thirty seconds. I was surprised to find that Sky, who appeared to be a healthy nineteen- year-old, had almost no energy flow for nearly five minutes. Finally, the first trickle of energy began, and slowly developed into a steady flow. Nearly three hours later, about an hour longer than normal, Sky's energy flowed steadily left to right, and I completed the session.

Sky seemed to be in a trance when she finally sat up on the table. Her entire being radiated an incredibly beautiful energy, and her smile revealed a different person from the one three hours before.

Then, Sky told me a part of her life's story that she had not revealed in our initial conversation. She had begun taking recreational drugs when she was fourteen, and she had tried almost every drug in the ensuing five years. She had totally ruined her life, and was alienated from her parents, who had told her not to come home until she was ready to straighten out her life. Sky said that the experience on my table had taken her to a level far higher than any drug had ever taken her, and that she now realized the error of her ways. She would never take another drug, as long as she lived!

Sky reflected that she felt as if she had just been born again. She was eager to return to her parents, whom she had not seen in more than a year, and to ask their forgiveness.

As with several others, I never heard from Sky again. Spirit reminded me that I am to divorce myself from the outcomes of my healing. In Spirit's timing, I may or may not ever know what Sky's life journey became, but, I received a measure of peace from realizing that my time spent with Zahra may have led to the divine resurrection of Sky's life.

A Stroke Victim's Recovery

Painting by Kay in 1938 at the age of 12 year after nuns taught her to paint in a parochial school in Iowa. This was her first painting. After her passing, the painting was loaned to me by her husband, Wayne. The painting hung in my healing space for about seven years and now hangs over my desk as I have written my life's journey.

Kay, a seventy-eight-year-old friend of forty-eight years, had a series of strokes in December 2004. She was hospitalized for most of the next six months, her condition worsened as more strokes occurred, and in 2005, she was sent home to die, with her husband as primary caregiver.

I called him to ask if he would consider energy healing, and he was most enthusiastic, so, and we scheduled a time for the next day.

When I arrived, I was not mentally prepared for Kay's condition. She was in a hospital bed in the front room, and she was almost comatose, unable to move, and barely able to mumble a few words. She did not recognize me or understand what I was there to do, and her eyes reflected fear.

As we lifted her to my table she began to sob, as many stroke victims do. When I placed my hands over her still body, her muscles began to twitch in many places.

From my prior experiences, the answer came to me that my energy was awakening her seven chakra energy centers, which were, in turn, awakening the sub-chakra energy centers throughout her body. Then, the message came to me to place my hands on her third eye chakra center, which extends from above and between her eyes to the medulla at the base of her brain. The energy flow commenced slowly at first, and then exploded between my hands, and her body began to move even more noticeably. (I adopted this technique for all my patients thereafter, spending an especially long time in the third-eye chakra center of migraine headache victims.)

I gave Kay two more sessions, and with each one, her body moved more, and she ceased to cry . By the fourth session, Kay had progressed to the point that she no longer needed the hospital bed. She recognized me, and was able to say my name. A few sessions later, she was able, with a walker, to stroll with her husband. The highlight for me was when she looked up from the table and said, "I like it when you put your hands on me."

Over the next fifteen months, Kay made significant progress. She was able to talk, and looked forward to each session. Kay lived for three years after her first session, with the last session given in extreme care.

From my experience with Kay, I was reinforced in my understanding that the seven chakra centers are the key to health. As aging, stress and other causes slow down the energy centers, the body becomes vulnerable to illnesses and the immune system weakens. Energy healing awakens the energy centers of the body, speeds up cellular production, and restores the body's ability to heal itself.

Our bodies consist of an estimated seven trillion cells and the body completely reproduces itself every year with billions of cells created daily. My energy healing experiences convince me that we all have immense control over the production of cells in our own bodies and thus our own healing. Normally, the first step in the healing process is to decide you want to heal and take charge of our own healing.

Elementals

Jerry was referred to me in January 2007, after she had suffered for more than a year with extreme right-side pain, which extended from her right foot all the way up the right side of her torso and to her head. Many specialists had examined her, but, none had arrived at a diagnosis. Numerous medications had left her with unpleasant side effects, but, no discernible relief from her pain.

My first step was to evaluate her energy field. As I brought my hands over her right side, I noted a cold blast of air, an energy blockage, in her right groin. I confirmed with her that it was all right to touch her to determine what was going on in that area.

When I put my hand on the cold spot, I discovered a very hard lump about an inch under the skin. It was like a piece of iron the shape of a slug, about three inches long. My energy exploded into the area, creating a strong throbbing over the cold spot. The area was soon warm, and the pulsation increased in intensity. Jerry felt the heat, and experienced an explosion of energy up and down her entire right side.

For more than fifteen minutes the area throbbed, as my hands grew hotter and hotter. As the session drew to a close, Jerry said that she was pain-free throughout her body, and that she felt a strong sense of peace and release.

I advised Jerry to have an ultrasound as soon as possible, to get a medical evaluation of her right groin area. The next week, when she came for another session, she told me an ultrasound had revealed that she had a gas bubble in the area of the hard spot. This did not make sense to me.

Jerry said that her pain had returned about five days after our first session. When I did an energy assessment, there was no cold blast where the hard spot had been the week before, and when I touched the area, the lump was gone. But, now I felt another cold blast of air about an inch below her navel, going straight up her torso. This lump was larger than the last one, about four inches long, and just as hard. Could this be the same lump in a different form? Again the area drained my energy, and the throbbing began. In a short time, Jerry's pain was gone.

The following Sunday, I visited the Beaverton healing group and talked to David, a longtime energy-healing enthusiast, about this experience. David knew right away what it meant. He said that Jerry had been infiltrated by negative forces; the hard spot was a collection of negative energy, like a black demon. That blob of energy was a parasite, it grew as it collected more evil, and caused increased pain to Jerry.

David guessed that Jerry must spend time around negative people. Correct! Jerry worked with young children as a mental health counselor, and she constantly took in the negative energy that penetrated them.

Positive energy always knows where to go, and my energy poured into Jerry, where the negative forces had accumulated, David said. After I chased out the black energy during the first session, the blob had moved to another location. When it was bombarded a second time by my positive energy, the black demon had quickly dissipated, and David surmised that this time it was gone for good.

The next week, when Jerry came in for her third session, I could find no blocked energy field. The demon had been cast out, and Jerry was pain-free! I was, once again, reminded that the power of the Holy Spirit is always stronger than evil in any form. As always, when I complete a session, I continued to build an energy shield around Jerry, to prevent negative forces from an attack in the future. Four years later, she was still pain-free, and I believe that she will remain so.

After my sessions with Jerry, I studied the topic of elementals -- black elementals, representing the evil and negative forces, and golden elementals, the positive force of the Holy Spirit. Two weeks later, I encountered a situation that helped broaden my understanding of these potent opposing energies.

I was asked to participate in healing a person who was inflicted with a rare, aggressive cancer that ordinarily kills within thirty days. The session was observed by a woman who "sees" divine energy, including the presence of Jesus. During the session, she observed the golden elementals that were healing the person, and she saw that Jesus assisted in the healing. She also observed that many angels, all the colors of the rainbow, participated as well.

Eight months later, the patient was pronounced cancer-free. That encounter, along with my experience with Jerry, opened a new world of understanding for me, assisting me to recognize that there are both black negative and golden positive energy forces in the world that are known as elementals.

The Colors of the Angels

I awoke at 3:00 A.M. on April 7, 2007, bursting with divine energy as the light of the nearly full moon cascaded into my bedroom. The bright purple colors of the plum tree danced across my bedroom, as a gentle breeze caressed the branches, reflecting the brightness of the moon and the streetlight above the tree.

The happenings of the last three days flowed through my mind, as my flock of angels revealed new insights to me. I knew that I must set tax season aside, and record the events as quickly as possible.

Saturday March 31 began at 4:00 A.M., as I arose to begin work on three tax returns that I had set as my goal to finish before 1:00 P.M., as that was the time I wanted to watch the first of three Oregon State University Beaver women's softball games over the next three days.

Little did I know what the angels had in mind for me this day!

My plans for the day were soon interrupted as angelic timing took control.

The first tax return proved more difficult than I had planned, and I soon realized that I was missing information to complete the return.

The second tax return, which also had more complexities than I had anticipated, was finally completed around noon. I was ready to assemble the return when I received a phone call that my daughter-in-law needed me to assist her in purchasing a car.

I abandoned my tax returns, switched gears, and searched the net for auto possibilities. The best buy was over a hundred miles away in Vancouver, Washington. Shortly thereafter, Edith, and my granddaughters, Elise and Danielle, and I drove north to search for a new car for Edith.

Several hours later, after searching through an inventory over three thousand cars, and not connecting with the car that we had come to investigate, we finally discovered the car that all four of us agreed was the car that we should buy.

Haggling began over the price, but, an hour later, we finally agreed, the seemingly endless paperwork was completed about 10:15 P.M., and we headed back to Oregon.

It was near midnight, as I settled into bed at my daughter's condo in Wilsonville where I had no plans to be when I awakened nearly twenty hours earlier to work on tax returns!

Almost immediately, I felt my back second abdomen chakra open to a white light about three inches across.

The second chakra center bubbled with energy, and amazingly, included about three vertebras. For five minutes the chakra center bubbled like a pot of porridge. The bright orange color of the chakra soon replaced the white. As in the past, when the chakra colors took control of my being, the brilliance of the orange color radiated in my mind that the beauty of the colors were beyond the mind's comprehension.

The message that I received from Holy Spirit was that the colors were really angels dancing in their angelic colors of the rainbow/chakra centers of my body.

The message from my angels was that I was about to encounter a divine healing event.

Sunday, after awakening at 6:00 A.M., I struggled to recover from the long day previously, and decided that it was time for breakfast. I called my friend Sherry, to ask if she planned to attend a Full Moon Ceremony Sunday night in Portland, eighty miles from Corvallis. Sherry was to attend, and she invited me to meet her friend, Cindy, who is an energy healer and an angelic reader.

I met Cindy, and as we talked, she asked if I would give a session to her son's mother-in-law, Tommy, who had been diagnosed with a rare aggressive cancer two weeks before. I agreed, and the next morning I found myself driving thirty miles from Portland to do a healing session with a person whom I had never met before.

When I met Tommy, I saw a woman whose energy field was dominated by fear and bewilderment. She looked dazed, as if she had been hit by a ball bat!

As I looked around her room, I saw an entryway that indicated the style of a woman with the highest degree of class. Then, I observed her daughter, about ten, who looked frightened, and appeared to be ready to burst into tears over the possible loss of her mother.

I immediately sensed that Tommy was a beautiful soul, whose energy had been drained in giving to the point that she had left herself vulnerable to cancer. She had already had her first chemo treatment, was exhausted, and fearful of what the future might bring.

Tommy's beautiful spirit radiated from her energy field, and I sensed that this woman had the will to heal, no matter her doctors' prognosis. The message that I received from Spirit was that a blend of our energy fields would produce a divine healing for her.

I carried my table upstairs to a remote bedroom, and set it up where Cindy, Tommy, a relative from afar, and I were ready to receive the healing blessings of the Holy Spirit. I explained to Tommy how GOD created our bodies with the built-in power to heal ourselves, how energy healing worked, and soon we were ready for the session.

As I worked on Tommy, I sensed the colors of the chakras float in and out of my being, I sensed her beautiful energy that exchanged with my energy, and at the same time, I was aware of countless negative entities and the dreaded chemo being cast out of her.

Several hours later, a smile of perfect peace radiated from Tommy's face. The stress in her face in the beginning was replaced with a serene smile that indicated that Tommy's body had produced countless healthy new cells.

Tommy's daughter entered the room, observed her mother, and from the look on her face, I immediately sensed that she thought that her mother was going to be all right.

When I finished, as is usual with prior patients, Tommy did not want to move, so as to preserve her tranquil state.

Later, Cindy who had observed the session and had participated in the session, related to me that she had observed many colorful angels arising from Tommy's chakra centers and she observed negativity being cast out of Tommy. Cindy also observed the presence of Jesus filling the room with his Divine Healing Power assisting in Tommy's healing.

This morning as I awoke and reviewed the divine events of the prior three days, the message came to me that when the colors are "seen" by anyone, what they are really seeing is the color of divine angels that dwell in everyone's chakra centers.

This explains why, when the colors of the angels appear in a person, their beauty is beyond comprehension. It is like a glimpse of heaven on Earth.

What is exciting is that everyone has the power to bring forth these angels, upon their acceptance and release of their minds to a higher power, as God created us all.

With hindsight, I would not exchange my healing session with Tommy for the entire Oregon State University softball season.

During the next eight months, I continued to send angelic healing to Tommy, laced with prayers of healing from the almighty.

UPDATE On December 19, 2007, I learned that Tommy had been pronounced cancer- **free**! Hallelujah!!!!

UPDATE September 21, 2008, I received the sad news that Tommy died on September 17, 2008, the cancer had returned with a vengeance, and chemo had not saved her. A part of me went to heaven with her, and I was sad that I had had only one opportunity to heal Tommy. As in the past, my message from Spirit was to divorce myself from the outcome.

I was given a mission, and that was to give Tommy a measure of peace and precious months before she passed into heaven.

Cindy participated in Tommy's healing, and she recorded her vision of the session:

I sent Tommy a letter from me, and also a transmittal from the Voice called God. Following this I had a vision. I wrote as I experienced the vision. The following is the vision.

Instead of an MRI machine, I see Tommy in a crystal cave of extraordinary beauty. Crystals-gold elementals-sparkling light of purity-vibrating ecstasy throughout Tommy's body. Actinic purification revelation of solar expression expanding conscious awareness of oneness with all of creation. Sonic bloom of God flame into the world of form changing molecular structure through Universes polishing the multi-faced diamonds of creative energy illuminating the God Self in all patterns of energy-transforming-transmuting-revealing pure love in its entire splendor.

With Tommy, I see Mother Mary Magdalene and Jesus. Vernon and I are holding hands with a Rainbow bridge flowing between the palms of our hands.

The souls expressing with Tommy in this life time are present and join hands with Vernon and me-creating a circle of energy flowing through our heart centers forming the rainbow bridge of connectedness around Tommy.

From the solar plexus of each of us, the pure love created by the rainbow bridge flows to Tommy and back again, a continuum. The angels are singing the Praises of God — Glory Halleluiah-the birth of Christ through every human- the true revelation of pure innocence proclamation.

As I "see" - this happening I know it's truly creating cellular regeneration of perfection.

I "hear" For three days all present will have miraculous revelations and manifestations.

Comments by Cindy

My feeling is her focus needs to be on Peace, Beauty, and Happiness with lots of laughter.

My experience has been when one focuses on fighting something or declaring war on something-i.e. cancer-that is where their focus is and their vibration is and that affects cellular vibration- to me it is a contradiction to Peace.

If anything, it is working with the ascended masters –Angels and personal healing team (white Brotherhood) that I introduce.

My Best Blessings Cindy

Part 7: Testimonials

From Randy

Dear Vernon,

Traci told me that you would like me to write down my experience I had at your energy healing session. She said you were compiling a book. Good for you. First off, I would like to thank you again for all the help you have given me. Traci is a very dear friend of mine. The two of you, have helped me get back on the road to my life. I have been depressed and overwhelmed in the past several months. When Traci recommended I receive a healing session, I was skeptical. Afterwards I was in disbelief. But my world seems to be coming together and I now have a lot of optimism. When I had the pleasure of your session, my confidence and positive attitude is getting stronger. I just wanted to prelude the description of my experience, with a heartfelt and sincere thank you.

Now on to my amazing experience:

It was October 4th of 2007. I never really talked to Traci about what went on in her sessions, other than she said she always felt so much better afterwards. I thought it was going to be more like a relaxing massage. Not the total out of body adventure, which I experienced. It started out on my way to your office I was thinking about all the worries I had facing me. I felt like I couldn't relax, and not stress out over them. But I told myself when I got there; I was going to not think about any of them. I remember lying down on the table and wondering more about what I could experience, when everything else just disappeared. I felt a little anxious and nervous.

When I lay down and you put my feet into the vibrating chi machine, I wondered how the machine was going to relax me. But as I started to open up my mind, I felt myself start to limber up and relax. As I started to let myself go with the motion back and forth, and not resist, I began to get comfortable with the energy level and feeling that was coming over me. I closed my eyes gently and felt myself start to drift in and out like I was getting sleepy. I was still totally aware of everything that you were doing and what was going on around me. When you started to try and open up my flow of energy you replied that you felt blocked energy flow. I didn't understand at first but it made sense as I thought more about it. I seemed to really open up when you were running the vibrating pads all over me. When I say open up, that's when I felt my energy in my body start to build. It seemed the more I was drifting away into a different plain, the more energy I was building up. I felt myself start to go numb all over like I could not feel myself lying on the table. It was as if I was floating and there was no gravity holding me down. I remember feeling as if I was not in my body and just an energy field emanating all around the room.

I remember when you put the crystal bowls on my chest I could feel them there but felt no weight of them. The feeling I got when you chimed the first one was outrageous. It started out as a chime and turned into a harmonic tone. When it changed, I felt as if my energy was entwined in the tone as it reveled around the room. Every time you did that exercise with the bowls I experienced the same effect but more intense with the different pitches.

As you were talking I could hear you and comprehend, but felt as if I were asleep. You explained the reason for the tuning fork to target certain areas of your body that needed healing. I didn't talk to you prior to my session about my health so you could not have known where I needed to be healed. When you chimed the fork and touched me with it I felt a tingle radiate down to my right kidney and a tingling sensation start there. I have two cysts in my right kidney that are a stage two concern to my doctor. They are the size of a softball and hardball and growing and changing slowly. We are watching them at this stage. I felt lighter tingles to other areas of my body. I realized later it was in areas of previous surgery or injury.

I remember hearing you tell Traci, that you wondered how I would feel after my nap, when I woke up. I wanted to say I wasn't asleep, but didn't because I didn't want to come out of the plain of energy I was immersed in. so I chose to stay in the conscious yet oblivious state. I felt as if I was on a journey of some kind out of my body and floating, yet I was all around the room, aware, present and part of what was going on. You slowed down on the things you were doing to me and I just felt out a sense of peace and tranquility that I have never experienced. When you started to bring me out, or wake me up as you thought, I felt like I didn't want to come back to reality. It was such a comfortable and peaceful feeling. When I opened my eyes again, I felt relaxed and not tired. When I wake up from a nap, I usually fight and feel like I should sleep more. When I came to, I felt as if I had slept for hours, refreshed and recharged. Who would have thought considering I was awake and told both you and Traci things you were discussing.

You sincerely have been blessed with a gift. I am glad you choose to share it with others. I have told Traci that when I give people back rubs it relaxes me, because I can feel my muscles opening up and relaxing. So I can appreciate what it does for you. Since then my life has taken on a calm feeling. I don't seem to let life's stressors get to me as much. I have a newborn confidence and excitement about what is to unfold for me, and a belief that it will all work out. I don't seem to have the negative energy consuming me as much.

Thank you for helping me get in touch with myself, and learning to appreciate life more for what it has in store, and less of what it is doing to me. Keep up the work and may God bless you. Randy

From Sara Wiseman

As a healer, Vernon Bowlby moves himself aside in complete service, to act as a Divine conduit of the highest level. The healing energy he channels is pure and true; miracles arrive to those who work with him.

—Sara Wiseman, Author & Intuitive

From Cathy

Good morning Vernon and Happy New Year!
I took my Ninety-year-old mother to the retina specialist yesterday for her third injection. He told her there was no noticeable improvement and if there wasn't any in six weeks he would discontinue treatment.

She told me afterwards that the only thing that really helped her was her session with you. She said that she really believes that a few sessions with you is the answer for the restoration of her vision. For a very long time following her session with you her back was pain free along with the discomfort in her ankles.

She hit bottom last night and put everything in God's hands. Considering some other new Earth healers here in Portland, She said the angels told her that you are the #1 choice for her. She really felt that and they confirmed it.

So, on my mother's behalf I am sending this e-mail to you to ask if you would be willing to work on her again when you come to this area. My best blessings to you and please give my best to your assistants! Cathy

From Jennifer

When I began seeing Vernon, I'd been suffering from six years of chronic headaches. I was living a life in which pain seemed to take away, over time, everything I loved to do: play with my young children, exercise, teach, write, and travel. I had lost my self-confidence, my ability to be spontaneous, and my reserves of patience. I felt stiff and "stuck"—physically and symbolically. In my very first session with him, Vernon eased some of that too-familiar pain in a way that no doctor, chiropractor, physical therapist, massage therapist, or acupuncturist had been able to for years. After each session, I left feeling healthier and more confident. Now, thanks to Vernon, I'm completely off all the preventive medications I was taking. I'm able to do everything I'd missed, and more. I'm no longer bound by pain; I've had tremendous teaching and publishing success; my family and I travel together and return each time to a new sense of peace in our home. I'll always be grateful for the way Vernon launched me back into life. Jennifer

From Joan

I was really pleased to hear from my husband about Vern's gift of healing. They play golf together and had told Vern about my shingles that was left untreated for a week thinking it was poison oak. My physician informed me that because it was not treated immediately the pain would likely linger for some time. I was excited about working with Vern and looked forward to my first session.

The following are my feelings and impressions from my four healing sessions.

Session one: Not knowing what to expect I was a bit tense for a few minutes but soon could relax and feel the healing take place. My first major feeling was after the Chi Machine had finished and I felt a bubbling sensation from my toes through the top of my head. When you shake a bottle of pop and all the fizz comes to the top describes the feeing. The rest of the session was focusing on whatever chakra Vern's healing hands were working on. I really focused hard on giving my body the will to heal. At the end of the session when I stood up my back felt really straight for the first time in years and the intense pain from the shingles was better.

Session two: I was able to cooperate mentally in the healing process and felt the flow from chakra to chakra. My back and neck continued to feel stronger at the end of this session. The pain from the shingles was now tolerable and the rash disappearing.

Session three: At the end of this session I almost jumped off the table and said "I feel 21 again". There was such a flow of energy thorough out my entire body. My shingles were almost gone with pain and rash was still diminishing

Session four: My upper back, shoulders and neck seemed to benefit the most from this session. When I do not stand tall with head back, I now get a slight pain in my upper back which seems to remind me to "stand up" and now it goes away when I oblige.

The healing session with Vern has been an incredible experience and left me pain free and standing tall once again. Thank you, thank you, thank you Vern, for sharing your energy and opening up for me much more than my blocked chakras. And thanks to you I am now learning to work with my own energy with a new perspective on health and healing. Joan

From Marion

Dear Vern,

Thank you so much for your expertise of turning a ninety-seven-year-old lady into an eighty-five- year old NEW lady!
It was a most memorable operation, AND so good!
I feel like I am born again - "new parts" and "fixed parts."

No Pain! No Swelling! Wow!

Corvallis certainly has changed since we first came. I remember when the Bowlby Building was built -- a big deal in developing Corvallis.

We miss Jim and Scotty -"the good old days" were so special, a beautiful town - everyone knew everyone.

Thank you, again, for making an "old lady" feel so well that it has encouraged her to "keep on trucking." Love, Marion

From Jack

In 2002, during the pre-op for a routine arthroscopic knee surgery ("old guy basketball repair") it was discovered that my white blood count was elevated.

The surgeon said the most likely cause was an uncommon leukemia known as CLL -Chronic Lymphocytic Leukemia. This was soon thereafter confirmed through a diagnostic blood test.

I was 53 at the time, toward the young end of diagnosis for this disease. My diagnosis was classic, as CLL is typically found through routine blood tests rather than any symptoms. One of the so-called "indolent lymphomas," CLL has many forms and is very complex. While not as immediately dangerous as ALL (Acute Leukemia), there are aggressive forms of the disease and it has historically been considered incurable in the long term.

I had the very good fortune to be referred to an exceptional oncologist, Dr. Peter Kenyon, who predicted - accurately as it turned out - that it would be about seven years before I would require treatment. Fortunately, I had a slowly progressing variant of CLL.

Accordingly, we (this now being very much a joint effort with my wife) entered a long period known as "watch and wait." For reasons having to do with the efficacy of repeated treatments, the traditional approach is to wait until treatment is required by symptoms, typically fatigue, persistent infections, and the like.

What I failed to do, although it only became clear to me in hindsight, was to truly take charge of my own healing. I had confidence in my doctor -justified, as it turned out -and a vague conviction that medicine would come to my rescue. I would await cure.

Alas, despite abundant hopefulness and early stabilization in my white blood counts, the vaccine eventually proved ineffective and my counts began to rise again. (Distressingly, they seemed to jump dramatically as if to make up for lost time.)

By mid-2008, it was clear that I was headed shortly for treatment. It was in this period that some providential spirit brought me into contact with Vern Bowlby. My wife casually overheard an acquaintance describing a healer who had cured his wife of a persistent and painful disability that resisted all medical treatment.

By the time I first saw Vern Bowlby, the CLL had progressed significantly and I was weakened, probably more than I realized. (Vern afterwards told me, as did others, how pale and ill I looked in this period.) Vern provided me energy healing sessions over the weeks before treatment, and then again during the five month treatment course.

This story does not have the miracle ending if by miracle you mean the lightning strike cure. Vern did not undo seven years of disease progression. I still required medical treatment within a few months.

What energy healing did for me was change the larger equation - the part I was playing in my healing - profoundly. After the first energy healing session - which ironically left me tired and sore despite the absence of physical contact - I began to realize I had been waiting to be healed. Vern helped my body energize to heal. I am convinced these few energy healing sessions - there wasn't time for more - revived my immune system, so that eventual treatment was powerful and (I genuinely believe) enduring.

Energy healing also fired up my spirit and my psyche, so that I could go through treatment optimistically, suffering uncommonly minor and infrequent side effects. Cautions that each treatment would leave me more weakened proved wrong - in fact, I was getting stronger daily. My hair didn't fall out.

Most of all, aligning my energy flows truly gave me the power to be, as Vern observed, "in charge of my own healing." I was no longer a patient being treated. I was focused on getting better, and I could and did express the instinctual messages my body was relaying. It felt right too. It was determination, not desperation. It was arising from inside.

Getting better and I could and did express the instinctual messages my body was relaying. It felt right too. It was determination, not desperation. It was arising from inside.

I think in retrospect my experience with energy healing - and a session Vern offered Alice - also helped her in the essential part she had in helping me get better. As she saw me grow more focused on healing, she became more determined and confident in her role as "care manager." It was an invaluable part of my treatment and recovery.

This idea is hard to express, and I am sure some will find it vague. I would have too, before experiencing it. For me it is very clear and very certain. I have a wonderful and very skilled physician. The nurses who treated me are the finest people in Oregon. The energy healing sessions with Vern helped me take what was offered by traditional medicine and put it to work in my life in a way that, looking back, feels nearly miraculous.

One year after treatment, the latest check up: "Your blood counts look fabulous."

Update June 20, 2013 -message from Jack

Hello Vern, I hope you are well and even finding time for golf in this crazy weather. I've been meaning to update you. I started on a new drug 8 weeks ago and have been feeling good. Yesterday we got the first CT scan since then and it showed -- for the first time ever -- reductions in the size of my abdominal lymph nodes. This hasn't happened since I got the damn disease! Of course we are really happy. I am convinced the energy healing kept me going and prepared me for this, so I remain very grateful to you! Jack

From Lark

I wanted to send a quick email before work. I am at a loss for how to thank you for your kindness and generous nature. You are a rare gift, and to spend so much of your time and energy helping people. I feel blessed to have been introduced to you and what you do.

Hugs, Lark

From Sue

Dear Vernon

There is no way I can thank you enough for the session this morning. It left me feeling amazingly better after I kind of woke up.
I am walking better and feel happier and more able to deal with everything that comes my way. My legs do not hurt as they have been.
My feet are actually warm!
Thank you again for your sharing your special gift of healing with me.
Sincerely, Sue

From Elise

Dear Vern,

I want to thank you again for your gift you give so freely and for helping me today. It is rare to see this level of generosity. I will be looking over the books you mention. Interesting, I'm feeling localized sensation in my spleen area; left upper quadrant. This corresponds to the "collapsed Earth" aspect I experience given the Chinese meridians and where I need to generate better energy flow.
Take good care. I still feel light as a cloud! Elise

From Lue

Hi Vern,

It was such a pleasure to meet you (twice!) and I wanted to say thank you for the wonderful session you did for me. It was really amazing and wonderful how opened and aligned I felt afterwards, and continue to feel. I think I went into a deep healing state, like a meditative trance -- I was aware of what was happening, but was so very relaxed, and tuning in to what was happening internally. It is such a beautiful state of being that I really didn't want to leave it and get up off the table! :) It was incredible to receive such a powerful session. Thank you and I'll be sure to contact you the next time I'm coming to town. Lue

Part 8: Mission Statement and My History of Healing

My mission statement and patient agreement signed before healing sessions is as follows:

I am not a doctor, nor am I licensed to do massage, or any other procedure, that requires a state license. I consider a session to be as friend- to -friend.

My first mission in the pre-session is to empower persons to heal themselves and to assist them to relieve pain, and "jump start" their bodies so that, within themselves, they can heal from any malady.

*I do not charge for healing, since I consider that the healing energy that I dispense is directly from the **Holy Spirit**. I consider myself merely the conduit of the flow of Divine Energy.*

To do energy healing, I have, since 1993, learned many techniques.

I have discovered that all energy healing methods accomplish the same thing, and that is to get meridians of energy flow to dissipate blockages created by stress, injuries, meds, chemicals, toxins, bereavement, and poisons that have accumulated in muscles throughout the body.

Deep tissue massage is often utilized to release poisons, toxins, and medication from the muscles to be released into the blood stream and out of the body, which is greatly enhanced by drinking alkaline water.

My sessions generally emulate that of one that I received in 1999, in Istanbul at a 1,500 year-old Turkish bathhouse. It had been one half massage, and one half energy healing. Sessions normally commence on the acupuncture table for thirty minutes, followed by an hour on the healing table, for a total of ninety minutes, unless there is significant pain, or if doctor has considered the patient terminal.

The **goal** is to evaluate each person as to their specific needs, and to apply procedures as I am guided by Spirit.

Knowledge and Understanding of how the body functions is as follows:

Chakras are to be fired up, or to say it another way – to restart/recharge the seven major chakra energy centers (which have a similar function as a car battery) with a strong emphasis on the thymus gland, that controls the immune system, distributes healing T cells throughout the body, and is "hard wired" to the brain, as well as all organs and muscles throughout the body. Each chakra controls a specific area of the body.

Balance energy flow- Eastern medicine discovered about ten thousand years ago that feminine energy flows on the left side of the body, and masculine energy flows on the right side. It was also recognized that the thymus gland was the key to body health.

When these two energies do not flow in tandem, the chakra center involved slows down, and results in a physical medical problem. (My granddaughter's two- inch- thick high school science book, that includes considerable information regarding the human body, does not include the word "thymus".)

Pain is the body's attempt to heal itself, and it should be blessed, rather than feared. Chronic pain occurs when the energy flow is blocked, and the body increases its attempts to heal itself, which results in increased pain.

Tumors and other growths can be located anywhere in the body, and they are the result of blocked energy, and in some cases, they are blobs of negative energy that have accumulated. Many times, I have located such growths that have been reduced substantially with gentle manipulations. Sometimes, they disappear entirely, and release energy to flow naturally.

Bottom-line- All physical shortcomings of the body can be cured by energy healing, when the patient accepts the empowerment to heal from the Holy Spirit.

I have experienced healings within persons of numerous forms of cancer, including leukemia, breast cancer, lung cancer, with tumor growths the size of pears, and in some cases, advanced cancer throughout the body.

Other specific healings include relief of all types of pain including migraine headaches, surgery recovery, shingles, fibromyalgia, death bed relief of pain and fevers, strokes, depression, mental illness, *chronic fatigue, tumors dissipated, and numerous other body malfunctions.*

The patient is to be in control of the session at all times, and if any procedure is uncomfortable, the patient can inform me immediately.

The patient has read the above mission statement, and understands the goal of energy healing, and the session to follow, and he/she accepts all responsibility from any adverse happenings, during or after a session.

Patient's signature _____

Date _____

Blessings- Vernon Bowlby

Christian Teaching and Energy Healing

The following comes from a handout at a therapeutic touch conference twenty years ago. It was written by the Reverend Tom Countryman. I believe that it was sent to me by divine Providence, as its content is invaluable to understanding that energy healing is scriptural.

I would like to extend full credit to Reverend countryman for its contents:

Traditional energy-based healing methods, such as therapeutic touch, can seem wonderful, or they can seem frightening. In the "modern" world, the idea of subtle energies that exist on the edges of our awareness, but, are not directly measurable by [current] scientific means, that we cannot prove, may be uncomfortable. What might seem surprising is that these healing methods are often regarded with suspicion by sincere and devout Christians.

Christians, who, by definition, believe in reality beyond measurement, should enthusiastically embrace such healing arts. However, the language of energy-based healing has spiritual overtones, and this raises a bothersome question: "What is the source of these healing powers?"

Ironically, Jesus was challenged with the same question, and even he was accused of having demonic power. Why, then, have some modern Christians echoed Jesus' enemies, and accused practitioners of energetic healing arts? The reason is simple: Christians often assume that the source of an extraordinary event (such as healing) is either God or an illegitimate (i.e. demonic) source. Christian theology teaches that Christians can access divine power by virtue of a unique relationship with God: a relationship marked by the dynamic presence of God's Holy Spirit. Since the healing attributes demonstrated by energetic healers are not limited to Christian practitioners, it is obviously not a power which accompanies the unique presence of the Holy Spirit.

Therefore, Christians often conclude that, since the healing is not really from the Holy Spirit, it is from that demonic source. However, this is a flawed conclusion. The Bible allows for another explanation of the healing power, besides the Holy Spirit or the devil.

Jesus had a great capacity to heal, as the gospel accounts report. Christians generally assumed that this healing power was available to Jesus only because of his divine nature and God One Begotten. But Jesus' healing ability can also arise from the fact that he was also fully human. Actually, from the standpoint of Christian theology, Jesus was the only person to have ever been fully human. Sin diminishes our humanity; Jesus, the Bible states, was without sin. Jesus, then, was the only person who ever lived who had access to the full potential of human life.

Therefore, Jesus' healing powers might be attributed to either his divine nature, or to his fully realized human nature. If it arises from his divine nature, then, every human being has an innate ability to heal. It also means that, as the person grows spiritually, becomes more Christ-like, and puts aside the dehumanizing power of sin, he or she could expect to be able to access the healing capacity.

Granted, the Bible clearly supports the premise that God, sometimes, effects healing by direct and miraculous means. The Scriptures also fully support the principle that the healing capacity is inherent in humanity.

Since humanity is created in the image of God (Genesis 1:27), and God can heal, it is reasonable to assume that the ability to heal is a human quality as well. This assumption is supported in the Epistle of James:

"Is anyone among you sick? Let him call for the elders of the church, and let them pray over him, anointing him with oil in the name of the Lord. And the prayer of faith will save the one who is sick, and the Lord will raise him up. And if he has committed sins, he will be forgiven. Therefore, confess your sins to one another and pray for one another, that you may be healed. The prayer of a righteous person has great power as it is working." James 5:14-16

My Ascension as a Healer

Step-by-step in my Christian non-stop ascension and still ascending:

- ➢ My Sunday school teacher Mrs. Sunday followed by Henry Sweigart
- ➢ My acceptance of giving two-thirds of the candy bar to my friend at age seven
- ➢ Acceptance of Christ as my personal savior at age twelve
- ➢ Full immersion in the Baptist Church in Goldendale, WA with my bride to be at age twenty-five
- ➢ Anointed as an Elder for Life in Calvin Presbyterian Church in Corvallis, Oregon at age thirty-eight
- ➢ Blessed with the Holy Spirit at age forty-one in Calvin Presbyterian church in Corvallis, Oregon
- ➢ Blessed with the Divine power to heal myself from a disintegrated Achilles tendon at age fifty-eight
- ➢ Blessed with the Divine power to access the power of the Holy Spirit to suspend gravity aged sixty-one and repeat this divine power three more times when requested
- ➢ Blessed with the opening of my chakra centers allowing me to receive the Holy Spirit and to receive Divine energy to heal others at age sixty-four
- ➢ Blessed with golden light in a dream at age sixty-five
- ➢ Blessed with the silver roman candle like showers of light throughout my body age sixty-seven

Does this mean that I can walk on water, or heal anyone upon my command? The answer is No. However, where I am on the ascension ladder allows me to request the power of the Holy Spirit, and the power flows through at the Holy Spirit's discretion.

Ascension Principles

All the above are just milestones in anyone's ascension. The acid test is to apply God's will in everyday life. Each day is a new step in ascension that requires daily prayer, as well as daily communication. For example, if a person feels anger, hate, envy, or dislike for anyone else, then they have not released themselves to God's control. A classic example of a person who is still in control of their lives, but, is not under God's, is an automobile driver who regularly displays road rage.

Unless there is an obvious reason, when a person asks for your presence and you deny them, you may deny God's presence and an opportunity for you to ascend.

Ascension is never- ending. Ascension goes on into infinity.

Ascension may take different paths for different people, as the gifts of the Spirit are bequeathed as determined by the divine. Patience is golden while you wait patiently for God's timing.

The more Christ-like you become, the more Holy Spirit empowers you with the nine gifts of Spirit.

At John 14:12 :

> "Truly, truly, I say to you, He that believes on me, the works that I do shall he do also; and greater works than these shall he do; because I go to my Father."

It appears to me, Jesus is leaving to go with his Father and before that the key words are: "He that believes on me, **the works that I do shall he do also, and greater works than these shall he do.**". It seems crystal clear to me what Jesus is saying and yet these words have been interpreted very differently by some people.

The Power of the Source to Heal

At Matthew 8:13 Jesus said:

> "Go, and it will be done for you, just as you have believed."

As I grew up in the Christian & Missionary Alliance Church in Hood River, I learned that this response was to a woman who had asked Jesus to heal her son.

Jesus had said that it was not necessary, as her faith in him was enough to achieve her desire. She had the power herself to heal her son. And so it was.

As stated in the above article by the Reverend Countryman:

> "Therefore, the healing power of Jesus might be attributed to either his divine nature or is fully realized human nature. If it arises from his divine nature, then every human being has some innate ability to heal. It would also mean that as the person grows spiritually – becomes more Christ-like and put aside the dehumanizing power of sin – he or she could expect to be more fully able to access the healing capacity."

When I healed my destroyed Achilles tendon in January 1990, I did not ask Jesus to heal me. What powers were within me that brought about healing in thirty minutes, instead of the minimum six months that the doctor had predicted?

From a spiritual viewpoint:

> ➢ I accepted Christ as my personal savior at age twelve and my physical body was cleansed of all sin. According to Matthew 8:13, I received the power to heal myself when I accepted Jesus.
> ➢ Anointed as an Elder in the Presbyterian Church for Life and with the capacity to heal others
> ➢ Blessed with the Holy Spirit
> ➢ Blessed by the power within me to heal my own leg in thirty minutes
> ➢ Blessed with the power of the Holy Spirit to open my chakra centers
> ➢ Blessed with the golden light of masculine energy
> ➢ Three times blessed with the silver light to enhance my feminine energy

In the 1960's, Dr. George Solomon of Stanford University, proved that our immune systems were highly sensitive to stress which led to the realization that the brain controlled the immune system, and was a separate function of the body, was a new theory to the medical profession.

Neuroscientist Karen Bulloch determined that the thymus was hard-wired to the brain.

Scientist David Felten expanded Dr. Bulloch's work, in that the brain controls all of the major functions of our immune system, including the thymus, spleen, lymph nodes, and bone marrow.

Candice Pert, Ph.D., discovered that certain brain chemicals called neuropeptides acted as messengers between the mind and the brain. These receptors can control the growth patterns of a particular cell, which ensures that, when a message is received, a new course of action will be taken. Neuropeptide "keys" are chemical carriers of emotion. Endorphins are natural pain-killers produced by the brain. These receptors are present in every major type of immune cell. It was determined that shifting moods can control and modify our immune systems. Dr. Pert called it "bits of brain floating throughout the body." She also determined that messages between the brain and the immune system are two-way streets. It is a biological fact that the immune system "takes" to the brain, and produces its own messengers, and it is a non-stop path of communication between the brain and the immune system.

To summarize, I was blessed with the spiritual powers, created by God, to heal my leg in thirty minutes!

Additional confirmation of the above doctor's research is in *Remarkable Recoveries*, a book written by Caryle Hirshberg and Marc Barasch whose research involved approximately thirty people who had been on their deathbeds, and who had recovered from their illnesses. The connection in all the cases was that these people had taken charge of their own healing. Their emotions had fired up their brains to communicate with their immune systems: they wanted to live, and not to die.

An Inquiry about my Status as a Healer

On March 4, 2014, before my LMS cancer diagnosis, I contacted a soul reader, who lived in another state, in regard to my status as an energy healer. I presently worked on a woman who was suffering with bereavement that I felt was enhanced by healing pads from Germany. My life's mission was to write a book relating my miraculous experiences with the Divine, and I needed insights from this woman.

What I received from the soul reader on March 6, 2014 exceeded all my expectations.

Now that you have read the story of my life's journey, does this make sense?

Healing at a New level

A transmission for Vernon

There is an Angel presenting itself to me this morning. It started to make its appearance March 4, 2014, when I accepted a request to perform a transmission for Vernon. It is making its - debut - It says, on my left - emitting the sensuous energy of the Divine Feminine quality in sparkling effervescent wings of white, wearing a vivid blue gown, with hair of spun gold and eyes of pure blue. As I gaze upon its beauty, its purity, it says, "I am reflecting the Truth of what is inside of you".

Who are you, I ask? "I am the Angel of Purification. I work with Vernon through his human energy system. The mat which he has been using is simply a manifested production of what is inside of him

- no more, no less. The occurrences he is experiencing are noteworthy for his documentary he is writing. The New level of healing is revealing itself through his queries. For Vernon - and you, sweet Cyndia, - through your pure desire to heal the atrocities committed against women, which resulted in the shutting down of the Divine Feminine flow through human activities that distorted the balance of the Divine Feminine and Divine Masculine - together you have manifested this session.

I have been awaiting this moment to speak openly and frankly with Vernon so that he may recognize me more fully and work more openly with me as his healing partner. I consider this my letter of introduction to him, however every time he uses his INDUCTION method, and it is I, the Angel of Purification, that partners WITH him. Mats aside, My Love resides WITHIN him. I am the aspect of the Divine Feminine that was cut off through a tortuous experience, however, Now I am fully integrating back into Vernon's expression of Wholeness - of his True Self - through the integrative process that has been determined to be the most effective one of all - restoring the Divine Feminine through the female clients who have the capacity to balance their fields of energy through receptivity. Vernon, while I take my leave now, Always know I am with you, within you....

(The Angel now hands the "microphone" to Jesus who has been waiting to speak)

"Yes, sweet Sister, it is I Jesus, Beloved Brother to ALL, wishing to add my WELL wishes, my Loving comments to Vernon's transmission for TRANSMISSION of Pure Love energy is precisely what Vernon is transmitting during his healing sessions - and this is his mission in this life time, and in doing so all of the transgressions against women that he personally experienced in any life time is being purified in this life time, bringing the past, present, and future together, reinstating the Divine Feminine to it's pristine quality of perfection in harmony with the Divine Masculine.

The bereavement that has been felt is in direct correlation to the Divine Feminine - which was cut off/shut down - however, that is all changing now - through the dedication of committed Souls such as yourselves who have chosen to re-embody during this lifetime to be part of a crusade that is taking over the Earth plane - the return of the Divine Feminine through every man, woman and child that is occurring now! The wave of bliss that is washing over Planet Earth is raising up consciousness and all life responds as it must. With every healing session performed by Vernon, this wave grows in momentum, saturating all Life with Pure Love. Healing the One heals the Whole. He is the conduit of this energy field, and he is more powerful than a million mats produced by man. And with that, I take my leave while leaving my Love, Jesus/Sananda.

There is a grouping in front of me representing the 5th Dimensional Body Elementals. They wish to have an audience with Vernon now. They speak in unison, as One Unit. "We work with the reconstruction of the human system during this time of Upgrades - new strands of DNA, new energy system upgrades taking over for the old patterns so that the new patterns of perfection can manifest with the greatest of ease and yes, comfort. This is not limited to humans as it involves ALL life in and on planet Earth, planet Earth, and all life beyond the beyond. All eyes are on Planet Earth right now and Her inhabitants. We give this overview so that Vernon's query can be answered from what is called The Bigger Picture.

Vernon, you have a team of high level Elementals working with you, along with a surgical team of experts from space crafts (one in particular), that hover over our Great Mother's body, planet Earth, right now. Disclosure will occur and the Truth will come out as it must and when it does, Vernon, your healing work will take off in a new direction you cannot fathom at this moment - however, that moment will present itself and you are fully and completely prepared for it. And with that, We take our leave....In Love, always In Love....

And now the "microphone" is in the Hands of Our Divine Mother - The Mother of ALL. "Yes, I wish a word with my Beloved son Vernon, for I watch over him - I AM within him, - his touch is My touch. He was born of My breast, and through his healing work, that which was cut off is now restored. There is no greater Love than a Mother's Love, and My Love for my children is what is being restored now - it is what is being remembered - it is what is re-surging in every cellular memory as these marvelous healings occur - and they are occurring through each of you who has taken upon yourselves this glorious task - of Love, and the remembrance of Me as your True Mother - The Mother of ALL - and in doing so, I, in the form of Mother Earth, return to My Pristine State of Perfection as does every one of my children, as does the nature Kingdom.

This is a time of great celebration as the Divine Feminine in full restoration merges with the Divine Male Counterpart to produce a New Race of Humans.

Vernon, there is so much more for you to incorporate in your documentary for it is the publication of your Soul's journey, a never ending Love story. So now you know the answer to your query - what God installs in our hearts is to fulfill HIS purpose - and that purpose was, is and always will be - LOVE! For YOU are the greatest Love Story of All! Now, go tell all your story - for your story is their story - you are all brothers and sisters in this together. The greatest Love story of all is being Lived Now as ALL of my children are coming Home to the full remembrance of who they are and from whence they have come." Your Loving Mother ~

Transmission transcribed by Cyndia
March 6, 2014

Vignettes

Divinely Sent

On September 1, 1972, my CPA partnership was dissolved, and I was in desperate need of a qualified accountant. I drafted an ad for the newspaper, and then prayed for a brilliant, congenial person who was quick to learn. The phone rang just as I planned to place an ad. The caller was a woman from a personnel agency in Albany, who said that she had an applicant that I might be interested in hiring. The applicant did not have a phone, but, she rented an apartment two blocks from my office. I went there and interviewed her, she came to work for me the next day, and became an exceptional employee, having all the attributes that I had prayed for, and she acquired her CPA certificate a year later.

The Vibration Awakening

In January 1991, I awoke at 6:00 A.M., with an unusual feeling. I arose from bed and moved to the couch. Within seconds, my body vibrated from head to toe. I had no idea what had happened, and for thirty minutes my body shook, with varying degrees of vibration. There was no pain, so, I knew that it was not a heart attack. When the vibrations ended, I was left with a feeling of bliss. I now believe that this was the Holy Spirit launching me on my spiritual awakening as a healer.

Eighteen months later, in July 1992, I came home from work at 5:30 P.M., with the same strange feeling. I lay on the bed and I immediately began to vibrate. Ruth considered calling 911, but, as there was no pain, she waited with me, as my body shuddered peacefully. Once again, the vibration ended in thirty minutes. This was the second phase of my awakening as a healer.

Since the first two vibrations that were so profound, I have continued to vibrate regularly about once a year.

Angelic Messengers

On the first of October 1995, I had a dream, with a profound message, that would impact me for many months. In this dream, I was with a tour group in Canada, and I laid my gloves on the railing in a hotel. An angel told me to be vigilant, but, some time later, seven miles from the hotel, I realized that I had left my gloves behind. The message that I received from the dream was that I should pay more attention when angels tell me what to do. The more that I opened myself to receive and to obey messages from angels quickly, the more messages I would receive, and they would be of great benefit to all concerned.

The next day, while I watched the World Series, I received a message that I should clean my gutters. I recognized that this might be a message from an angel, and I decided that I would use the time between innings to go outside and remove leaves from the gutters. Three innings later, the gutters were clean, and I had only missed TV commercials. Then, I received the message to put away the deck furniture. Again, I obeyed, and by the end of the game, I reveled in the satisfaction of having accomplished my chores in the time that I would have wasted. Since then, I have enjoyed a constant flow of messages from angels, which help me make decisions that support my own best interests, as well as God's will.

In October 1993, about eight months after my facial pain began, which included roaring in my ears, Ruth and I traveled to Greece and visited Delphi, known as the ancient healing center of the world, where a major energy vortex exists. As I went to sleep that night, I had extreme roaring in my ears, but, the next morning, the noise had departed, and it never returned.

Praying for Peace

In early 1994, I received a strong message that I should pray for peace throughout the world. Although at first, this seemed overwhelming and remote, the task became more personal when Ruth and I traveled with a local church choir on a tour of England, Wales, and Scotland. Ireland had been in a state of religious and political conflict for twenty-five years. The message was clear that I should pray for peace and forgiveness in the hearts of the men of Ireland, who perpetuated the strife. Each morning during our trip, I awakened to pray for peace in Ireland, and I knew that I was joined by millions of others around the world. I continued to pray when I returned home, and on August 31, 1994, which would have been my brother, Wayne's sixty-eighth birthday, peace was finally achieved.

The message then came that I should pray for peace in Bosnia. On November 23, 1995, my sister Lillian's sixty-seventh birthday, a peace treaty was signed in Dayton, Ohio, to end the war in Bosnia.

Was it a coincidence that both wars ended on my older brother and older sister's birthday's or was it a response to my prayers?

Depression

One woman came to me and said that she had been clinically depressed for three weeks. When she told me how many medications had been prescribed for her, and how the pain and depression increased, despite the medications, I realized how archaic Western medicine has become. Medications do not heal! The best that any medication will do is to mask symptoms. I gave the woman a two-hour session, and an hour later, another healer and I gave her a joint session. Throughout these sessions, her entire body quivered, as the energy centers began their recovery from being stifled by the medications and stress. I believe that her chakra centers were revived, and that her immune system began to heal. When we had finished, she said that she felt that she had just been born again.

Over the years, new techniques of healing have flowed to me that help me with specific needs. For mental problems, including depression and strokes, I have learned to place my hands on the third-eye chakra and the medulla.

Declaring War on Illness

When a person receives a frightening diagnosis from a doctor, or suffers chronic pain, the first step is to declare war on the illness. The person with a dysfunctional body must act like a general at war. Facts must be accumulated, and game plans plotted on how to fight a battle to win.

There is no single solution to any illness. As the general in charge, one must constantly search for more information, and change the game plan as new information is received. The doctor is just one of many resources. A successful battle is rarely fought on one front, nor should one focus on only one approach to healing.

Reiki

Reiki is a Japanese technique for stress reduction and relaxation that also promotes healing. It is administered by "lying on hands" and it is based on the idea that unseen life force energy flows through us, and is what causes us to be alive.

The word Reiki is made of two Japanese words: Rei, which means "God's Wisdom or the Higher Power," and Ki, which is "life force energy." Reiki is actually "spiritually guided life force energy." A treatment feels like a wonderful glowing radiance that flows through and around you. Reiki treats the whole person, which includes body, emotions, mind, and spirit, creating many beneficial effects that include relaxation and feelings of peace, security, and well-being. Many patients have reported miraculous results.

Reiki is a simple, natural, safe method of spiritual healing and self-improvement that everyone can use. It has been effective in virtually every known illness and malady, and it always creates a beneficial effect. It also works in conjunction with all other medical or therapeutic techniques to relieve side effects and promote recovery.

Born to Heal

I have been told by several spiritual readers that I was born to be a healer. Although I did not start my healing practice until I was sixty-two years old, I feel that my healing touch was developed in other ways prior to that age. I remember that in elementary school, students would come to me to help settle disputes. That was a kind of healing, as they knew that I would come up with a fair judgment for all parties.

I also healed people financially through my accounting practice. People came to me with nearly impossible situations, and we always found solutions. Many extremely complex cases were resolved through discussions with one of my women accountants. Now, I recognize that process: we exchanged masculine/feminine energy, and that took us both to a higher level, and a very simple solution. I always felt as though the end product was divinely sent. The mind can erect invisible barriers, and the divine has no such barriers

Non-Believers

I understand that some people are resistant to the idea of energy healing. Some members of my own family have a difficult time believing in the work that I do, although they cannot help but recognize that there is something unusual in the way that I bounce back from injuries and illness. I show them the thank-you letters and testimonials that I receive, and they acknowledge them politely. But, it is hard to overcome the influence of a society that places its faith exclusively in the Western medical establishment.

I was an elder for six years in a church that I attended for forty-five years. But, when other church members heard about my healing path, they thought it was wrong. I performed a healing session on one parish member, and she was thrilled with the results. When I discussed my healing experiences with one of the staff, he dismissed my healing experiences as "new-age stuff," and ignored my reply that the Bible has numerous references to healing. Jesus said at John 14:12: "Truly, truly, I say to you, He that believes on me, the works that I do shall he do also; and greater works than these shall he do; because I go to my Father."

My Healing Hands

Even as a young child, I knew about the energy in my hands. I learned that I could focus my mind and hands together, with extreme intensity, and I would exceed other children picking beans and strawberries. I used that speed and concentration all the way through my teenage years. Later, I was employed by Hickey's Market as a meat cutter, where fast hands were a necessity for safety, as well as productivity. My reputation at Hickey's led to a job as head meat cutter at Safeway, in Goldendale, Washington (which led to meeting the love of my life!).

For the last twenty years, I have used that intense connection between my mind and my hands to channel healing energy. If I think about healing, my hands immediately commence to have a strong energy flow! My fingers start tingling, my palms get hotter, and they turn red. Little white spots appear, and it looks like my blood boils!

Patients love it when I put my hot hands on the source of their pain. There is an instantaneous transmission of warm, healing energy, which eases the blockages in their bodies, and ignites their immune systems. Through my hands, the infinite power of Spirit flows into their energy centers, and gives them strength to overcome the negative forces that have been in control. To have been blessed with this power from the Holy Spirit is the most amazing gift imaginable.

Spirit's Gift to Us

Almost all physical deficiencies of the body can be cured by energy healing when the patient accepts the empowerment to heal from the Holy Spirit. I have experienced healings of numerous forms of cancer including leukemia, breast cancer, lung cancer with tumor growths the size of pears, and in some cases, advanced cancer throughout the body. I have also helped to relieve all types of pain including migraine headaches, surgery, chemotherapy, shingles, fibromyalgia, and bereavement. People have come to me with strokes, depression, Parkinson's, mental illness, chronic fatigue, and auto-immune diseases. I never know what the outcome will be when I begin, but everyone receives some relief of pain and spiritual growth.

The Wisdom of Mary Baker Eddy

About seven years ago, I went to Powell's Books in Portland, Oregon, and came home with three books. I read two of them, and the third sat on my bookshelf unopened for about four years until divine timing determined that it was time to read the book. I found Mary Baker Eddy's masterpiece of research and writing to be one of the most powerful books I have ever read. The book was first owned by residents in England and found its way about 5,000 miles to me. Her book confirmed what I had learned about healing over a 20-year period of time. *Science and Health, with Key to the Scriptures,* first published in 1875, defines the fundamentals of the Christian Science religion.

Mary Baker Eddy lived between 1821 and 1910. She was sickly throughout her childhood and early adulthood, and tried many alternative healing practices of the times, including mesmerism, electric shock therapy and morphine. When she was forty-five years old, after a bad fall and serious spinal injury, she experienced a miraculous healing, which she attributed to reading the Bible. She spent the next years studying the scriptures, and developed a religious philosophy based on self-healing through prayer.

Christian Science explicitly rejects drugs and Western medical treatments. Pharmaceutical companies products were just becoming popular at the time Mary Baker Eddy was developing the fundamentals of the religion, and the home remedies that people had been using to self-heal were losing ground to a more drug-centered approach. Mrs. Eddy was severely persecuted for her opposition to the medical establishment. She believed as I do that people have the power to heal themselves when they put their faith in God as infinite Spirit.

Although I generally agree with her, and I try to avoid taking any kind of pharmaceuticals, I feel that the Christian Science faith goes a bit too far with its prohibition of doctors and medications. My approach to illness is to search for as many remedies as possible, keeping an open mind to all options. Given my history of injuries, heart issues and cancer, it is clear I would not be alive today if it were not for Western medicine! But I believe, as did Mrs. Eddy, that your own healing thoughts are the most powerful tool to enhance healing on the planet.

In her book, she reflects that silent prayers are far more powerful than audible prayers. On page 7, she states Audible prayer is impressive...but may embrace too much love of applause to induce or encourage Christian sentiment. She also states on page 15, The Master's injunction is, that we pray in secret and let our lives attest our sincerity. I marvel at the speed and clarity of corporate prayers spoken which I believe are a direct gift from the Holy Spirit and provide an essential part of unification of prayers to everyone present.

Healer of the Golden Light

In July 1994, I had another awakening dream. I slept on my side in my own bed. My spirit arose from my body to the ceiling in the northwest corner of my bedroom, to observe myself lying in bed. A golden spiritual body arose from my body to lie horizontally over me. My spiritual body shimmered in shades of gold. Suddenly, about two feet from my body, hundreds of golden Roman candle-like explosions sent streams of gold into my body, making it vibrate in sparkling gold. This continued for some time. Finally the explosions of gold stopped, and the golden body flowed into my physical body, as I continued to sleep on my side.

I awoke with the dream indelible in my mind, and with a clear interpretation of the dream. The message was that the Holy Spirit had just ordained me as a healer of the golden light!

A Dream of Energy Balance

In May 1994, I had an amazing dream. In this dream, I was in Canada at a rustic resort, and I was being married to the most beautiful woman I had ever seen, who wore a beautiful white gown. We were outside the resort, and we welcomed a line of fifty couples. I introduced my bride to each of the one hundred guests, and as I did, a flood of information about the life and personality of each person came to me. When I had introduced the last person, I awakened, regretfully.

I searched for an interpretation of the dream. A week later, it came to me in another dream. I received the message that, to become balanced, a healer must possess an abundance of both masculine and feminine energy. The interpretation was that I was marrying my feminine self! The fifty couples represented the balance of masculine and feminine energy.

Vibration Flow

In 1996, I had visited a Turkish bathhouse in Istanbul, where I had received a massage from a young monsieur, who utilized an amazing vibration technique on me. I asked him if he could teach me this technique. He responded that it could not be taught, that it was an ancient form of healing, and that Spirit gifted chosen people with the blessing. Eight years later, at the Beaverton healing group in divine timing, a woman, who had never visited the group before, sat down beside me. Instantly, her energy took me to another level, and I received the vibration flow that I had experienced from the young Turk. Since that time, that vibration has flowed through me in all my healings.

Part 9: My Journey with LMS Cancer

Sometime before 2004, a single normal cell multiplied uncontrollably in my right forearm and created the first cell known an LMS cancer.

Once created, the cell ignored signals to stop accumulating and created a mass known as a tumor.

I discovered this cell, no bigger than a BB, in the summer 2004. Over the next three years, I consulted several physicians regarding the removal of the growth, and they said, "Don't worry about it."

On May 1, 2007, I awoke with the message from Spirit to have the tumor removed, and I consulted a surgeon. On June 30, 2007, the tumor was removed, and it was determined that the surgeon had removed all the margins around it.

On July 12, 2007, I received a call from my doctor, who said that the tumor was a very deadly cancer known as LMS.

The Leiomyosarcoma (LMS) is a rare cancer of the soft tissues of the body, which strikes about four in every one million people.

A search on the internet indicated that there were only three medical institutions in the United States that dealt with this cancer. They were located in Boston, Houston, and Seattle.

On August 22, 2007, a doctor at the Seattle Cancer Care Alliance removed a substantial amount of tissue around the site of the LMS cancer. All of the tissue was cancer-free.

A review of the internet indicated that over ninety percent of the time, the LMS cancer returns in the same spot within two years.

Right on cue, in June 2009, a tiny tumor commenced to emerge. In July, we called the doctor in Seattle and scheduled another appointment. Upon seeing the tumor, about the size of a BB, he told us that it would be the smallest tumor that he had ever removed, and that we should go home and wait until it grew larger.

On July 22, 2009, the growth was removed and it was LMS cancer.

In September 2009, I commenced a series of thirty-five radiation treatments on my forearm.

In November 2010, I had a CT-scan that indicated that I was cancer-free.

For the next thirty months, I was monitored by the oncology department every six months. No blood tests, CT-scans, or other diagnostic procedures, were performed during this monitoring period.

On October 31, 2013, I reported that I had four suspicious growths that I wanted removed. The remark was made to wait and see until the next monitoring on May 7, 2014.

In February, 2014, a biopsy was ordered.

On March 19, the biopsy revealed that the LMS cancer had returned.

On April 3, I had a PET scan.

On April 4, we met with a nurse assistant, who gradually told us that my cancer had metastasized into my shoulders, with additional tumors in my left leg, as well as a major cancer in my left hip bone, a growth of nearly six inches and other growths were on my liver.

She also stated that I had stage 4 cancers, with the type that has no cure, and I was immediately eligible for hospice and a disabled card for my car, as the cancer in my leg could cause my bone to break at any time, with devastating results.

To see your entire body, with its countless tumors, look as if it was riddled by a machine gun or a shotgun, is a mind-numbing experience.

The PET scan did not determine if the cancer was in my brain, as sugar is immediately transferred to the brain after ingestion. Therefore, an MRI was ordered for Monday, April 7th, to determine if the cancer had metastasized to my brain.

The oncologist suggested that my life expectancy was about six months, and that chemo might extend my life by several months, but, I would suffer many side effects. I chose not to have chemo.

On Tuesday, April 8, we met with an oncologist, who told us the good news that my brain was cancer-free.

On April 23, I had a CT-scan that established in more detail exactly where the cancers were in my body.

On May 30, a second CT-scan indicated that there was almost no change in the tumors, with the exception of a small increase in the large tumor on my liver.

July 30: I have no chronic pain, and I have no symptoms that anything is wrong with my body. I am super-charged with energy, perhaps from all the prayers people send me from all over the country!

July 31, 2014: I received a phone call from the oncology office to tell me that the blood tests showed a normal liver!

August 15: a third CT-scan revealed that most tumors had increased in size by over thirty percent.

September 10: I have only occasional minimal pain. The large growth on my liver has now protruded below my ribs, and it presses on my heart, intestines, bladder, and stomach, but, I have high energy.

Part 10: In Retrospect – The Recap of My Journey

How can it be that an eight year-old, raised in a loving family, during the Great Depression, under conditions that would now be considered primitive?

- ➢ Would Graduate second of a select group of over one hundred soldiers from Army Leadership School?
- ➢ Would graduate near the top of his class at the University of Oregon?
- ➢ Would teach at Oregon State University for ten years?
- ➢ Would be the first to pass the CPA exam, and the first of his college class to receive his CPA certificate?
- ➢ Would form Professional Corporation #1 in Oregon, which is still in existence after forty-four years?
- ➢ Would establish a CPA firm, and as a sole owner in a small town, perform accounting work across the nation?
- ➢ Would counsel clients on how to earn a profit in their businesses which resulted in millions more profit, and with the related income taxes paid?
- ➢ Would counsel with other CPA's across the United States in regard to timber and Christmas tree tax law, without remuneration?
- ➢ Would counsel unknown people, without remuneration, to extricate themselves from situations with the IRS, and other dire financial situations?
- ➢ Would counsel hundreds of college students over ten years, with no expectation of personal return, except for blessings received from spirit?
- ➢ Would write a tax manual on a subject so complicated that no one had ever done it, before or since, that would be recognized by the IRS as the best source for information for tree growers?
- ➢ Would travel across the United States over thirty times to give classes to CPAs and tree grower conventions?

➢ Would employ several hundred employees over twenty nine - years, pay many thousands of dollars of payroll taxes, and give his employees a twenty-five percent of salary pension contribution, which would fully vest in six years?

➢ Would achieve his fourth grade school manifestations to visit nearly all the Civil War battlefields, and China?

➢ Would build an office building with over eight thousand square feet with two hundred dollars out of pocket?

➢ Would become a land developer and real property landlord?

➢ Would own a four hundred acre timber and Christmas tree plantation free of debt?

➢ Would own a premier mountain home and a premier ocean home?

➢ Would become an energy healer, and heal people from many afflictions without remuneration?

➢ Would heal himself in thirty minutes from a destroyed Achilles tendon which the doctors predicted would take six to eight months to heal?

➢ Would become a founding director in a local bank, and would serve on its board of directors until the bank was sold fifteen years later, at a substantial profit to the investors in the bank?

➢ Would become a part owner of a radio station?

➢ Would visit all fifty states of the United States?

➢ Would visit over forty countries around the world?

➢ Would have two hole-in-ones on the same golf hole about 175 yards away in about seventy years of playing golf?

➢ Would give away most of the wealth accumulated during his lifetime?

➢ Would raise a family, aided by his wife, of three children, who have made significant contributions to mankind, and with grandchildren on the same path?

➢ Would assist his grandchildren to achieve their dreams?

➢ Would pay close attention from messages from above?

➢ Would attribute his success to a strong belief in the Almighty for guidance?

➢ Would attribute the majority of his success and longevity to his powerful Guardian Angel, and the flock of angels who watch over him?

➢ Would write a book to share his life's journey with others, which includes his present battle for his life with a metastasized cancer, and to share, as well, his walk with Jesus with whomever Spirit dictates?

What were the conditions that created these opportunities?

Could it be that I have mirrored John 15:5? "I am the vine, ye are the branches: He that abideth in me, and I in him, the same bringeth forth much fruit: for without me ye can do nothing."

Clearly, by divine Providence, I have lived a charmed life. My life journey has been as if I were born with a "silver spoon in my mouth", and from the beginning, I have been guided by Saint Michael.

Seven Factors That Made Positive Contributions to my Life's Journey

1. A democracy founded on the principle that the United States was a Christian nation, and that has always been central to American identity.

2. My parents commenced my religious education at an early age, and I was blessed by the presence of Mrs. Sunday, my Sunday School teacher, when I was about three years old, followed by Henry Sweigart, from age three on through high school.

3. My mother, who always preached to us that "The world was our oyster", and that there were no limitations on what we could accomplish in life

4. My many angelic guides, who protected me from harm, and changed the course of my life, repeatedly, with far better plans than I could have ever accomplished upon my own.

5. My acceptance of messages from Spirit early in life, which exponentially resulted in my constant ascension, with more and powerful blessings.

6. I was a dreamer, and whatever I dreamed, I could do, fostered by the lazy days of my youth, while I lay in the tall grass with my faithful dog, Buster. In my dreams, there were no limitations, or fears of what the future might bring.

7. Outstanding grade school teachers, who challenged me to unlimited problem analyses, aided by *The Grit* newspaper.

The Big Picture of My Life

By nature, I always like to stand back, look at the big picture of my life, and think about the mysteries left unsolved.

Why was I born in Constantine, Michigan?

The decision of my parents to traverse over 2,200 miles to Michigan on shoddy roads, in a two-seater car with my mother four months pregnant, with a four- year -old and a twenty-two month-old child, must have been a traumatic event for both my parents.

My dad's in-laws, and especially my grandfather, Frank Simpson, had always wanted a son, and their first-born was a boy, who died at birth. He was followed by five daughters, and my grandparents must have been extremely dismayed, and full of emotional stress, when their first grandchild, my brother, Wayne, left Oregon for Michigan, perhaps removed permanently from their lives.

My parents, exhausted from their trip to Michigan, must have been desperate when they arrived in Three Rivers, planning to live with my dad's brother's family temporarily, only to discover that there was no job for my dad, and that they lacked money and a home of their own.

Apparently, great grandmother Blanchard came to their rescue, and she provided a home for them near Constantine, Michigan, where she was born, as was my dad, and followed by my birth.

The question becomes, was there a divine power that determined that I was to be born in the only Constantine in the United States, or, was in all a coincidence?

Was there a relationship between Constantine the Great and Archangel Saint Michael which led to my birth in Constantine?

Constantine the Great built a magnificent basilica north of Constantinople to honor Saint Michael, which became the model for all future basilicas throughout the Roman Empire.

Four years after becoming a Christian at age twelve, I attended St. Marks Episcopal Church Youth Group on Sunday nights, and I became enthralled with the powers of Saint Michael that were available to anyone upon their request.

As I now look back over my life, it is no surprise that the powers of Saint Michael, who constantly sent messages to me, and which I obeyed immediately, became a significant part of my life's journey.

My survival of many near-death events, that defy all human logic, suggests that there was a powerful Guardian Angel watching over me.

In the story of the road to Prineville, I quickly obeyed a series of messages that may have led to one or more people's lives saved by Saint Michael that night, without their ever knowing it. In the process,

Saint Michael transferred his powers to suspend gravity to me, enabling us, with no physical strength, to move the rock from the road.

At my request, three more times, Saint Michael granted me the power to suspend gravity, without any physical strength, and to move heavy objects.

In January 1990, either the Holy Spirit or Saint Michael granted my request to heal my destroyed Achilles muscle in thirty minutes, instead of six to eight months. It really does not matter how I was granted the power to heal myself. What does matter is that, by request, divine decree allowed my body to be healed in record time, and thus, my ascension as a healer was begun.

Over three years later, after my heart angioplasty, books and classes in healing methods flowed to me, as my physical body began its ascension as a healer.

This ascension was followed by my next twenty years' power to heal several hundred people, as granted, again, by the power of the Holy Spirit, or, by Saint Michael's healing power.

June was on her deathbed in July 1998, when she prayed for Saint Michael to heal her, and I believe that Saint Michael sent me to divinely end her pain and suffering, and to transfer her to heaven in peace. It may indicate that it was Saint Michael who granted me the blessing of healing.

What is ascension anyway? My belief is that ascension is accepting divine messages, with a goal to become more Christ-like on a daily basis. The ascension is never-ending, as no one will ever become as perfect as Jesus.

My favorite way to say it is, "Until I die, I am in the infancy of learning to be like Christ."

Along life's journey, as one does progress along the path, the Holy Spirit may bestow heavenly gifts in divine timing, and in divine patience, which determines whether one has really surrendered oneself to God, or if one pretends.

It is always easy to be a Christian ninety-nine percent of the time, when no decisions are being made, or there is no stress in one's life. The acid test is the one percent of the time when decisions are being made, and how one reacts during those stressful times.

My interpretation is that when you accept Christ as your personal savior, it is like a down payment on becoming a Christian. What really counts is for one to cast out negative thoughts, such as hate, anger, worry, depression, hopelessness, anxiety, over-cautiousness, and an inability to make simple decisions. What all these feelings have in common is one's degree of self-centeredness.

The antidote to these feelings is NOT medications, which Mary Baker Eddy determined after a nine- year study of the Bible. What medications may do is to expand negative thoughts, and which may mask the real culprit of unpleasant emotions, and give temporary relief, but, does nothing to resolve the harboring of negativity within a person.

We all have the choice of free will. We choose to have the attitude to degrade others in order to upgrade ourselves. But, help others to rise, and you ascend with them. To give, without expectation of a return, is the ultimate way in which to overcome negative feelings.

When I chose to give away two thirds of my candy bar, I was filled with positive emotions, and my body CREATED powerful compounds within my body that became a seed of exhilaration. A way of life was shown me, which enlightened me on how I could ascend to become more Christ- like, and how I might receive more spiritual gifts.

Saint Michael's message from God is love for our fellow human beings. When one gives freely to someone else, without expectation of return, one is, in a sense, obeying the message from Saint Michael, which I identify as a Golden Saint Michael Moment. A person become more like Jesus the more his/he mindset is to place others above self, and life tends to flourish. A Golden Saint Michael's Moment can be as easy as a prayer for another.

Giving away two twenty dollar bills with no expectation of return other than to increase my rate of ascension, as determined by the Holy Spirit, is another classic example. There was no human reward, but, instead, a powerful spiritual reward that pays perpetual dividends.

We all have the power to **create** endorphins in our brains, which can eliminate pain, and which contributes to the overall health of our bodies. This is more powerful than any medication produced by a drug company.

One might consider that committing an act of kindness to someone, without an expectation of return, might be considered a Saint Michael Moment, and it might lead to benefits exceeding of one's wildest dreams.

With hindsight, it appears that a divine force planned my life from its beginning: my birthplace, my childhood, my Christian education, my Army career, my wife, the love of my life, my family, my ascension as a healer, completed by my being filled with the Holy Spirit. How else to explain my college career, my love of the Christmas tree business, which grew from a hundred or so trees harvested from public lands to over

80,000 trees harvested from my own land, my CPA career, my publishing career, my university teaching career, my investment career, my travel adventures, my constant experiences with death, my healing blessings, with extraordinary displays of divine happenings, that defied all human timing.

My life has been that of a tightrope walker crossing the Grand Canyon on a greased rope, hands tied behind my back, blindfolded, walking backwards, and with a strong wind blowing, but, with the knowledge that I was completely safe. I took countless blows to the skull, any one of which could have killed me, I was twice saved by my dog from drowning, driven 1.2 miles asleep at fifty-five miles per hour in heavy traffic, with many other harrowing close calls to death by auto, skied the impossible ski run, survived death by disease, and many other times that I could have, should have, died, but, I am still alive.

But, I'm not to leave before I have completed a book on my life's miraculous journey for others to ponder.

By age thirty-one, Alexander the Great had conquered the known world by 350 B.C., and he considered his god critical to his success.

In thirty years, by 308 A.D., Constantine the Great had changed five hundred years of Roman pagan worship, and established Christianity, attributing his success to his acceptance of Christ as his personal savior.

My belief is that the key to my life's success was that I listened, discerned, and responded to messages from Saint Michael and a flock of angels, which led to more messages, which created an exponentially rewarding life.

The message that I receive from Spirit is that God has a plan for every human being and awaits one's decision to accept his plan or deny His plan.

What is powerful in this story is that Saint Michael and a flock of angels await everyone to send divine messages to whoever requests them.

Final Thoughts

The bottom line is – I have lived the American Dream. I learned early in life to attack any situation with intensity, to do the best job that I could do, with the realization that the more I produced what others needed, the more successful I would be.

Along the way, I learned to give of myself, without expectation of monetary return, with the same vigor that I would if it were a profit-making endeavor.

I believe that I have met John Kennedy's statement of, "Don't ask what your country can do for you, but ask what you can do for your country."

I trust that anyone who reads my book will have a "light bulb or two" flash on, that, any day, I may die, and I will then be able to thank my angels personally for the fun journey that they have given me.

Since I was old enough to count my blessings, I have been aware that I have had more than my share of divine Providence.

I believe that anyone can request the presence of angels. That is one of the primary reasons for this book: to share my experiences, and through those, to encourage others to call upon the boundless reserve of divine Providence. I am convinced that every one of us has the choice to call on the unlimited power of the angels at any time. We can access them by prayers from our hearts for divine guidance, heeding the messages that we receive, and by focusing our energy on the goodness we must share with everyone we meet.

I bless the Lord for this nearly pain-free time in which to fulfill my life's mission of writing this book: my final teaching experience. My last wish is that my story will enrich your life, beyond your wildest expectations!

And, as my mother used to say "The World is Your Oyster." Your Life is Your Choice!

Love and Hugs to All from the Hands of Vernon!

Vernon and his grandson, Andrew view the sunset in Depoe Bay, Oregon, while Zelda was looking for food in September 2014

Andrew plans to become a teacher, following in the footsteps of his aunt, Catherine, and his grandfather.

Vernon is looking to the sunset days of his life.

Appendix

Letter to IRS

Please read only with a clear mind, early in the morning, with a pencil and paper for notes. I realized in my first two letters to the IRS that I gave them detailed information which should have convinced them that Kate was innocent. I switched in my third letter from a left brained approach to a right brained approach. The IRS agent conceded the day he received my letter and Kate received payment for the wrongful withholdings from her paychecks.

Jim Jones   January 7, 2007
Taxpayer Advocate Service Fresno, Ca 93776
Re Case Number 3781770 Kate Jones
Subject: The **Nails** in the Coffin of Kate

On Thursday, January 4, 2007, I spent the day skiing. As I skied the slopes, my mind wandered on how vulnerable all young people are, as Kate Jones was at nineteen.

As young adults, they are automatically supposed to know all the intricacies of the ever-changing Internal Revenue Code, the most complicated document in the history of the world, even though they have never read a single page of the tax law which is the law of the land.

If they make one innocent mistake, they are subject to countless potential penalties, at the option of the IRS, such as Kate's $1,300 penalty, assessed by the IRS in October 2001.

In Kate's case, she signed an IRS settlement statement, in the belief that she would go to jail if she did not sign it. The threatening power of the IRS, forced her to sign the agreement, under extreme emotional duress.

The Kate Jones case reads like a Hitchcock movie, with Kate as the victim. Had Kate died after her attempted suicide, shortly after she signed the IRS settlement agreement, no one would ever have known of the "Nails in her Coffin" outlined below.

The players, in 1999, when this emotional melodrama began were:
- Kate aged nineteen
- Jim Lake aged forty, a janitorial businessman for most of his adult life
- Vicky Linn, in her sixties, the partner of Lake, in business since at least 1989.
- Jenny Kent - a licensed Arizona CPA
- An unknown IRS agent

In November 2006 -Vernon Bowlby CPA, aged seventy-five is divinely sent to attempt to free Kate from an unfair tax burden that belongs to others.

Nail #1: The opening scene

On April 17, 2000, Lake drove Kate to the office of Jenny Kent, CPA. Kate has no clue that she is being driven to an office, where she will be betrayed by Lake, and which will commence nearly seven years of emotional financial hell.

Lake Pointed to where Kate is to sign her tax return. Kate signs and never looks at the tax return and is never given a copy. Lake will have completed his plan to transfer a portion of the 1999 tax liability of himself and Linn to Kate.

Lake's plan of tax evasion, to transfer his obligations to Kate, began on 05/25/99, when he manipulated Kate into filing for a Maricopa county business license, with the assumed name of Austin Cleaning Service as the one hundred percent owner.

On 01/13/2000, Lake pressured Kate to file for an Arizona business license registration as the one hundred percent owner of Austin Cleaning Service. Lake paid for the licenses from his own funds.

(Lake had previously enticed Catrina Martin, a part-time employee of Lake, into filing with the Arizona business license registration as the one hundred percent owner of Austin Cleaning Service on 06/12/98, with the apparent intent of transferring a portion of his 1998 tax liability to Martin)

Kate met with Jenny Kent (for the first time), who has prepared Kate's 1999 tax return for Kate to sign. Also attending the meeting is Linn. The return is prepared from information provided by Lake. Since Kate had no funds, Kate now believes the taxes due of $1,774 were paid by Lake.

Nail #2

Jim Lake schemed and planned to use Kate as the victim to evade his own income tax liability, as well as, apparently, Linn's tax obligations.

Kate called Lake for assistance to respond to the $23,160 IRS notice for increased income and the related tax, penalties and interest. Lake refused Kate any information with the comment that, "Those records were his." Kate had never seen a bank statement of Lake's business.

Lake knew that he had Kent prepare 1099s to be issued to himself and Vicky Linn for the same $23,160 amount!

He knew his victim, Kate, was unknowledgeable to respond!

Lake was obviously protecting himself from IRS scrutiny!

Lake & Linn may not have reported the 1099s as income with the intent of making Kate the owner of their business to the IRS.

The allocation of the income in Lake's handwriting is proof of the intent of the preparation of the 1099s.

(It is unknown if Lake filed the 1099s with the IRS!)

Nail #3

Vicky Linn, a partner of Lake since 1989 or before, based upon the allocation of income between herself and Lake for the year 1999.

Linn co-conspired with Lake to have Kate report a portion of her apparent partnership income in 1999. Linn was present in the meeting when the 1099s were prepared and her allocation of the income was indicated by the 1099 as determined by Lake.

Nail #4

Jenny Kent prepared Kate's 1999 income tax return reflecting the allocation of the $64,131 of gross income in Lake's handwriting from the 1099 from Broken Maintenance. Jenny reports gross income of $40,971 on Kate's schedule C. Jenny prepares a 1096 with $23,160 of gross income and related 1099 to Lake of $7,580 and $15,580 to equal the 1099 from Broken of $64,131.

Jenny Kent, who had prepared Lake's tax returns for several years, errored when she prepared Kate's schedule C. She should have reported the gross income of $64,131 less amounts reported by others of $23,160 to a net of $41,971.

If this had been done, the 1099 from Broken Maintenance would have matched Kate's tax return and there would not have been an additional assessment and penalty to Kate.

The entire procedure of issuing 1099s to Lake and Linn for a portion of the 1099 does not pass the "smell test" and should have been a clue to Kent that Kate should not have reported any income from Lake and Linn's business.

Does it make any sense that Kate, aged nineteen at the time, could suddenly become the owner of a business (for one year only) to employ a forty- year- old man, who had been in business for many years, and a sixty- year- old plus woman, who also had been in business for many years?

Nail #5

The 1099 originally issued by Broken's Maintenance in the amount of $64,131 to Catrina Martin, and later changed by Lake to Kate's name, arrives at an IRS office, and does not match Kate's gross income reported on her schedule C, in the amount of $23,160, the same amount as the 1099s prepared for Lake and Linn by Kent.

It is not known which 1099 was received by the IRS for the match up. It might have been a corrected 1099, issued by Broken Maintenance (if so, most likely at Lake's request) or the copy changed by Lake, reporting the income as Kate's, or the changed copy may have been filed with Kate's tax return. (Broken Maintenance provided 1099s to Kate for several years, but 1099s were not available for 1999.)

The IRS issued Kate a proposed tax assessment increase of $6,499, plus a $1,300 accuracy penalty, plus $758 of interest. (The accumulated interest now exceeds $3,000 on the tax assessment and penalty after numerous payments by Kate.)

Kate attempted to secure information from Lake to dispute the assessment. Lake refused to give her any information, and told her the accountant had made a mistake, and that she owed the taxes.

Kate had no experience with the tax law. She did not have a copy of her 1999 tax return. She had no idea who had prepared her 1999 tax return, and she was at a complete loss as to what to do. Kate pleaded with the IRS agent, that it was not her income, **to no avail**.

Finally, after being told by the IRS agent that she had **no options**, Kate went to an IRS office, and signed the settlement agreement only because she thought she would go to jail, if she did not sign.

Kate was in such a stressed state of mind at the time of the signing, that she has no idea whether the person she met during the signing was a male or a female.

Shortly after signing the settlement agreement, Kate attempted suicide, and she was admitted to an Arizona mental facility. Kate thought that this was the only option out of the IRS assessment.

The Conclusion

The stated mission of the Internal Revenue Service is:

"To provide America's taxpayers top quality service by helping them understand and meet their tax responsibilities and by applying the tax law with integrity and fairness to all."

The first question is: what did Kate knowingly do to deserve a $1,300 accuracy penalty?

The second question is: did the IRS apply the tax law with integrity and fairness to all?

It appears that the system, in this case, was geared towards the collection of revenue, rather than fairness to Kate.

(This situation is contrary to my experience in fifty years of public accounting, with the many IRS agents whom I have found to be professional and fair, it would appear that Kate's situation is one that has "fallen between the cracks".)

This is especially true, when it is considered that the IRS agent could have called the CPA who prepared the return, and the mismatch would have been resolved without an assessment.

If this had been done, Kate would have been spared the emotional nightmare that has gone on for six and one-half years.

What is the role of Vernon L Bowlby CPA in this case?

Why would anyone spend over three hundred hours of time, over two months, surfing the net for governmental licenses at 3:00 A.M. in the morning, sending and receiving countless emails to governmental agencies, and others, writing and rewriting letters to the Taxpayer Advocate Service, and piecing together a scenario that happened seven years ago, to a person that he had never met, who lives nearly thirteen hundred miles away, without any remuneration?

Do not ask my wife; she thinks I am crazy!

My view is that, when people with problems are divinely sent to you for extrication, to be indifferent makes you part of the problem.

I believe that indifference to others in need is lethal to any civilized society.

The bottom line is - as in one of the Four–Way Tests of Rotary

"Is it fair to all concerned?"

Kate has not been treated fairly in this case. I suggest that it is time for an exoneration of Kate's IRS debt, which was a mistake, and a conspiracy in the first place.

If murderers and rapists, who have been incarcerated, and who are freed when DNA tests prove them innocent, and the IRS mission statement is honored, Kate should be freed from this unfortunate emotional turmoil, and a refund should be issued to Kate for all amounts paid the IRS, plus interest.

Vernon L Bowlby, CPA   Corvallis, Oregon

There is no doubt in my mind that spirit led me to Kate and then sent me the messages to clear her from the wrongful IRS assessments.

All names have been changed to preserve the privacy of the persons involved.

About the Author

This is the story of a boy raised during the Great Depression and how his family survived. Vernon tells of his acceptance of messages from angels and the guiding force of his life. These messages empowered him to find the love of his life, to graduate from college and to become a CPA, to raise a family, to teach at a university, and to survive many near-death situations. In addition, these messages enabled him to author a tax manual, and to travel to fifty states and forty foreign countries. But, most importantly, his angels inspired him to become a physical healer, who would contribute countless hours, without expectation of return, to whomever he believed was divinely sent to him.

Vernon's journey reflects the gift to him from the Holy Spirit, a divine message that, over the next forty-one years, he should record his miraculous journey in a book for others to ponder.

Now, Vernon faces the biggest challenge of his life: a diagnosis, on April 3, 2014, of stage 4 metastasized cancers. He refuses to accept current medical solutions, and he has, instead, written this book, continued his life, which includes playing golf in high temperatures, and relied upon his angels' messages to guide him through the rest of his journey.

He lives in a retirement community with his wife, Ruth, and he has enjoyed a fifty-eight year marriage.

Like many others, Vernon has discovered grandchildren to be one of life's greatest joys.

Bible Quotes

Title Page, Matthew 5:16, King James Bible

Page 65, Proverbs 22:1, English Standard Vision

Page 66, Mathew 5:16, King James Bible

Page 80, John 3:16, New International Version

Page 168, Luke 6:31, New International Version

Page 184, John 12:35-36, New International Version

Page 221, James 5:14-16, English Standard Version

Page 222, John 14:12, American King James Version

Page 223, Matthew 8:13, International Standard Version

Page 232, John 14:12, American King James Version

Page 241, John 15:5, King James Version

Bibles

King James Version. New York: American Bible Society, 1999.

English Standard Version. Wheaton, Illinois: Crossway Bibles, 1952

American King James Version. New York: American Bible Society, 1999.

New International Bible. Colorado Springs, Colorado: Biblica, 2011.

Footnotes

Forward   Archangel Michael played .....
Wikipedia®

Michael does not want to be......
The Miracles of Archangel Michael xii
Doreen Virtue Hay House, Inc. 2009

Michael, like other angels.....
Ibid page 66

Michael watches over everyone.....
Ibid page 81

The Bible describes Michael.....
Wikipedia®

The Michaelion was one of the.....
Wikipedia®

Page 161   To me, the most powerful words.....
Page 260, *Anatomy of the Spirit*
Caroline Myss,
Harmony Books, New York City, 1996

Page 176   Ellen White, a prolific Adventist writer.....
Page 142 Ellen White, The Ministry of Healing
Pacific Press Publishing Co. 1942, Boise, Idaho

Page 174   Evil spirits can take hold.....
Ibid page 6

Page 178   We all have a choice- to reject or receive
Science and Health with a Key to the Scriptures
Mary Baker Eddy published by the Trustees under
the Will of Mary Baker Eddy, Boston, Mass.1934

Page 236/247   Ibid.

Page 180   This story remained in the cobwebs.....
Tamara Eberlein, May 14, 2014 in Daily Health News

Page 180   The article highlighted the research.....
Dr. Mark Hyman the founder of the Ultra
Wellness Center in Lenox, Mass.
Ultra Mind Solution, New York, Dutton books,1995

Page 182   From an interview with Dr. Melissa Lem.....
David Suzuki Foundation, April 24, 2013

Page 227   In the 1960's. Dr. George Solomon.....
Page 22 The Immune Power Personality
Henry Dreher: Dutton Books 1995

Page 227   Neuroscientist Karen Bulloch.....
Page 24 The Immune Power Personality
Henry Dreher: Dutton Books 1995

Page 227   Candice Pert, PhD.....
Page 26 The Immune Power Personality
Henry Dreher: Dutton Books 1995

Book Ordering Information

This book is available for purchase from Amazon.com as well as bookstores across the country upon request.

Further distribution options are being explored, and updates will be posted to http://VernBowlby.com.

www.ingramcontent.com/pod-product-compliance
Lightning Source LLC
Chambersburg PA
CBHW060256100426
42742CB00011B/1766